THE POLITICS OF THE PRISON AND THE PRISONER

In recent years there has been a resurgence of interest in the role of the prison as a source of political ideas and site of political engagement, as well as in the prisoner's quest for citizenship. The rising number of prisoners has increased fiscal burdens, which has meant that imprisonment has become a more important political issue. There is also greater interest in the prison as a site of political activism and in the generation of radical political ideas within the prison context and the formation of political networks within prison which extend beyond the prison walls.

This book considers the prison as a site of political protest, discusses the quest for citizenship and the denial or negation of citizenship in prison, examines the discovery of politics in prison and the role of the prison in increasing political awareness, explores the treatment of political prisoners and reflects on the prisoner as a political problem for politicians negotiating pressures from the media and the public when addressing prisoners' demands.

Drawing on a range of contemporary and historical topics such as prison riots, radicalisation and the denial of voting rights, and including discussion of cases from the UK, US and Russia, this book examines the prison as a political institution and as a site of both politicisation and political protest. This book will be of interest to students and academics engaged with prisons, penology, punishment and corrections.

Susan Easton is a Barrister and Professor of Law at Brunel Law School. She has lectured and published in both sociology and law, specialising in prisoners' rights, and has taught in UK prisons.

THE POLITICS OF THE PRISON AND THE PRISONER

Zoon Politikon

Susan Easton

Routledge
Taylor & Francis Group

LONDON AND NEW YORK

First published 2018
by Routledge
2 Park Square, Milton Park, Abingdon, Oxon OX14 4RN

and by Routledge
711 Third Avenue, New York, NY 10017

Routledge is an imprint of the Taylor & Francis Group, an informa business

British Library Cataloguing-in-Publication Data
A catalogue record for this book is available from the British Library

Library of Congress Cataloging-in-Publication Data
Names: Easton, Susan M., author.
Title: The politics of the prison and the prisoner : zoon politikon / Susan Easton.
Description: 1 Edition. | New York : Routledge, 2018. |
Includes bibliographical references and index.
Identifiers: LCCN 2018001453 | ISBN 9781138946019 (hardback) |
ISBN 9781138946033 (pbk.) | ISBN 9781315671031 (ebook)
Subjects: LCSH: Prison–Political aspects. | Prisoners.
Classification: LCC HV9069 .E275 2018 | DDC 365–dc23
LC record available at https://lccn.loc.gov/2018001453

ISBN: 978-1-138-94601-9 (hbk)
ISBN: 978-1-138-94603-3 (pbk)
ISBN: 978-1-315-67103-1 (ebk)

Typeset in Bembo
by Out of House Publishing

For Berkeley, Blue, Bunny, Celeste, Rafferty, Swift, Monty and Woody

CONTENTS

ACKNOWLEDGEMENTS

Some of the ideas in this book were first presented in papers at conferences organised by the British Society of Criminology, the Howard League and the Inner Temple. I am grateful to participants for their comments. I have also benefited greatly from discussions on the issues raised in the book, with colleagues, especially Christine Piper, and with students, past and present, including those I have taught inside prisons. I would like to thank the anonymous reviewers of the original proposal for this book for their suggestions. Any errors, of course, remain my own. My thanks also to my editor at Routledge, Hannah Catterall, for her help, to the production staff for their assistance, to Rebecca Willford and Andrew Devine, and to Esmond Easton Lamb. I would also like to thank Brunel Law School for giving me research leave to work on the book.

Susan Easton
December 2017

TABLE OF STATUTES

TABLE OF CASES

1

THE PRISONER AS A *ZOON POLITIKON*

Introduction

This book examines the prison as a political institution in the light of recent developments. The relationship between imprisonment and the political and economic structure of society was considered in the 1930s by Marxist writers, including Rusche and Kirchheimer (1939) and Pashukanis (1978), and also in the 1970s by Althusser (1971), and its disciplinary power by Foucault (1975). Although criminalisation has been analysed within the context of the changing mode of production and class relations, for example, by Hay et al. (1975) and Thompson (1979), the focus was on the way punishment is shaped by the needs of capital accumulation, rather than on prisoners' efforts to assert their citizenship rights.

While the economic role of carceral expansion is still receiving attention from modern writers such as Wacquant (2012), there is in addition a resurgence of interest in issues surrounding prisoners' quest for citizenship and in prisoners' rights and the role of the prison as a source of political ideas and a site of political engagement, and increasing recognition by the courts of prisoners as citizens. The political dimension has become more topical and pressing as the level of disorder inside prison has escalated. There has also been heightened concern over the threat from prisoners radicalised in prison and the site of prison as an incubator of dangerous ideologies. The role of the prison as a source of radicalisation has also become more important in recent years and of greater concern to governments and policy makers in the context of security concerns. Interest in the prison as a political institution has increased.

So this book is intended to contribute to the debate on prisoners' role within democratic society and on the responsibilisation of prisoners and the issues are considered in the context of the need for prison reform. It develops ideas first explored in an earlier book, *Prisoners' Rights: Principles and Practice*, which examined the elements which have shaped the emergence of the prisoners' rights movement and the experience of imprisonment (Easton 2011).

Over the past few years, we have seen increases in the numbers being imprisoned, making it harder for prisons to fulfil their rehabilitative goals and which have reduced them to warehousing or containment roles. These pressures have been felt in the US as well as the UK, as the excessive use of imprisonment has imposed fiscal burdens and become a more important political issue. There is also currently greater interest in the prison as a site of political activism and in the generation of radical political ideas within the prison context and the formation of political networks within prison, which extend beyond the prison walls. Despite the improvements in prison conditions since the 1990s, there is a danger of those advances being undermined by the loss of staff, the impact of drugs and increasing violence.

Lord Woolf, in an interview on the anniversary of the Strangeways riot, stressed the importance of taking prison out of politics.[1] While it is true that treating prison and prisons as a political issue as part of the law and order debate, has impeded prison reform, we should not ignore the political nature of imprisonment. Political meddling and ideologies have impacted on prison conditions and regimes, often to their detriment, for example, in relation to prisoners' voting rights. As we shall see, prisons and prisoners have often proved an embarrassment to politicians as they try to exceed each other in their hostility to prisoners and toughness on law and order issues.

It will be argued, however, that politics is inextricably linked to imprisonment and the political dimension deserves attention for a number of reasons. First, there may still be elements of resistance and confrontation in modern prisons although not collective rebellions on the scale of the Attica or Joliet riots. Moreover, even if prisoners are not actively resisting their confinement, this compliance does not of itself suggest acceptance and may be punctuated by sporadic incidents of violence. Certainly recent manifestations of discontent have illustrated this. Two thousand sixteen was a year of riots in Birmingham, and other prisons. There were also tensions at Hull, when prisoners were transferred there following the Birmingham riot. These incidents were not unexpected, given the increases in the prison population, and cuts in staffing and a rise in prison violence. This disquiet has continued with further incidents in 2017. We also find a political awareness of citizenship in its broadest sense, manifesting itself in campaigns for enfranchisement, but also in active citizenship and peer support, as well as through engagement in education.

The term 'politics' originates from *politicus*, the Greek word for citizen, and politics relates to matters of the state or government. Politics will be construed broadly in the forthcoming discussion. It does not refer to politics in the narrow sense of support for a particular party or to politics as the study of power, but means being part of the polis in the Aristotelian sense of a *zoon politikon,* a political animal. For Aristotle, citizenship is defined, in his *Politics*, as participation in judging and ruling and in the *polis*, private interests are subordinated to the public interest. In the Aristotelian model, the citizen, as a political animal, looked to the good of the community rather than his own narrow interests. Moreover, participation in the political life of the community could itself create virtue in moving beyond self-interest.

Since Aristotle, the notion of citizenship has been subject to debate and arguments over the extension of citizenship to previously excluded groups and whether it should include social rights (Marshall 1950). It has been championed by the Left who have seen citizenship as a means of promoting equality and by the right who have focused on the citizen as a consumer. A Speaker's Commission on Citizenship in 1990 considered the matter and argued for the development of active citizenship and the need for training on citizenship as part of education.[2]

Political action, in the following discussion, will be understood to include the active citizenship of peer mentoring and participation in prisoner councils, as well as the formal expressions of political ideas or engagement in the democratic process. So, for example, several serving prisoners submitted evidence to the House of Commons Justice Committee (2017) in its review of prison reform.

A range of activities in prison will therefore be examined from this standpoint. While prison life has been subject to numerous ethnographic studies, the focus here will be specifically on what we can learn of the role of politics inside prison, how inmates may engage in political behaviour and assert themselves as citizens, despite the ways in which prison as an institution and the wider society seeks to undermine that status. In exploring these issues, insights from a range of disciplines, including political thought, social psychology, criminology and human rights law will be used.

Prisoners' rights

The discussion of prisoner politics inevitably raises questions about prisoners' rights in general and the specific rights safeguarded by the European Convention on Human Rights. As we shall see, the use of the Convention to further prisoners' rights claims has aroused the ire of successive governments and has become a weapon in the UK government's critique of the Strasbourg Court.

But this fails to take account of the extent to which these claims in the past have been unsuccessful in that court, for a variety of reasons, including being out of time, or failing to exhaust available domestic remedies. Claims have also been thwarted because of the weight given to competing demands, including the needs of the administration for security and good order, efficiency, cost-cutting and risk management. There is plenty of scope within the Convention for some of the rights to be legitimately qualified in the interest of the public, including national security, and the prevention of crime. Several of the rights protected by the Convention are qualified, for example, Article 8, which protects the right to private and family life, Article 9, which protects freedom of thought, conscience and religion and Article 10 which protects the right to freedom of expression. So Article 3, the right not to be subjected to torture or inhuman or degrading treatment or punishment, which is not qualified and is non-derogable, even in times of war or public emergency, has proved to be of greater value in protecting prisoners than Article 8. States are also afforded a margin of appreciation in which to devise arrangements which they see as appropriate to the local context. Despite the image purveyed by critics of the Convention, in fact the data shows that the majority of claims do not proceed or succeed and the cases where the UK has been found to be in breach are relatively few, compared to other states such as Russia. In the period 1959–2016, 23,781 applications concerning the UK were referred for judicial consideration, while 21,599 were declared inadmissible or struck out. For the Russian Federation, the figures were 140,731 for judicial consideration and 129,694 ruled inadmissible (European Court of Human Rights 2017: 5). The number of judgments finding at least one violation were 312 for the UK and 1,834 for the Russian Federation. However, the highest number of findings of violations were against Turkey with 2,889 judgments and Italy with 1,791 judgments (ibid: 6).

The domestic courts have also given considerable leeway to the prison authorities in dealing with prisoners detained under the Terrorism Act, as well as ordinary prisoners where the courts tend to defer to the prison's judgments where risk assessments are in question.

But even where rights are recognised by the courts – here and in other jurisdictions – a major barrier to implementation will be resources. There have been cases where prisoners have succeeded with their rights claims, and the courts have ordered reforms, but these have not been implemented, because there are insufficient funds. This has been a recurring theme in riots in the US where the courts have demanded change in a number of areas, as we shall see in Chapter 2, but the prison administration has failed to introduce those improvements, because they are too burdensome in imposing economic and administrative costs. This has contributed, in some cases, to the development of disorder as prisoners' expectations have been raised and then dashed.

Many of the Strasbourg Court's judgments on penal matters are against poorer, less economically developed states. While European penal law – including the Convention and the European Prison Rules – is widely seen as setting the highest standard for penal systems, their effectiveness in achieving improvements in practice is limited in less wealthy states or states where the government is unwilling to invest sufficient resources in penal reform.

For example, in modern Russia, where the state is a signatory to the European Convention as well as the European Convention on the Prevention of Torture, there have been insufficient resources and a lack of political will to effect substantial change and human rights violations persist in Russian prisons. Since the 1990s they have been measured against western standards.[3] Piacentini (2004) interviewed Russian prison officers on their views of human rights and found some prison officers welcomed human rights as a way of making prisons more humane, some equated them with more paperwork, while some resented them as shaming Russia, and were nostalgic for the past. Others were critical of European bodies for finding fault with Russian prisons, whilst giving no financial support to address the problems, while some officers saw human rights discourse as mere window-dressing. However, as van Zyl Smit and Snacken (2009) have pointed out, the

European Union has provided support for a programme to train prison officers in human rights ideals in areas of South Russia marked by conflict (van Zyl Smit and Snacken 2009: 382). But clearly the challenges remain of under-resourced prisons and a system where prisoners are, in many cases, held far from home. However, in some respects, the Russian penal system goes further in recognizing prisoners' right to family life, for example, by allowing conjugal visits and extended family visits. The positive impact of European penal standards has also been felt in the establishment of a prison ombudsman in Russia.

Closer to home, Dickson (2010) argues that the Convention was of limited value in the Northern Ireland conflict. As well as the margin of appreciation and qualifications, the deference of the Commission and the Court to governments limited its effectiveness. While the Commission was not overtly hostile to prisoners, human rights jurisprudence was not then as developed as it is now. However, given the evolution of Convention jurisprudence since the late 1990s, it is likely many of those earlier cases would be decided more favourably towards prisoners now.

But this is not to downplay the contribution of Irish political prisoners who brought successful challenges which benefited other prisoners. For example, Campbell and Fell were involved in a protest at Albany prison in 1976, over the treatment of another prisoner and charged with disciplinary offences under Prison Rule 47, including prison mutiny. Father Patrick Fell was a Catholic priest convicted for his involvement in IRA activities in Coventry in the early seventies. Campbell and Fell were denied legal representation at their disciplinary hearing, although they lost over 500 days remission and were not allowed to consult lawyers privately. The Court upheld most of their complaints under Article 6(1), as the decision of the Board of Visitors was not made public, and under Article 6(3), because of the denial of legal assistance.[4] The case contributed to helping other prisoners receive legal advice when accused of breaching prison rules. However, there were also cases in the 1970s and 1980s when prisoners were complaining of harsh conditions and the Commission and the Court rejected them, especially if it was thought that the cases were simply propaganda for political groups, such as the case involving members of the Baader-Meinhof group or the Red Army Faction.[5] Moreover, it is clear that the Commission and the Court have been more comfortable dealing with procedural rather than substantive issues. The Court, in recent years, has resulted in a number of decisions which address key issues facing prisoners and implications for the length of detention, for example, in demanding reviews for prisoners given whole life sentences in *Vinter and others v UK* App Nos. 66069/09, 130/10 and 3896/10 (9 July 2013) and *Hutchinson v UK* App No. 5792/08 (3 February 2015).

Moore and Scraton (2014) are also critical of rights discourse because it assumes it is possible to improve prison conditions and to give prisoners dignity without challenging prison as an institution, or analysing the structural conditions which lie behind the routes into prison. Focusing just on reform means we do not move beyond the prison, or understand its role or structural determinants. This raises the problem of abolitionism versus reformism which has preoccupied critics of imprisonment, but as Moore and Scraton acknowledge, concentrating just on abolition ignores the plight of those there now. So a humane environment for prisoners needs to be pursued without reinforcing prisons' permanence.

Notwithstanding, the criticisms of European human rights law from prison reformers, it offers a way of critiquing prison systems from an external standpoint. Moreover, in the current political climate, abolition is very unlikely, the best we can hope for is a reduction through creative policies, such as justice reinvestment, making prisons more effective and bolstering struggles for citizenship. At the same time, we need to protect the role of human rights in raising and upholding standards of imprisonment.

Key themes: seeking citizenship and denying citizenship

A range of issues are explored in this text to illustrate the ways in which the prison and the prisoner can be viewed through a political lens and the ways in which the prisoner may develop towards a *zoon politikon*. Chapter 2 considers the prison as a site of political protest, with reference to a range of responses, including prisoners' unions, prison strikes and prison riots, including Attica and Joliet in the US and Strangeways and Birmingham in the UK, where the prisons were taken over by prisoners for a temporary period. As we shall see, prisoners may respond to their confinement in a range of ways, from acceptance and resignation without protest, or use legitimate methods of protest, while others may react violently to their conditions of imprisonment. Protests may include hunger strikes, as used in the past in Northern Ireland, and more recently in immigration removal centres, no-wash protests also used in Northern Ireland, and the withholding of prison labour, which has occurred recently in the US. More individualised and strategic responses may involve engineering one's segregation to obtain transfer to another prison. Prisoners' reactions may also shift over time. Resentments and tensions may also be directed inwardly through self-destructive behaviour, including self-harming or drug use. Prisoners' unions which seek to improve conditions will be examined, looking at PROP in the UK and recent European developments. The rise of the prisoners' rights movement also offers a significant means of challenging conditions, so the right to association will be considered. However, barriers to the collective organisation of prisoners will be discussed, including the impact of drug use and the individualisation resulting from the Incentives and Earned Privileges Scheme.

While there may be local, institutional and individual factors which precipitate a riot, common themes and antecedents can be identified, including a response to regime change, a failure to deal with complaints, crises of legitimacy, administrative failures in dealing with discontents, and deprivation. While 1990 is seen as the year of the most dramatic riot in the UK, at Strangeways prison in Manchester, obviously riots have occurred both before and since then, in a wide range of prisons, with differing levels of security and with differences in the composition of their population. Incidents of disorder on a lesser scale have erupted since the 1990s, but in the last few years have become more frequent, despite the fact that prisoners are now subject to greater surveillance and control. The more recent riots have occurred in context of falling staff numbers and rising prisoner numbers, more time spent locked up, cuts in prison budgets, increasing prison violence and the availability of new psychoactive substances. While riots are primarily associated with men's prisons, examples of riots in women's prisons will also be referred to, as well as women's participation in strikes and occupations. As we shall see, women respond to imprisonment in a range of ways, including the establishment of alternative identities. In the US, major riots including Attica and New Mexico, are considered. However, while tensions have persisted in US prisons, in the context of mass incarceration, riots have declined, principally as a result of strategies of increased surveillance, segregation of disruptive prisoners and better staff training to manage incidents of disorder before they escalate into full-blown riots. As in the UK, specialist rapid response teams are used to combat riots in their early stages. Riots may be seen as rudimentary political activity, but also, in some cases, as simply enjoyment of rioting or an opportunity to settle scores or steal drugs.

A further shift has been the increased use of prisoners' rights litigation to challenge conditions which has achieved some success, for example, in relation to indeterminate sentences. Many of the rights achieved in the UK through challenges in the Strasbourg Court have also been secured in the US, through litigation and in response to violent protests. Nonetheless, in both jurisdictions prisons remain volatile. Rights litigation obviously provides a safer and more productive route to change and reference will be made to key cases, including the Pelican Bay case, but as we shall see, barriers to litigation in recent years have decelerated this process.

Chapter 3 discusses the quest for citizenship in prison, examining a variety of ways prisoners pursue citizenship, including volunteering, peer support and participation on prisoner councils, as well as engagement in campaigns for voting rights in prison, both here and in the US. The role of education is also considered in the development of the prisoner as a *zoon politikon*. Although much of the discussion of prisoners and citizenship in recent years has focused on the campaign for voting rights, the expression of citizenship is clearly wider than this and there are broader and valuable means of expressing or performing active citizenship. For example, the increasingly significant role of peer mentors and volunteers in prison, including involvement in literacy programmes, helping with the teaching of English to foreign national prisoners, participating in Listener schemes and providing assistance to older prisoners, which is becoming more important given the rising number of older prisoners, will be examined. As we shall see, there are various ways prisoners can become involved in prison and community projects, including prison radio and assisting community projects outside the prison. Volunteering and education may be seen as key elements in the development of the prisoner as a *zoon politikon*. The range of volunteering opportunities has expanded considerably in recent years. They may have positive effects on inmates, as well as the recipients, in improving prisoners' self-esteem and self-confidence. Volunteering also promotes social inclusion, undermines isolation and allows prisoners to take responsibility. It can also relieve staff of burdens and arguably contribute to desistance, in fostering a new sense of self. Prisoners may be involved as peer mentors in literacy schemes. Education is also an important means of developing citizenship skills and is being given more attention in the light of the Coates Report (2016). Prisoners may pursue their courses following national curricula and thereby increase their links to the outside world. Citizenship courses may be used to promote awareness of responsibilities. However, barriers to educational advancement will also be discussed.

The role of prisoner councils, as a means of developing citizenship skills, will be examined, as they give participants experience of the democratic process by standing for election, representing other prisoners and contributing to decision making. However, their powers are limited and while some of the key issues which concern prisoners, such as discipline, are excluded from consideration, some improvements to prison life and prison regimes may result from the work of the councils. In the elections for councils, prisoners stand for parties with specific agendas and demonstrate to their electorate the importance of voting and assessing candidates on their manifestos. Prisoners' campaigns for voting rights are discussed as a key dimension of the quest for citizenship, with reference to the UK and the US, where the denial of the vote is more extensive and where there are significant disparate impact issues. Although these campaigns have not succeeded in achieving significant change, they demonstrate prisoners' demands to be treated as 'political animals'.

Developing the above routes to citizenship, it is argued, may have positive benefits and even if they impose some financial costs on prisons, in the longer term they may actually save money and give social benefits in re-integrating prisoners and improving employability, allowing prisoners to develop new skills and an alternative identity which is an essential element of desistance. These avenues or pathways also give prisoners a voice and are important elements of the politicisation of prisoners and offer an alternative to more violent methods of expressing discontent.

The loss of voting rights is examined in more detail in Chapter 4, which focuses on the denial or negation of citizenship in prison, with the prisoner's exclusion from political as well as social life. The experience of other jurisdictions, including the Republic of Ireland and the US, will also be considered. While the UK position is less draconian than that of the US, sentenced prisoners are still not permitted to vote. Despite a successful challenge to the UK's denial of prisoners' voting rights in the Strasbourg Court in *Hirst v UK* in 2005, where the Court ruled that the UK law infringed Article 3 of Protocol No. 1 of the European Convention, and the recommendations of a Joint Parliamentary Committee in 2013 for limited change, and the protection of the right to vote in international human rights law,[6] most sentenced prisoners are currently not permitted to vote. Parliament made it clear, when it voted on the issue in 2011, that the ban should remain.

Whether this civil death of prisoners is appropriate in modern democratic societies and whether it can be justified in terms of the purpose of punishment will be discussed. The implications of disenfranchisement for the social exclusion of prisoners will be considered, as well as the disparate impact of the disenfranchisement on specific groups. The social death of prisoners has been justified by governments because they are deemed to have breached the social contract and therefore have lost the right to contribute to how a country is governed. As we shall see, the UK's strong defence of disenfranchisement runs counter to the wider trend of restoration of the vote to prisoners, which reflects the greater recognition of prisoners as citizens and the impact of prisoners' rights jurisprudence and the increasing cosmopolitanism of rights jurisprudence. Given the current levels of incarceration in the UK, large numbers of prisoners are affected by the automatic ban which the Strasbourg Court has argued is disproportionate, bearing no relation to the gravity of the crime.

We will examine jurisprudence in both the domestic courts and the Strasbourg Court in the period since *Hirst,* and the many discussions of the issue over the past twelve years, including the Consultation Papers in 2006 and 2009 and the findings of the Joint Parliamentary Committee, which reviewed the question of prisoner voting, taking evidence from a range of sources, including prisoners and prison governors, and reported in 2013. As we shall see, the Committee did recommend some limited change, affecting a relatively small number of prisoners, namely those serving less than twelve months, and it was mindful of both the obligations to comply with the Strasbourg Court's judgment and the importance of the sovereignty of Parliament. But this recommendation has not been accepted. The UK government's initial tactic was to delay compliance – a tactic favoured by all administrations since *Hirst*, then to actively resist compliance and to justify this by appeals to both Parliamentary sovereignty and public opinion. The most the government is willing to concede in future is to allow prisoners on day release to vote outside the prison, which affects very few prisoners.[7]

The government's intransigence has been bolstered as the votes for prisoners question has become enmeshed with its broader critique of the Convention and its clashes with the Strasbourg Court, with the government threatening to withdraw from the Convention. Its hostility to human rights has focused on prisoners. The views of the government have become more entrenched inhibiting the prospects for radical change.

Arguments for and against re-enfranchisement will be discussed, including the impact of the vote on the integrity of the democratic process particularly if prisoners vote together or en bloc, the problems of linking voting rights or universal rights generally to deservingness and voting to virtue, whether and how disenfranchisement can be justified as an additional punishment, and the implications for retribution, deterrence, rehabilitation and public protection. The positive benefits of restoration will also be considered, namely promoting the reintegration of prisoners and strengthening their sense of citizenship. The significance of voting or participation in political life in promoting virtue is stressed as the prisoner, as a *zoon politikon,* looks beyond his own self-interest.

The question of the disparate impact of felon disenfranchisement will be explored, with specific reference to the US, where there is a disproportionate impact on young black males, who have very high levels of disenfranchisement which may extend beyond release, because of prior criminal convictions. While there has been some relaxation of these laws in some states, there remain numerous 'lost voters', because of the very high incarceration rates and the large numbers serving long sentences.

While there is a trend towards re-enfranchisement worldwide, the UK and US positions on prisoners' votes are at odds with this trend. Moreover, the way the issue has been handled by UK governments has made prisoners' votes a more controversial and significant issue then it might otherwise have been. A more measured approach which made clear the advantages and absence of risk, could have reassured the public and may have made Parliament more receptive to change. In contrast, in the Republic of Ireland, for example, the law was amended without political or public opposition.

Political awareness in prison

Chapter 5 examines the discovery of politics in prison and the role of the prison in consciousness-raising and increasing political awareness. Reference is made to the prison as a potential and actual source of political radicalisation, in relation to Islamist extremism. Possible strategies to address radicalisation and methods of deradicalisation will be discussed. While individuals already politicised may develop their political ideas further in prison, such as Bakunin and Kropotkin in nineteenth-century Russia and Angela Davis in twentieth-century America, it is also clear that many prisoners become politicised for the first time while in prison and, in some cases, because of their experiences in prison. The presence of key figures from a political movement in prison may also mobilise other prisoners.

In recent years prisons have become more strongly associated with radicalisation, with prisons seen as sources of recruitment for al-Qaeda and other groups around the world, and there has been more interest in developing measures to combat this. There have been several examples of prisoners radicalised in prison in Europe and the US as well as the UK, so the experience of Spain, the Netherlands and other European states and the US will be discussed, including the formulation of policies to address the problem. The role of prison in the deradicalisation process will also be examined. In the UK, with the rise in offenders serving shorter sentences for preparatory offences, this has meant more TACT prisoners, that is offenders convicted under the Terrorism Act, in the ordinary prison estate. The recent increase in terrorist attacks has made the problem of combating radicalisation even more pressing for governments to address.

The role of the prison has been addressed by the UK government's counter-terrorism strategy, as well as by the House of Commons Home Affairs Committee and the Acheson Review, which visited a number of prisons, spoke to prison chaplains, identified elements of the threat, and considered ways of dealing with the problem (Ministry of Justice 2016b). The Prison and Probation Service has revised its extremism prevention strategy in light of the Review. As we shall see, a number of interventions have been formulated here and in other states using a range of different methods. A new Extremism Risk Guidance tool has also been formulated.

The implications of separation or integration of terrorist prisoners for the radicalisation of other prisoners are discussed. As we shall see, there are arguments for and against segregation but special units to hold extremist prisoners have recently been established in the UK. Attention is also given to the process of deradicalisation in prison, the rejection of extremist ideology and disengagement from involvement in future terrorist activity. The existing body of theory and research on desistance from offending may also be useful in developing deradicalisation programmes. What emerges from recent findings is the importance of having well-run prisons, with adequate levels of staffing and safety, to combat radicalisation. Unsafe prisons may mean offenders are more likely to seek safety from others, and overcrowded and disorganised prisons make it easier for prisoners to radicalise others and for behaviour to pass unnoticed. So the problem has to be addressed in the wider context of prison conditions and prison disorder discussed in Chapter 2. Muslim prisoners' concerns over their differential treatment in prison because of their faith are also considered.

The discussion then moves on, in Chapter 6, to the treatment of political prisoners. Imprisonment has been used as a means of silencing political opposition frequently in the past, most notably in the twentieth century. The use of prison for this purpose is still evident, despite greater international monitoring and surveillance of detention and the formal ratification of human rights instruments. The relationship between political prisoners, imprisoned for their political beliefs or views, or where there is a relationship between the offence and a political objective, and non-political prisoners will be considered, with reference to the specific contexts of the Gulag in Stalinist Russia and the more recent Northern Ireland conflict.

Political imprisonment will be discussed with reference to the anarchist prisoners, Bakunin and Kropotkin, in Tsarist Russia, but the twentieth century is obviously the key era of political imprisonment, reaching its peak in Nazi Germany and Stalinist Russia. Although it is now harder to imprison citizens for their political ideas because of international human rights law and greater scrutiny and the availability of other methods used to silence opponents, political imprisonment still persists. Modes of punishment of political opponents will vary, depending on the legal, political and economic context. This chapter also considers the perception of the function and role of the prison within political theory with reference to Marxist and anarchist theory, as well as their differing attitudes towards prisoners.

As we shall see, the relationship between political prisoners and 'ordinary' prisoners is complex, as some political prisoners have tried to distinguish themselves from non-political prisoners, while others find common ground. Furthermore, ordinary crime may be politicised and offenders may become politicised in prison, especially if prison regimes are repressive. The presence of political prisoners may also influence others, as occurred in the late 1960s and 1970s, with the imprisonment of civil rights activists whose presence affected other prisoners and contributed to the demands made in the Attica riot.

It might also be argued that all imprisonment is political in so far as it reflects social inequality and deprivation, and those in prison are mostly socially excluded and powerless. The contrast between the two groups – political and non-political prisoners – should not be overstated as ordinary prisoners in the 1970s engaged in litigation which improved the treatment of all prisoners. Furthermore, some former political prisoners have gone on to campaign for prisoners' rights on their release.

However, the experience of the Gulag is examined as an extreme example of the state's treatment of political prisoners and to show the arbitrary nature of the distinction between the two groups as theft, for example, could be defined as a political act if the goods were taken from state property. The differential treatment of 58-ers – those sentenced under Article 58 of the Criminal Code – and ordinary prisoners or *zeks* will be discussed, as well as the legacy of the Gulag for modern Russian prisons.

The question of whether we should distinguish political prisoners, imprisoned for political beliefs or political actions, from the 'ordinary' prison population and whether the former group should be treated differently is also explored, with reference to sectarian political subcultures in Northern Ireland. Here the camps in which paramilitary prisoners were held became the site of their wider and immediate political struggle. There are clearly differences between Northern Ireland and the Gulag. In Northern Ireland, prisoners were demanding political status as a means to improved conditions and recognition of their political aims. But in Russia the classification was unsought, widely feared and often meant worse conditions. The campaign for political status in Northern Ireland developed when special category status was taken from paramilitary prisoners in 1976. This led to resistance and conflict, including hunger strikes. These strikes attracted worldwide criticism and mobilised support for the prisoners and their political beliefs. While prisoners of war have received formal protection through successive Conventions, political prisoners have struggled to receive recognition in the UK.

Northern Ireland is also interesting because political prisoners played an important role in the peace process, in moving towards peaceful struggle and democratic means rather than armed struggle. This also had positive effects on their subsequent treatment under the Good Friday Agreement. Political status may affect not only the treatment of prisoners while incarcerated, but also their prospects for release as occurred there after the Good Friday Agreement. The role of amnesties and the early release of prisoners is obviously very controversial and has also resurfaced in recent debates over the failure to prosecute those suspected of committing serious crimes during the Troubles.

The specific issue of whether terrorists should be treated under the ordinary criminal law or under separate special emergency laws and powers and counter-terrorism provisions will also be discussed. This is a particularly pertinent issue in Northern Ireland, where there was an array of measures to deal with the threat from sectarian groups, including emergency provisions, non-jury trials and supergrass evidence. Whether these measures were necessary will be considered.

Although the majority of political prisoners have been men, there have also been many examples of women imprisoned for their political deeds in the UK, including the suffragettes and women in the Northern Ireland conflict, as well as women imprisoned for political views and activities in the US and Russia. The experience of female political prisoners and their relationship to non-political women prisoners will be discussed.

Prisoners, politicians and the public

Finally, Chapter 7 considers the prisoner as a political problem for politicians, who negotiate pressures from the media and the public when addressing prisoners' demands. How politicians and the public view prisoners will be explored, as well as the media's treatment of prisoners' rights claims. The impact of budgetary constraints on the treatment of prisoners is also referred to, in the context of the politics of mass incarceration in the US. In California there have been reductions in the prison population driven by the Court and a realignment policy to move supervision of non-violent and non-sexual offenders from state to local level.

Governments' attempts to reconcile the pressures of public opinion, conveyed via the media, with budgetary constraints on punishment, and with pressures from international human rights standards, will be discussed. Governments committed to penal austerity still have to respond to that pressure and in the European context, to demands from the Strasbourg Court, although this has proved problematic, leading to conflicts between Strasbourg and the UK courts.

These pressures have had a significant impact on the prison system in the UK, as cuts have been imposed by closing smaller prisons and cutting staff, leading to problems of instability. There has now been some recognition of this, with recent increases in staff levels, but current staff numbers have still not reached earlier levels. But it is also difficult to satisfy demands for harsh punishment even if crime rates do fall. It is difficult to pursue strong decarceration policies if the public do not support them. This also raises the issue of whether public opinion is well informed and based on accurate information. Research on sentencing, for example, suggests that the public may accept prevailing sentencing levels as legitimate if given accurate information.

As we shall see, the public is not homogenous, and there may be differences between different sections of the public on their levels of punitiveness. On key issues of prisoners' rights, there may be some limited support for change here and in the US. The media's treatment of prisoners' rights claims will also be considered. The negative impact of the media in its depictions of prisoners in inflating demands for punishment will be reviewed. Given the lack of contact between the public and prisoners or prisons, the media will be a key source of information. Sensationalist reporting may make it harder to secure support for reductionist policies and strengthen support for punitive and expansionist policies. The popular media has been a strident voice, notably in debates on prisoners' rights, including voting rights and on prison austerity. Engaging the media in reporting on positive developments to promote penal reform is crucial and could be used to challenge punitive attitudes.

However, attention will also be focused on the positive aspects of the media, including its role as an element of normalisation inside prison, while assisting prisoners' transition to the outside world by giving information on life outside. We will also examine prisoners' own relationship to the media, which may be important in raising issues of concern and highlighting problems in prison. In addition, prisoners' access to social media has enabled them to seek to make their voices heard, while inside and on release.

Conclusion

Discussion of the politics of the prison and the prisoner raises a number of issues, including the role of the prison as an incubator of radical political views and a site for political struggle and the reasons for the increasing levels of violence within prisons. As well as considering violent expressions of prisoners' resistance to their imprisonment, we also need to identify alternative ways of channelling discontents and demands and to facilitate opportunities for active citizenship.

There have been some positive developments, with increased interest in prison safety, a White Paper, *Prison Safety and Reform* (Ministry of Justice 2016a) and a report from the House of Commons Justice Committee on prison safety in 2016 (House of Commons Justice Committee 2016). In addition, the Coates Report has argued for more weight to be given to prison education (Coates 2016). The Prisons and Courts Bill introduced in response to the White Paper, included some useful provisions. It gave a new statutory purpose for prisons. Clause 1 stated that the aim of prisons is to protect the public, reform and rehabilitate offenders, prepare prisoners for life outside prison and maintain an environment that is safe and secure. Interestingly it did not refer to punishing offenders. The Bill also strengthened the powers of the Prison Inspectorate and of the Prisons and Probation Ombudsman by giving them a statutory basis.[8] So if the Inspectorate reported concerns, the Secretary of State would have to respond within twenty-eight days. But Part I of the Bill was lost when Parliament was dissolved for the 2017 General Election and has not been revived. Other aspects of the Bill were less welcome. For example, the proposed development of prison league tables was seen as unfair and demoralising to staff especially at a time of staff shortages and high staff turnover. The Bill also contained nothing on suicide or on self-harm, which reached a record high in the twelve months ending June 2017.[9] It did not address the key problems of overcrowding, understaffing and violence in prisons. In an open letter[10] in August 2017, Andrea Albutt, the President of the Prison Governors Association highlighted the continuing difficulties of rising numbers, indiscipline and understaffing, and staff retention and the daily problems faced by staff in carrying out their duties.

The House of Commons Justice Committee, in its latest report on prison reform, published in 2017, stressed the need to avoid variations in treatment or levels of security (House of Commons Justice Committee 2017). It also noted that it had seen no evidence that governor empowerment, favoured by the government, would lead to better outcomes. The Committee was also concerned over holding governors accountable for reforming offenders, given the movement of prisoners between establishments and the number of parties involved in the process of rehabilitation. It was also unconvinced of the need for league tables, which it concluded, 'are not a useful means to compare prison performance or drive improvements' (ibid, at para 47).

The Justice Committee is also conducting an inquiry, *Prison Population 2022: Planning for the Future*, which will examine who is in prison and expected to be imprisoned in the next five years, why they are there and why they return, and whether the Ministry of Justice and prison services have a credible approach to accommodating the anticipated changes. In the meantime, the social and economic costs of imprisonment remain high.[11] Insufficient attention is paid to reducing the level of imprisonment, for example, by developing community punishments, investing in women's centres and developing alternatives to deal with younger offenders. In its response to the Committee's Report, the Government[12] has said that it will try to speed up the process to deal with the Prison Inspectorate's concerns, including establishing a unit to track how the Inspectorate's recommendations are being implemented. It also stresses that it has put in place more training for governors to prepare them for their new role, new performance measures and that it is subjecting prisons to greater scrutiny. A new urgent notification protocol[13] has been introduced and has already been used by the Chief Inspector of Prisons to draw the attention of the Secretary of State for Justice to problems in HMP Nottingham and to demand a response. However, while the government's focus has been on deregulation and devolution of powers, the fundamental problems of understaffing, underfunding, violence and overcrowding have persisted. A recent report from the Inspectorate has highlighted the continuing poor conditions in many establishments (HMIP 2017). The implications of these issues for the politics of the prison and the prisoner will now be explored in more detail.

Notes

1 *Inside Out*, BBC Northwest (25 May 2015).
2 For further discussion see Commission on Citizenship (1990), Murdoch (1991) and Beck (1996).
3 See King (1994), Piacentini (2004), van Zyl Smit and Snacken (2009).
4 *Campbell and Fell v UK* App Nos. 7817/77 and 7877/77 (28 June 1984).
5 *Ensslin, Baader and Raspe v Germany* (1978) 14 DR 64.
6 Under Article 25 of the International Covenant of Civil and Political Rights, Article 2 of the Universal Declaration of Human Rights and Article 3 of Protocol No. 1 to the European Convention.
7 HC Deb, 2 November 2017, Vol. 630.
8 Clauses 2 and 4.

9 www.gov.uk/government/uploads/system/uploads/attachment_data/file/654498/ safety-in-custody-stats-q2-2017.pdf, accessed 29 November 2017.

10 http://prison-governors-association.org.uk/wp-content/uploads/2017/08/Bulln724H. pdf, accessed 29 November 2017.

11 The costs for 2016–17 were £38,042 per place and £35,371 per prisoner:www.gov.uk/ government/uploads/system/uploads/attachment_data/file/653972/costs-per-place- per-prisoner-2016-2017-summary.pdf, accessed 30 November 2017.

12 https://publications.parliament.uk/pa/cm201719/cmselect/cmjust/491/491.pdf, accessed 29 November 2017.

13 www.justiceinspectorates.gov.uk/hmiprisons/wp-content/uploads/sites/4/2017/11/ HMIP-MoJ-protocol-amend301117.pdf.

2

POLITICAL PROTEST IN PRISON

Introduction

This chapter considers the prison as a site of political protest, with reference to a range of responses, from the formation of prisoners' unions, hunger strikes and roof protests, to full-scale prison riots, where prisons are taken over by prisoners for a temporary period, in the UK and in the US. The Attica and Joliet riots, as well as more recent developments, are considered. Prisoners may engage in a variety of forms of disruptive behaviour to achieve their aims. They may participate in violent rioting, attacking staff and other prisoners, damaging their cells and prison property and may completely take over the prison. In an extreme case, at Pavon prison near Guatemala City, a prison originally intended as a farm prison, was taken over by prisoners in 1996 and was not recaptured until 2006. The prison has been described as a republic and a feudal state with drug lords in control.

Resistance may also include engaging in no-wash protests – as occurred in Northern Ireland – participation in strikes and industrial sabotage. Without resorting to a full-scale riot, prisoners may alternatively go on the roof, or on the netting, in order to seek publicity for their grievances. They may also deliberately behave disruptively to obtain a move to a segregation wing, as a step towards achieving the goal of transfer to another prison. Resistance may also take a more individual expression, through a range of responses from hunger strikes to minor acts, such as the example given by Ugelvik (2014) of prisoners cooking certain foods. The pains of imprisonment may be reflected in the self-destructive behaviours of drug use and self-harm, and ultimately suicide. Another example of resistance in the past has been by acquiring tattoos. For Russian prisoners, tattoos can signify the type of crime, the length of sentence, or gang membership, but tattoos can also be used by prisoners to punish others. Prisoners may form gangs or join gangs with links to

gangs outside, and in some states, notably the US, prison gangs have wielded considerable power within the prison structure.

Prisoners may respond in a range of ways to what Sykes (1958) describes as the
'pains of imprisonment', as prison life offers continuing challenges to overcome
and their response may change over time. Some will simply want to serve their
time as painlessly as possible, without trouble and may accept their conditions of
imprisonment without protest and if they have issues to raise, may use formal,
or informal complaints procedures. If we approached this from the standpoint of
Merton's typology of deviance, these prisoners would be seen as conformists, as
they accept the goals of the regime and the legitimate means of achieving those
aims (Merton 1938). As well as using the complaints system, prisoners may also
participate in prisoners' councils or forums, to raise concerns, although, as we shall
see in Chapter 3, some of the key issues which frustrate prisoners such as disciplinary matters, are excluded from discussion, with councils focusing instead on
matters such as the availability of goods in the prison canteen. Others, who might
be described as innovators, may seek creative and illegitimate alternatives to negotiate prison life, while retreatists may withdraw into themselves, rather than resisting
or embracing prison life, while rebels may reject legitimate means of achieving
their own goals. These responses may shift over time, so a prisoner who begins
by complying may later rebel. Moreover, a lack of overt rebellion does not necessarily mean acquiescence or normative compliance. For example, older prisoners
are often viewed as more passive and easier to manage, but as an older prisoner
interviewed in a Prison Reform Trust study, remarked: 'old and quiet we might
be thought of but we can also be "old, cussed and angry"' (PRT 2008: 7). A range
of behaviours will therefore be considered, from peaceful to violent responses, in a
wide range of establishments, in the UK and in the US.

Prisoners' unions

One non-violent way prisoners have tried to improve their position is through
the formation of prisoners' unions. These are organisations or action groups of
prisoners who act together to improve their situation and may campaign on issues
relating to prison conditions, but may also act as trades unions, protecting the rights
of prison employees. They are found in a number of states, but in the UK, an early
example of a prisoners' union is PROP, an acronym for Preservation of the Rights
of Prisoners, which was active in the early 1970s. Members of PROP were active
inside prison, as five PROP members were incarcerated, while outside supporters
campaigned for their release. PROP was set up by prisoners and ex-prisoners to
improve the treatment of prisoners and to protect their rights and interests at a time
when prisoners' rights were not as well established as they are now. While prisoners'
unions are usually seen as a left-wing manifestation, PROP welcomed members
holding any political views, and the majority of prisoners who joined in fact were
not left-wing radicals. Most left-wing groups in the past generally have shown
relatively little interest in helping ordinary prisoners, but have focused on political

prisoners, as we shall see in Chapter 6. Slogans demanding freedom for political prisoners would not necessarily win the support of other prisoners, but PROP supported all prisoners. It tried to resist being a political party and being diverted into other political causes, as was made clear in the minutes of PROP meetings (PROP 1973).

One reason the group emerged was because some individuals concerned about prison conditions had attended a meeting of other political groups, but had been unable to raise the issue of solidarity with prisoners. PROP resisted identifying specific groups of prisoners as political, but wanted to focus on all prisoners. Those PROP prisoners who had been incarcerated wanted, on their release, to help others left behind in prison. The founding of PROP was therefore significant, because this was the 'first time a group of ex-prisoners had launched a public campaign proclaiming their unequivocal solidarity with all prisoners and their "Rights"' (PROP 1973: 2–3). The first national prisoners' strike was in 1972 when prisoners in thirty prisons acted in solidarity with PROP's aims and in support of other prisoners. PROP encouraged and supported this solidarity at a time when there was little interest in or public support for prisoners' rights and at a time when European Convention jurisprudence on prisoners' rights was limited. PROP was particularly concerned about internal disciplinary procedures, as prisoners at that time could be tried and punished without legal representation. It also published reports on the riots in Hull in 1976 and in Wormwood Scrubs in 1979 (PROP 1976, 1979). However, despite PROP's efforts, there were few major changes in prison conditions until after the 1990 riots. While prisoners still face problems in relation to access to legal aid, disciplinary procedures and procedural justice are now much improved, following the development of judicial review of disciplinary and complaints procedures in the 1970s and 1980s, as well as the impact of Article 6 jurisprudence from the Strasbourg Court, and the impact of the Woolf Report which reviewed the reasons for the 1990s riots (Woolf and Tumim 1991).

As well as campaigning for improved conditions, PROP organised prison strikes and demonstrations. The group was also interested in discussing the role of imprisonment per se. However, PROP received relatively support from other political groups, as when the latter did venture into debates on the criminal justice system, they were principally motivated by their own treatment by the police. So the emergence of PROP on the scene was a significant development. The investigations into the Angry Brigade and treatment of the Stoke Newington Eight had, in the 1970s, raised questions on the Left about the police's political role and concern over the targeting of left-wing activists and groups by the police, but there was far less interest in the treatment of ordinary prisoners. Although it is understandable that groups will focus on their particular members who are incarcerated, it is surprising that ordinary prisoners received relatively little attention, especially as these 'political prisoners' in some cases shared cells with ordinary prisoners. Of course, the prison population was much lower then, in the 1970s, less than half of the current level. But while the modern context and debates on the political implications of mass imprisonment were missing, there was also an abolitionist movement here and in the US. However, some political activists moved into community campaigns, such as claimants' unions, despite the disapproval of their contemporaries for engaging in reformist rather than radical activities. Generally the Left's publications in the 1970s were focused on the civil liberties of those apprehended by the police, rather than the plight of prisoners. While much invective was directed at the police, there was little discussion of prisons. Since the late 1960s, the criminal has been viewed through various tropes in radical criminologies, from the inner-city Robin Hood, romantically viewed as robbing the rich to help the poor, the victims of class injustice, while white-collar and corporate crime is ignored, to the exploiter of his community, in left realist criminologies, which recognise the impact of crime on working-class communities and see offenders' behaviour as undermining those communities.

In that period, the late 1960s and early 1970s, it was also quite hard for political groups to publish material highlighting poor conditions, as there were far fewer self-publishing opportunities than there are now, although some independent material did emerge, for example, Brian Stratton's *Who Guards the Guards?* which looked at conditions in Parkhurst before the riot there in 1969. Within criminology, Cohen and Taylor's *Psychological Survival*, published in 1972, examined the experience of long-term imprisonment using unstructured interviews and the ways prisoners negotiate and resist the constraints of imprisonment, while Mike Fitzgerald, who was also the press officer for PROP, discussed both the PROP campaigns and the wider implications of the prison system in his *Prisoners in Revolt* (Fitzgerald 1977). Also, in the late 1970s, some inmates wrongfully convicted of crime campaigned for their release from within prison and these cases came to be seen as politically significant, notably the Birmingham Six and Guildford Four convicted in 1975 and the Maguire Seven convicted in 1976, and the revelation of these miscarriages of justice and quashing of their convictions in 1989 and 1991, were instrumental in leading to new safeguards for all suspects and defendants. Political prisoners have also benefited from improvements in the criminal justice procedures, including police interrogation, for example, the advances in the Police and Criminal Evidence Act 1984 following the recommendations of the Royal Commission on Criminal Procedure in 1981, and changes in the rules governing criminal evidence following the reports of the Criminal Law Revision Committee in 1972 and the Royal Commission on Criminal Justice in 1993.

Anarchist groups have taken more interest in prison issues and the Anarchist Black Cross has supported political prisoners in a range of countries and published papers on prison conditions and has been interested in the politicisation of ordinary prisoners. Its magazine, the *Black Flag: Bulletin of the Anarchist Black Cross*, was first published in 1970.

As well as the development of the prisoners' union, the 1970s was also important for the rise of the prisoners' rights movement which reflected the increasing rec-ognition of the prisoner as a citizen, echoed by developments in the public law jurisprudence of the period. While formal prisoners' unions such as PROP, may have had limited impact in changing prison conditions in the 1970s, there were also challenges to the prison administration through the courts and by direct action, both of which did lead to changes which have benefited all prisoners. For example, a Republican prisoner, Patrick Fell, successfully challenged the treatment of prisoners in the context of disciplinary proceedings, in the Strasbourg Court, using Articles 6 and 8, resulting in improvements to prisoners' rights in disciplinary procedures.[1]

A further key right within the spectrum of prisoners' rights is the right to freedom of association. Prisoners enjoy this right under Article 11(1) of the European Convention which states that 'Everyone has the right to freedom of peaceful assembly and to freedom of association with others, including the right to form and to join trade unions for the protection of his interests.' But this is a qualified right, so Article 11(2) provides that 'No restrictions shall be placed in the exercise of these rights other than such as are prescribed by law and are necessary in a democratic society in the interests of national security or public safety, for the prevention of disorder or crime, or the protection of health or morals or for the protection of the rights and freedom of others…'. The right is also protected by the European Prison Rules: 'Prisoners shall be allowed to associate with each other during exercise and in order to take part in recreational activities (EPR 27.7). These Rules do not explicitly refer to the right to join trades unions or political organisations, although they do stipulate that: 'Prison authorities shall ensure that prisoners are able to participate in elections, referenda and in other aspects of public life, in so far as their right to do so is not restricted by national law' (24.11).

The right to form associations under Article 11 has been used principally in relation to trades unions, but could also cover political parties and professional associations and has been invoked in relation to political demonstrations. For example, states, have a positive duty to ensure that lawful demonstrations may proceed without violence. It also covers the negative right not to join an association. However, it does not protect the right to strike.

There is relatively little Article 11 jurisprudence in relation to prisoners' contact with other prisoners. The European Commission of Human Rights did address the issue in *McFeeley, Nugent, Huntley v UK* (1981) 3 EHRR 1961, where the prisoners had complained that their separation from other prisoners breached Article 11. The Commission noted that Article 11 concerns the right to form or be affiliated with a group or organisation pursuing particular aims, including the right to form or join a trade union, but not the right to join other prisoners: 'It does not concern the right of prisoners to share the company of other prisoners or to "associate" with other prisoners in this sense' (at para 114). The fact that the prisoners had been subject to cellular confinement at certain times reflected their decision not to wear prison uniforms and to go 'on the blanket' and their decision not to undertake prison work as part of their political protest. McFeeley had been removed from association because he had been trying to establish himself as a leader of the other prisoners and his removal had been approved by the Board of Visitors, under Prison Rule 24, as he was considered a threat to good order and discipline. Surveillance of the prisoners and searches and restrictions on family visits, because of the refusal to wear clothes, were deemed to fall within Article 8(2).

The prisoners at the Maze prison had protested at changes in the regime which meant loss of association with others in the prison, as well as close body searches. The complainants had also challenged their treatment under Articles 3 and 8, on a range of issues, including slopping out and having to use chamber pots within the view of prison officers and limits on visits, and interference with correspondence.[2] But the Commission found that the treatment did not reach the level of severity required for inhuman and degrading treatment. They also noted that some of the conditions were a result of the prisoners' own decisions not to wear clothes as part of their protest at the state's refusal to recognise them as political prisoners. For example, prisoners had elected to slop out without clothes as part of their protest. Close body searches, in the view of the Commission, were also reasonable and necessary.

The right to association under Article 11 is not breached in relation to segregation or separation of prisoners for reasons of good order and discipline. Dickson (2010) refers to a Northern Ireland case, *Re Conlon's Application* [2002] NIJB 35, where Conlon argued unsuccessfully that restrictions on his association with others breached Article 11, but the Court found it fell within the restrictions in Article 11(2). Provided there is objective justification, the separation of extremist prisoners in UK prisons, as currently being introduced, is also likely to fall within Article 11(2).

Freedom of assembly is linked to freedom of political expression. Domestic law on the freedom of assembly treated it as a residual right, so the individual was free to exercise the right, unless the law prevented him from doing so and it could be restricted on public order grounds. There are also statutory rights of workers to belong, or to choose not to belong, to trade unions. Public processions can be prohibited and conditions can be imposed on public assemblies under the Public Order Act 1986 (ss 13 and 14). Organisations may be proscribed under the Terrorism Act 2000, if they are deemed to be involved in terrorism and it is proportionate to do so. Even where the right to freedom of assembly is strongly defended, for example, in the US, where there is a constitutional right protected by the First Amendment to the Bill of Rights which states that 'Congress shall make no law… abridging freedom of speech, or of the press, or the right of the people peaceably to assemble, and to petition the government for a redress of grievances', the right may still be balanced against public order interests, as in the *Skokie* case.[3]

John Hirst, a former prisoner and campaigner for prisoners' rights did set up an Association of Prisoners with Ben Gunn, with a webpage, Prisoners Voice, and a blog. Hirst has also contributed to *insidetime* the national newspaper for prisoners and detainees, which is published monthly and delivered free to all prisons, special hospitals and to many secure units and hostels.[4] It began in 1990 and the paper now has an estimated readership of 50,000 per issue. The organisation also publishes information on all aspects of prison life on its website, to which prisoners contribute regular updates. Any profits from the paper are given to the New Bridge Foundation which organises befriending services for prisoners.

However, with the current larger prison population and fragmenting effects of drug use and the IEP scheme, it may be even harder to organise prisoners into unions, so campaigns in the UK have in recent years focused on specific issues, such as books for prisoners and votes for prisoners.

Prisoners' unions have also emerged in other European states. In the Netherlands, the Union for Lawbreakers or *Bond voor Wetsovertreders* (BWO), has also been actively campaigning for prisoners' rights. It began in 1972 and has campaigned on a number of issues, including in 2013, the display of suspected shoplifters being posted on the Internet[5] and has been supported by forty-five publicly financed lawyers. Rita Verdonk, who later became the Minister for Integration and Immigration, was active in the BWO when a student, in the early 1980s.

In 2014 a group of prisoners at Tegel prison in Berlin formed a trade union, the *Gefangenen-Gewerkschaft Bundesweite Organisation* (GGBO), specifically to campaign for freedom of association, as well as a minimum wage for prisoners and for a pension scheme, without which, they argue, many elderly prisoners will be released into poverty.[6] The prisoners were working in prison workshops and the prison kitchen, but were excluded from the German national minimum wage and from the state pension scheme. At that time they earned between 9 and 15 euros a day and the minimum wage was then 8.50 euros an hour. The group registered as an association without legal status. The group included Oliver Rast, who was then serving a sentence connected with his membership of the radical group, Militante Gruppe, which carried out arson attacks on government buildings, but he has since been released. By the end of 2015, the organisation had expanded to over 800 members in forty German prisons. It also formed a section in Austria and has made contact with unions outside the prison.[7] There was a hunger strike at Butzbach Prison in December 2015, in support of the GBBO's demands.

The right of prisoners to form a union was also considered by the United States Supreme Court in 1976, in *Jones v North Carolina Prisoners' Labor Union* 433 US 119 (1977). Union meetings were prohibited by the Department of Corrections and union members were not allowed to solicit others to join. When prisoners challenged this, the Court ruled that prisoners did not have a right under the First Amendment to join the union. One reason the court took this view was that it thought that doing so would make prison riots more likely. Yet this has not been validated by subsequent experience. In none of the major riots in the US in the 1970s and 1980s studied by Useem and Kimball (1991) were prisoners' unions or rights groups' actions a contributor to or catalyst for the riot. On the contrary, in one case, they tried to stop the riot and at Attica and Michigan, the prisoners most willing to engage in negotiations were those least likely to harm hostages. Associations or unions may also be beneficial in building mutual trust between prisoners as conflict between prisoners is a major source of violence within prisons. Prisoners' unions may therefore contribute to the stability of prisons rather than undermine it.[8] Prisoners' labour unions have been set up in Washington State and Missouri to fight for better working conditions but have no official recognition. The Prisoners Rights Union, active in California during the 1970s, campaigned for prisoners' rights on a range of issues including indeterminate sentencing, civil rights and the right to organise, and published its magazine *The Outlaw* from 1971 until 1979.[9] It also engaged in litigation to improve prison conditions.

A further dimension of resistance is industrial action. As well as riots, prisoners may engage in strikes to protest against their conditions and low rates of pay. A prison strike in the US in September 2016 was organised by prisoners and activists from the Industrial Workers of the World (IWW) or 'Wobblies', who have well-established links with prisoners as workers, to coincide with the forty-fifth anniversary of the 1971 Attica riot. There are conflicting accounts of the number of participants, but the indications are that it attracted support from 20,000 prisoners from eleven states, including Florida, South Carolina and Texas.

The prisoners were protesting against their low pay and poor working conditions and because they were being used to provide cheap goods for private companies. But strikes have been conducted over a long period since the late 1940s in the US. The Attica riot in 1971 was preceded by a strike in the prison's metal shop. There was also a strike in Georgia in 2010, when prisoners claimed that they had not been paid for their work. The 2016 strikes were coordinated outside by the IWW who set up an Incarcerated Workers' Organizing Committee. This Committee acted as a liaison between workers on the outside and prisoners trying to organise and unionise inside prison, to support prisoners challenging their work conditions and low wages. The organisation is also concerned with the issues of patriarchy, racism and challenging the criminalisation of the working class. It has stressed the importance of mutual aid and solidarity between the working class and prisoners, or as they describe it, an alliance between wage slaves and cage slaves. Prisoners can become full members of the IWW within prison but are not required to pay subscriptions and IWW members outside provide support to prisoners and ex-prisoners.

In addition to industrial strikes, there have also been hunger strikes at Guantánamo Bay in 2013, in 2014 in Arizona and other states, and in 2015 at immigration detention centres in Washington State. In the UK there have also been hunger strikes at Yarl's Wood Immigration Removal Centre in 2015, where the strikers demanded the release of the widow of a man who had died there, as well as at Harmondsworth IRC in 2015 over poor conditions and at Brook House IRC in 2016. In the past, hunger strikes were also used by the suffragettes as part of their fight for women's voting rights and by prisoners, including Bobby Sands, during the Northern Ireland conflict, as part of their struggle for recognition as political prisoners (see Chapter 6). In the conflict there were a range of protests, including no-wash protests as well as hunger strikes, in which the body itself became a weapon in the struggle and a means of physical resistance.

Prison riots in the UK

Another and more common extreme response to conditions of imprisonment, of course, is the prison riot, which has a long history in the UK and overseas. The most notorious UK riot was at Strangeways in 1990, but other states have experienced large-scale riots. Fifty-two prisoners were killed at Topo Chico prison in Monterrey, Mexico in 2016, in clashes between drug cartels there. In Brazil in January 2017, over fifty-six were killed and six prisoners were decapitated at Anisio Jobim Prison Complex near Manaus in battles between rival drug gangs.

The definition of a riot is not fixed, but a minimal definition is when a large number of prisoners take control over a large enough area of the prison, for a significant amount of time. What some might see as a riot, may be seen by the prison administration or by governments, as merely an incident of disorder. The classification of an event as an incident of disorder, rather than a riot, may reflect the desire of managers to downplay riots or mutinies. Riots may begin with an explosive incident, but then the prisoners involved become more organised and the riot spreads, with more joining and confronting those in authority, until the riot is terminated. This is usually followed by an inquiry into its causes.

The motivation of rioters may vary: for some prisoners rioting may relieve the boredom of prison life and offer excitement; alternatively, it may be seen as a means to challenge intolerable conditions. For other prisoners, a riot may be an opportunity to settle old scores which is why the eruption of riots may be more feared by prisoners than the prison authorities. Some prisoners may reluctantly join the riot because they are afraid of recrimination by other prisoners if they do not do so, or anxious that they may be targeted by rival groups in the prison.

In the UK there have been relatively few riots, given the size of the population, the prevalence of violence and the persistence of problems of overcrowding and understaffing. Given that a prison population will by definition contain offenders who are already undeterred by a risk of punishment and will include many individuals with violent histories and that offenders are then herded together, suffer deprivations and may be treated with a lack of respect, it may be surprising that riots do not occur more frequently. However, as we shall see, prisoners' may respond to the deprivations of prison life in different ways and internalise their violent emotions by self-harming, or seek solace in drugs. Moreover, there are strong disincentives to riot when it may result in additional days added to their sentences. A prisoner convicted of prison mutiny may also be transferred to a less desirable prison in terms of location and facilities. Although Foucault famously observed that 'where there is power there is resistance', this does not necessarily always follow in the context of imprisonment (Foucault 1990: 95).

Often riots may occur in response to a change in regime conditions, or the failure to deal with complaints or grievances. But other factors include weak organisation and administration, poor management, availability and accessibility of drugs, weapons or alcohol, high staff turnover and under-staffing, which will usually mean prisoners spend more time in their cells, and, in some cases, overcrowding. Prior tensions and a history of violence between prisoners as individuals, or as members of gangs or groups, have also been seen as contributory elements in some cases.

Although England and Wales experienced a year of prison riots in 1990, there have been incidents before and since, albeit not on the same scale as the 1990 riots. The phenomenon of the prison riot received little attention from criminologists until the 1990s. However, while order has been contained for the most part, riots erupted again in 2016 and 2017, in the context of cuts in prison budgets.

In the 1930s there was a riot at Dartmoor Prison in 1932, at a time when the prison was very sparsely populated and the total prison population for England and Wales was much lower than it is now. At the time of the incident, 442 prisoners were held in the prison which had a capacity of 935 cells, so clearly overcrowding was not a factor. Although the incident was brief, lasting only one and a half hours, more than 150 prisoners took over the prison, inflicting physical damage on it, as well as lighting fires and looting food and cigarettes. Brown (2007) reviewed the available documentary evidence and argues that the riot arose because of grievances, as a new governor had made changes with the effect of limiting visits and educational classes and restricting working hours because of falling staff numbers. So the regime had deteriorated as a result of these measures. At the subsequent trial of the rioters, prisoners complained about staff brutality, poor food and the ineffectiveness of the complaints system. Prior to the riot, there were concerns over the mistreatment of a vulnerable prisoner, but the officers had been exonerated. While there were specific grievances, prisoners in the act of rioting also experienced elation and excitement, as well as rage and frustration. In the aftermath of the riot, prisoners who did not take part, or who had helped the officers, were subject to reprisals by other inmates. The media coverage also condemned the prisoners who included members of a well-known criminal gang. Brown (2007) could see no evidence of what Carrabine (2005) has described as fatalism in prisons, when the power order in prison in seen as immutable, but rather found prisoners were ready to challenge the regime.

After World War II, riots occurred sporadically. There were riots at Parkhurst in 1969 and in the 1970s at Gartree, Hull, Brixton, Albany and Parkhurst (King and Elliott 1977). There were also riots in Northern Ireland in the 1970s when prisoners at the Maze Prison in October 1974 set fire to part of the prison. This was followed by riots outside in the city of Belfast. In 1978 there was a riot at Gartree and in 1979 at Wormwood Scrubs, at Albany in 1983, at Haverigg in 1988 and at Risley again in 1989. In 1987 there were riots in Scotland at Peterhead Prison, where the riot lasted five days until the SAS were sent in, and at Barlinnie prison.[10] These riots affected the physical infrastructure of the prison, but also meant an increase in security and disciplinary measures because of fears inmates would escape.

The most spectacular riot was in 1990 at Strangeways, where prisoners took over the prison and the riot lasted from 1 to 25 April, resulting in damage to property as well as physical assaults and injuries and a fatality. The prison was damaged and riots spread to five other prisons. Sex offenders were targeted by the rioters during the riot. These riots were heavily scrutinised, with various explanations and theories including overcrowding, poor physical conditions, poor relations with staff, industrial action by staff which affected the quality of regimes, dispersal policies, the presence of volatile and disruptive prisoners, excessive security and insufficient procedural justice. However, riots also occurred in less crowded and more modern prisons. Certainly in the 1980s, conditions were poorer than now, with no national operating standards and the European Prison Rules were not adopted until 1987. The European Committee for the Prevention of Torture (CPT) had also criticised conditions in three prisons, Brixton, Leeds and Wandsworth, as inhuman and degrading (CPT 1991). In 1986 there was an overtime ban by prison officers which meant that prisoners spent more time in their cells which caused resentment and contributed to the generally volatile atmosphere in prisons.

A major inquiry into the riots was conducted by Lord Woolf and Lord Justice Tumim. They interviewed prisoners and officers, and the findings and recommendations of the Woolf Report published 1991 did lead to many changes in prison regimes (Woolf and Tumim 1991). The Woolf Report noted the poor relations between the prison staff and the prison department, the new working conditions and loss of overtime and the understaffing of prisons with staff overworked and dissatisfied. Some prisoners had been transferred to Strangeways, from other prisons, because they were disruptive. There had also been an increase in numbers at the prison. Prisoners were spending more time in their cells because of the additional demands on staff. There had also been incidents before the main riot which showed tensions were high, although staff seemed unprepared for the riot which eventually erupted.

The Woolf Inquiry acknowledged the poor physical conditions prevailing the time, but saw the key issue as the sense of injustice and unfairness felt by prisoners. Because incidents of disorder have been found in modern and Victorian prisons, overcrowded and uncrowded prisons, holding different types of prisoners, it is hard to attribute the riots to one particular cause. But for the Woolf Report the perception of unfairness was a key issue.

At that time, the Boards of Visitors dealt with disciplinary matters and could impose punishments including extra days, but they were not seen by prisoners as independent. Prisoners felt that their complaints were not dealt with fairly and there were also resentments over transfers and segregation.[11] Woolf therefore recommended fair, independent and speedy grievance and disciplinary procedures, as well as improvements in physical conditions, the provision of constructive and purposeful activities, improvements in home leave and visits and the introduction of national operating standards.

The Report concluded that the riots had been the result of an imbalance between security, justice and control and argued that the Prison Service needed to find the right balance between these elements, in order to achieve stability (Woolf and Tumim 1991 para 1.148). It had to address security issues, the prevention of escapes, and to improve control, to prevent prisoners from causing disturbances, but it also needed to ensure justice, by which it meant treating prisoners fairly and with humanity (para 1.149). Providing justice, it argued, will enhance security and control. Justice includes giving prisoners reasons for decisions which affect them and better complaints and disciplinary procedures. The Report also recommended establishing a Prisons Ombudsman.

Following the Report, many of these recommendations were implemented. The Boards of Visitors, now re-named Independent Monitoring Boards, lost their adjudicative function in 1992, with further improvements in procedural justice resulting from the impact of successful challenges in the Strasbourg Court. National operating standards were introduced in 1994, but are not legally enforceable. The first Prisons and Probation Ombudsman was appointed in 1994. The Ombudsman's Reports have highlighted the key problems prisoners experience and made recommendations for improvement which have also had an impact. However, the recommendation to use smaller community prisons so prisoners can stay near their homes has not been implemented. Rather, the move in recent years has been towards larger and fewer prisons. Nor was the recommendation of a statutory limit on overcrowding implemented.

The offence of prison mutiny is prohibited by the Prison Security Act 1992 which was enacted following the riots. Section 1 provides that:

(1) Any prisoner who takes part in a prison mutiny shall be guilty of an offence and liable, on conviction on indictment, to imprisonment for a term not exceeding ten years or to a fine or to both.

(2) For the purposes of this section there is a prison mutiny where two or more prisoners, while on the premises of any prison, engage in conduct which is intended to further a common purpose of overthrowing lawful authority in that prison.

(3) For the purposes of this section the intentions and common purpose of prisoners may be inferred from the form and circumstances of their conduct and it shall be immaterial that conduct falling within subsection (2) above takes a different form in the case of different prisoners.

(4) Where there is a prison mutiny, a prisoner who has or is given a reasonable opportunity of submitting to lawful authority and fails, without reasonable excuse, to do so shall be regarded for the purposes of this section as taking part in the mutiny.

The Act also increased penalties for offences relating to the escape of a prisoner.

But incidents of disorder have persisted in recent years, albeit on a lesser scale than the Strangeways riot. There was disorder at Portland Young Offenders Institution in 2000, riots at Lincoln in 2002, at Hindley in 2005, at Haverigg and Stoke Heath YOI in 2006, at Ashwell in 2009 and at Cookham Wood and Moorland in 2010. At Moorland the disorder lasted three days. It began in the Young Offenders wing, but then spread to the adult wing, resulting in injuries and assaults on officers and other prisoners and damage to the prison. In 2011 there were riots at Littlehey Young Offenders Institution and at Ford Open Prison, where prisoners also set fire to the prison.

In 2013 in the 'mackerel mutiny' at HMP High Down in Surrey, prisoners barricaded themselves in their cells and damaged them, in protest at cuts in food and other changes, following the introduction of a new regime. In a demand note they complained that they were not given enough exercise or food, or time in the gym and were 'banged up like kippers'. They agreed to come out if they were given mackerel and dumplings. In November 2013, a group of prisoners took over the wing at Maidstone, a Category C prison, for four hours and destroyed it, following changes in the prison regime which meant that they spent more time in their cells. A Tornado riot squad was used to restore order.

There was also a serious incident of disorder at HMP Oakwood, which one officer described as a riot, in January 2014. This was a new prison run by G4S, which housed 1,600 prisoners, and which had been much lauded as a reform prison. A group of prisoners barricaded themselves into part of Cedar Wing and booby-trapped it. The incident followed a prisoner being locked in his cell for threatening a member of staff. Twenty prisoners were involved and the incident lasted for nine hours before a Tornado riot squad regained control of the wing. Six prisoners were convicted of violent disorder. There had been a history of easy access to drugs by prisoners, as well as issues over staffing levels. In the past few years concerns over safety and disorder in prisons have intensified. The Report of the Prison Inspectorate in 2014 also noted that there had been more incidents of prisoners going onto the netting, in the hope that they would be placed on seg-regation and then shipped out to prisons with better conditions or nearer home (HMCIP 2014: 10). Concerns have also been raised over an increase in assaults by the Prison Inspectorate and others. On 27 January 2016, the House of Commons held a debate on prisons and probation. Andy Slaughter MP reported that:

> The prison riot squad was called out 343 times last year – once a day on average – compared with 223 times the year before and 118 times in 2010. Alcohol finds have nearly trebled since 2010. From mobile phones to drugs and legal highs, the list of what people can smuggle into prison at the moment is elastic. According to one prisoner at HMP Oakwood, a prison that the previous Lord Chancellor called 'an excellent model for the future' – [*Official Report*, 5 February 2013; Vol. 558, c. 114.] it was easier to get drugs than soap… Earlier this month, seven officers reported suffering ill effects from inadvertently inhaling legal highs.[12]

In June 2016 there were incidents at Erlestoke Prison in Devizes while an inspection of the immigration detention estate also gave cause for great concern, highlighting problems at Yarl's Wood Immigration Removal Centre (HMCIP 2016: 10). The atmosphere was also tense at Morton Hall IRC in 2017 where there was anti-social behaviour and violence (HMCIP 2017: 10).

There was also disorder at HMP Lewes at the end of October 2016, where there was a six-hour disturbance, in which rioting prisoners damaged cells and offices. There were only four staff on the wing, and they were obliged to retreat. At Lewes, as in many other prisons, there were problems with under-staffing and with prisoners gaining access to drugs. This was followed in November 2016, by a riot at HMP Bedford, where 230 prisoners got out of their cells, stole keys, broke into medicine stores and started fires. Two prisoners were hurt, but no staff were harmed. Eventually the riot was brought under control, but it took six hours and fifty prisoners were transferred from the prison after the riot. The Prison Inspectorate had previously noted easy access to drugs at HMP Bedford, but also that prisoners had spent too much time locked up.

There were also problems in 2016 at HMP Northumberland, a Category C private prison run by Sodexo since December 2013. A reporter for *Panorama* working undercover as a prison officer found easy access to drugs and a lack of security, with some prisoners keeping cutting tools in their cells.[13] Officers reported being unable to manage the prison properly as their numbers were so low, due to cuts in staffing, and that they felt threatened by prisoners. There had previously been problems there, in March 2014, when fifty prisoners took over a wing and refused to go back to their cells; their demands included longer working hours and more time out of their cells, which had been reduced because of staff cuts.

The most serious riot in 2016, was at HMP Birmingham at Winson Green, which was also the worst riot since Strangeways in 1990. The prison experienced twelve hours of rioting, with estimates of 400 to 600 prisoners involved in the melee, in which a prisoner was assaulted. The riot started in two wings, but then spread to another two wings. An officer was attacked and his keys were stolen, when he was trying to lock a prisoner in his cell. Prisoners were then able to get into the administration office. Prisoners contacted the BBC on mobile phones during the riot and blamed poor conditions, including poor food and health care, and that too much time was spent in cells because there were insufficient staff. The riot was also used to settle drug scores, and prisoners in the sex offenders wing were very scared of reprisals. Specialist Tornado units and dog units were sent in to restore order. Following the riot, 240 prisoners were transferred, fifteen of whom went to Hull, where it was feared that they would incite a riot there. Six prisoners were later convicted of prison mutiny. There had already been tensions at Hull with assaults and the destruction of CCTV cameras, staff cuts and prisoners on lockdown. The MP for Hull in December 2016 had reported that the prison was on the brink of a riot.

There was also concern over possible copycat riots elsewhere in the prison estate. On 23 December 2016, sixty prisoners took over a wing of Swaledale, a Category B prison. Tornado teams were used to restore order. The prison had experienced high levels of violence and there were other tensions over problems with family visits which were threatened by staff shortages.

Tensions persisted at prisons in 2017. In the Mount, a Category C men's prison in Hertfordshire, there were two consecutive days of rioting in the summer of 2017 when prisoners took over part of the prison. A Tornado team restored order on both days. There had been increasing violence at the prison in the period preceding the riots and staff shortages had led to more time spent locked up. There were also problems at HMP Erlestoke, another Category C men's prison in August 2017. A smoking ban had resulted in an increase in tobacco smuggling, but there had also been increases in the use of spice and in levels of violence before the disorder. There was also disorder at HMP Haverigg and Featherstone where smoking bans had been introduced. There was a further incident at Birmingham in September 2017, when prisoners refused to leave their cells and flooded them. Order was restored within seven hours and twenty-eight prisoners were transferred. There was also a riot at Long Lartin High Security prison in October 2017.

The contexts of the riots in recent years have demonstrated a number of common features, including access to drugs, understaffing and a loss of authority by staff as fewer staff control greater numbers and too much time is spent in the cells. In some cases overcrowding has exacerbated the problems of stretching staff resources. Grievances have included problems of organising family visits, particularly if prisoners are allocated a prison far from home, and a lack of education and training places.

Despite the relative peace of the first part of 2017, the Prison Officers Association warned that there will be more violence unless the numbers are increased. The scale of the problem can be seen from the figures. There were 25,000 prison staff in 2010, but by 2016 this had fallen to 18,000 and the decline did correlate with the increase in riots. There is also a problem of retaining existing staff in the current turbulent context. Although it is illegal for prison officers to strike, officers did withhold labour for certain tasks for twenty-four hours in 2017, in protest over the lack of safety in prisons, but an injunction was granted forbidding future action. There has been an increase in staff recruitment since then, although staff numbers have not reached 2010 levels. The government announced in 2017 that it would lift the 1 per cent public sector pay cap for prison officers. Despite the substantial changes introduced after the 1990 riots, in a lecture reflecting on progress in the twenty-five years since Strangeways, Lord Woolf (2015) expressed his concern over the current state of the prisons, exacerbated by staff shortages, high incarceration rates and the move towards larger prisons with prisoners held further from home.

Reports of the Prison Inspectorate and the Prisons and Probations Ombudsman have also highlighted the increasing levels of violence in prisons in England and Wales, as well as the rising suicide rates and rates of self-harm, which can be seen as individual manifestations of distress. The Prison Inspectorate has noted that prisons in England and Wales 'have become unacceptably violent and dangerous places' and recorded an increase in self-harm and suicide on the previous year (HMCIP 2016). In the calendar year 2015, there was an increase of 27 per cent in self-inflicted deaths, 25 per cent in incidents of self-harm and 27 per cent in assaults compared with the previous calendar year (ibid: 8). Furthermore, the incidence of serious assaults rose by 31 per cent (ibid). The Report found violence increasing in almost every men's prison on which it reported. It notes that '(I)t is clear that a large part of this violence is linked to the harm caused by new psychoactive substances (NPS) which are having a dramatic and destabilising effect in many of our prisons' (ibid: 8). These drugs, often referred to as Spice or Black Mamba, contain synthetic cannabinoids and may lead to mental health problems, including psychosis and paranoia, while prisoners who incur drug debts may be subject to violence and bullying from dealers and, in some cases, may self-segregate to avoid the violence resulting from their use. Serious violence continued to increase in 2016 with a total of 26,002 assaults, of which 3,519 were serious. This constituted a 27 per cent increase on the previous year (HMCIP 2017: 22). There was also a 38 per cent increase in assaults on staff, with 6,844 incidents in 2016, of which 789 were serious (ibid). There were 103 suicides in 2016–17, a 10 per cent increase on 2015–16, and 40,161 recorded instances of self-harm in 2016, compared with 32,313 in 2015, a 24 per cent increase (ibid: 20).

Similar patterns were identified in the report of the Prisons and Probation Ombudsman. Self-inflicted deaths in prison increased by 34 per cent in 2015–16 compared to the previous year (PPO 2016: 7). The Ombudsman noted that this rise in suicides and increases in violence and disorder 'are evidence of the urgent need to improve safety and fairness in prison' (ibid.). There were six homicides in prison in 2015–16, which was the highest number since the Ombudsman began investigating deaths in custody. In 2016–17 self-inflicted deaths increased by 11 per cent and four apparent homicides were investigated (PPO 2017: 17). The impact of new psychoactive substances was also noted: 'our investigations suggest that the use of NPS, like other drugs, can be closely associated with organised crime, debt, bullying and violence, with attendant risks to vulnerable prisoners, of mental ill-health, suicide and self-harm' (PPO 2017: 34).

The current context of staff problems, combined with high imprisonment rates – the highest in Western Europe – and levels of overcrowding as well as the new drug problems, create a volatile atmosphere in prisons. Examples are given of prisoners climbing onto roofs or netting to obtain a transfer because they did not feel safe in their current prison. Despair at ever being released can increase the risk of suicide and self-harm for some prisoners serving indeterminate sentences. For example, James Ward, who self-harmed in prison, was an IPP prisoner sentenced for a minimum of ten months for arson in 2006, but his release was not approved by the Parole Board until 2017.

The Ombudsman received 5,010 complaints from prisoners in 2016–17, investigated 2,568 cases and found in favour of the complainant in 38 per cent of those cases (PPO 2017). Twenty-nine per cent of completed investigations concerned complaints from high security prisoners, although they comprised only 7 per cent of the prison population. However, the Ombudsman was less likely to find in favour of the complainant in such cases, in 32 per cent of cases compared to 41 per cent in other men's prisons (ibid: 19). The Ombudsman receives a large number of complaints, mostly from adult male prisoners, covering a range of issues from minor matters, to allegations of staff misbehaviour. But he makes the point that many of them could have been resolved at the prison without needing referral to the Ombudsman (ibid: 12). A clear and effective complaints procedure with proper management of complaints in prison is essential to deal with grievances.

The Prison Inspectorate has reported that prisoners are still spending too long in their cells with not enough purposeful activities. There may be insufficient activity places, or those places may not be filled because attendance is erratic, or because of staff shortages which affect the movement of prisoners around the prison. The expectation is that prisoners should be unlocked for ten hours per day, but HMCIP found in their survey of adult male prisoners that only 14 per cent of prisoners said this was the case (HMCIP 2017: 38).

The House of Commons Justice Committee in its Report, *Prison Safety*, also highlighted the continuing problems of insecurity in prisons (House of Commons Justice Committee 2016). It referred to a letter from the Chair of the Prison Officers' Association, which reported that the use of specialist squads to deal with incidents including hostage-taking and concerted indiscipline, had reached unprecedented levels. It also highlighted the increases in self-harm and self-inflicted deaths, recorded in the Ministry of Justice's Safety in Custody statistics, as well as increases in incidents of disorder. An officer was attacked by a prisoner she was escorting to court in 2015 and had died from her injuries. Attacks on staff have increased, but so have the number of serious incidents of disorder, including fire incidents and incidents at height, when prisoners go onto the netting on prison wings. The Report concludes that the problems are linked to understaffing, which undermines dynamic security. While more officers are now being recruited, it is not sufficient to meet the need. Staff resources are important if staff shortages mean more time locked up or popular activities are curtailed. If understaffing persists in the context of overcrowding, rising levels of assaults and violence and rising drug use, then the prospect of future riots will increase.

These issues were further considered in the Conservative Government's White Paper *Prison Safety and Reform*, published in 2016 which committed the government to spending more on new prisons, recruiting another 2,100 staff which, in addition to the 400 previously announced, would increase numbers by 2,500 by the end of 2018 (Ministry of Justice 2016a). Further ameliorative measures proposed included new drug tests for psychoactive substances and the use of body cameras by staff, the introduction of no-fly zones over prisons to prevent the delivery of drugs and mobile phones by drones. There have already been several convictions in relation to smuggling of such items into prisons by unmanned aerial vehicles (UAVs).

Some of these changes have been effected. Governors are being given more autonomy in relation to Release on Temporary Licence (ROTL) and regarding education budgets. In addition, the White Paper referred to boosting staffing through a new graduate recruitment scheme which is now in operation[14] and by recruiting staff from the armed forces through a 'Troops to Officers' scheme. New performance measures for individual prisons are also being introduced. Body worn cameras have been piloted in prisons and act as a deterrent to disruptive prisoners and may assist the implementation of sanctions and are now being rolled out across the prison estate.[15]

While some of the problems of staffing were addressed by the White Paper, the envisaged expanded staff levels remain below 2010 levels and the problem of staff retention was not addressed. The Psychoactive Substances Act 2017 creates a new offence of supplying psychoactive drugs and it is aggravated if it is committed in a custodial institution (ss 5 and 6). Testing for spice has been included in mandatory drug testing since late September 2017. NOMS has also been replaced by HM

Prisons and Probation Service in April 2017 and it is intended that there will be a greater focus on rehabilitation.

Riots have received more attention since 1990, but even before then commentators were attributing riots to a number of causes including deprivation and the impact of disruptive prisoners and changes in perceptions of legitimacy following regime changes. For Woolf, the key to prison stability was legitimacy and a similar approach is taken by Useem and Kimball (1991) who also combine deprivation and disorganisation approaches. Since the Report was published, security and control have been given considerable attention while justice has been addressed primarily through the expansion of prisoners' rights jurisprudence but where they conflict, security is usually given primacy by the courts.

Whether prisoners' grievances erupt in political or violent protest may depend on a number of factors, including the local conditions and the wider environment. Tensions and conflicts in prison may be expressed in fights, conflicts and in interpersonal rather than political manifestations, or tensions may be directed inward towards self-harm and suicide, or prisoners may retreat into drug or alcohol use. Others may get involved in political campaigns, such as voting rights or books for prisoners campaigns. But even if prisoners do not resist, this does not necessarily mean they are satisfied. Although one might expect riots to occur more frequently in high security prisons which hold more violent and dangerous prisoners, in fact, as we have seen, disorder may be found in a range of prisons from category D open prisons, such as Ford, in category C prisons, for example Northumberland, and category B prisons such as Bedford, as well as high security prisons. For example there were incidents at Gartree and Parkhurst, when they held category A prisoners and more recently at Long Lartin. It is true that Category A prisoners held in the high security estate are by definition more resourceful than other prisoners and if serving longer sentences may be more frustrated by their conditions and have more to gain from any improvements in conditions. But they are usually held in less crowded and better conditions than prisoners serving shorter sentences in local prisons. They will also have the time and, in some cases, the skills and resources to negotiate change in more peaceful ways, for example, through legal challenges which will give a greater return on the investment of their time, than would be possible for shorter sentenced prisoners. Most of the prisoners' rights litigation has been initiated by those serving longer sentences.

However, prisoners' experiences and opportunities in prison are increasingly individualised which will have implications for organised or collective resistance. There are strong incentives to comply within the Incentives and Earned Privileges Scheme (IEP) and in the context of achieving favourable parole decisions. The IEP Scheme was set up in 1995 with three levels: entry, standard and enhanced and is a framework for earning privileges through good behaviour. Further restrictions on privileges were introduced in 2013, with a new entry level for prisoners in their first two weeks of their sentence.

Prisoners have to demonstrate that they are committed to change through the IEP scheme, on Offending Behaviour Programmes and at Parole Hearings.

The opportunities for ROTL and other privileges will depend on their behaviour so there are powerful disincentives to vigorous resistance to prison regimes. Compliance may be achieved through the sanctions and rewards of the IEP scheme. Rehabilitation is also proved by individual responses, rather than collective ones. But while the IEP scheme may be an effective control mechanism, it can also generate frustration if prisoners are held too long at a lower level. If privileges are withdrawn and prisoners are downgraded on the scheme, this can itself generate resistance and undermine compliance and commitment. The Prison Inspectorate found that 42 per of prisoners in their survey thought that they had been treated unfairly under the IEP scheme (HMCIP 2017: 25). So compliance cannot be taken for granted.

As well as the fragmentation of prisoners' resistance through the IEP scheme, prisoners are also subject to increased surveillance and control. Offenders are now more heavily scrutinised and managed than they would have been in the 1990s, for example, by mandatory drug testing and the increased sharing of information between prison establishments and other agencies. The focus now is less on coercion and more on dynamic security, so prison staff are more aware of issues and, as we shall see in Chapter 3, prisoners' forums may also provide a way of dealing with grievances at an earlier stage. Coercive practices and bullying by officers have been tempered by increasing controls over staff discretion, the impact of centralised policies and a greater focus on procedural justice, for example, an improved complaints procedure. Discontents may be negotiated by other means than active rebellion, through formal and informal complaints procedures as well as through legal challenges and rights claims. However, while a range of formal and informal procedures are available to address complaints and grievances, they may not resolve issues. Prisoners may not complain because of fear of repercussions, or lack confidence that the issue will be addressed properly. For example, prisoners experiencing racist comments may not complain because it happens so regularly, or because they do not think that they will be dealt with fairly (HM Inspector of Prisons 2005).

The substantial improvements after Woolf, including the work of the Prisons and Probation Ombudsman, as well as the Decency Agenda, and the impact of prisoners' rights litigation, have diminished the extreme pains of imprisonment and provided more avenues for expressing discontent. There has also been more micromanagement of officers as part of the managerialism shaping public institutions, as well as an increased focus on performance indicators and targets. As the culture of prison officers has changed with increased focus on decency and respect, there is less overt hostility from staff and less confrontation.

Prisoners are controlled and scrutinised through less physically coercive means such as CCTV and body worn cameras, but this also means that staff are surveyed as well, which may affect their behaviour. The use of electronic surveillance and control may also reduce opportunities for resistance. An extreme example here would be the supermax prisons in the US where prisoners are segregated and isolated, with no contact with other prisoners. Although prisoners may resist by using their bodily fluids as weapons, their room for manoeuvre is very limited. In this context, the prisoners' rights movement has been used as a way of negotiating and improving the most extreme conditions, so the plight of prisoners in the segregation unit was included in the Pelican Bay litigation.[16]

UK prisons and European prisons are generally seen as more humane than those in the US, both in terms of prison conditions and the extent of imprisonment. Since the 1990s, UK prisons have been less oppressive as the impact of managerialism and the decency agenda, as well as the impact of European human rights law and the European Prison Rules, have meant that conditions have come under greater and regular scrutiny (van Zyl Smit and Snacken 2009 and Easton 2011). In its latest report, for example, the CPT has highlighted its concern over the levels of violence in UK prisons (Council of Europe 2017).

Crewe (2009), in his study of Wellingborough prison, found no collective or organised resistance, which he attributes to the prevalence of the individualist outlook. However, he acknowledges that 'Prisoners can be galvanised into purposeful action by political convictions, particularly when these are reinforced and supported by a wider ideological community' (2009: 96). So an example here would be Republican prisoners in the Maze during the Troubles. But in Wellingborough, the individualism of the IEP scheme for the most part fragmented prisoners' solidarity. Prisoners were unwilling to risk losing their privileges by supporting others' protests, were aware of the offence of prison mutiny and knew that resistance would have adverse effects on their prospects of release and their conditions inside prison. Leisure time was spent watching TV and using play-stations, which prisoners themselves recognised were a means of calming and dividing prisoners. Prisoners usually ate in their cells even when they were able to eat outside their cells. He also attributes the weakening of prisoner solidarity to the use of hard drugs, as drug users were seen as unlikely allies as they were deemed untrustworthy. Moreover, there were new sources of status for male prisoners such as ownership of consumer goods, which was replacing more traditional masculinist sources of status such as violence and physical prowess.

However, he notes that a more authoritarian regime is more likely to lead to rebellion, and denial of home leave or access to courses could aggrieve prisoners. There may also be sources of identity such as ethnicity, or religion, which is a key source of identity for Muslim prisoners, who had the most collective outlook with a cohesive group identity and a strong shared interest in world politics and similar views on UK foreign policy. They were also more likely to challenge the prison administration than other prisoners. Crewe also found differences between black Africans and black Caribbeans, and between first and third-generation African Caribbeans prisoners, with older prisoners critical of the younger generation. There may also be pockets of minor acts of resistance. He gives examples from Wellingborough of prisoners moving furniture around, or Muslim prisoners praying together on prison landings, and prisoners sticking pornographic pictures on the walls. The prison closed in 2012, although there are now plans to build a new prison on the site.

Ugelvik examines how prisoners 'within the constraints of a prison wing, take liberties, construct free areas, find and explore secret means of escape, and creatively and productively put up resistance to, through and against the everyday routine forms of power in the prison' (2014:4). The prison he studied was a men's prison. He uses a Foucauldian-informed analysis to study the social field constituted by the prison wing of Oslo prison, Norway's largest prison. Prisoners responded to the pains and constraints of their incarceration in a variety of ways, including making a complaint and taking it 'all the way' to the highest level, refusing to give a urine sample for a drugs test, and using secret alternative food, such as covertly making filter coffee, or frying eggs in their cells. As he says 'prisoners make themselves into free men through the various covert practices of illegal or semi-legal alternative food preparation that goes on behind closed cell doors' (ibid: 13–14). Prisoners also transformed their cells into a substitute home with pictures and drawings and invited other prisoners in as guests to share illicit food. His study is an analysis of 'doing freedom' through acts of resistance which may be far from the confrontations of riots and strikes, but still constitute a way of negotiating the power of the prison in their everyday lives. Even the use of drugs and alcohol which might be seen by observers as a form of retreatism, may be seen by prisoners as a way of challenging the power of the prison by providing a symbolic escape.

Resistance, says Ugelvik, can take a variety of forms, confrontation, or a refusal to participate or cooperate, all of which deny the legitimacy of power of the prison. By taking liberties within constraints, prisoners become temporarily free. As he says: 'The capable bricoleur is the master of his surroundings and transforms them to his benefit' (Ugelvik 2014: 240). These forms of micro resistance can function, he argues, as a safety valve, releasing tensions and make prison life more bearable. This may explain why there are so few riots and why prison order persists, despite the physical imbalance between prisoners and officers in terms of their numbers and criminal histories.

Prison riots in the US

Prisons riots in the US, like the UK, have a long history, with some examples of extreme violence. Obviously, there are differences in the structure and organisation of the penal system, current levels of incarceration and penal austerity. One significant difference is a more developed gang culture within prisons in the US which reflects and consolidates gang power outside prison. Gang leaders have been used by the prison regime to control other prisoners. Skarbek (2014) argues that prison gangs operate as informal governance institutions, offering prisoners a way of protecting themselves, to settle disputes and also regulate prisoners' behaviour and control illicit goods within the prison. Despite efforts to break up their power, prison gangs have survived these challenges. Even during periods of social stability, riots have occurred. For example, there was a flurry of riots in the early 1950s. Hartung and Floch (1956) note that the number of riots in 1952 in the US was greater than in any previous year. The majority of these riots, they argue, were in response to the harshness of prison life, poor food, housing and the brutality of prison officials, or a combination of these factors. While there had been some improvements, in some states conditions were still very poor. However, in other cases, poor conditions were not a factor, but reflected a combination of the concentration of different types of inmates within the prison and the restriction on informal self-government of the prison by a new administration. Some maximum security prisons had in the past been stable because of the informal inmate structure which amounted to a semi official self-government, in which inmate-assistants and inmate-clerks performed many of the duties of the prison, both custodial and administrative, including allocating jobs and distributing privileges, although they also smuggled in alcohol. Discipline problems were also dealt with informally. But as this informal structure was eroded in many prisons, inmate-leaders lost their powers, there were no incentives to control other prisoners and unrest increased. Hartung and Floch conclude that 'Some form of inmate self-government, whether unofficial or official, is necessary for the maintenance of peace in a modern maximum custody prison' (1956: 57). One step in this direction, which will be considered in Chapter 3, is the role of prisoner councils. While their powers in the UK are limited they do offer a local democratic structure.

Of course since the 1950s, there have been a number of changes in prison and in ways of negotiating the pressures of prison life. Most strikingly, the courts in the US have become more willing to engage in the scrutiny and oversight of prison conditions, while in the 1950s a 'hands off' approach to the courts prevailed, in which prisoners were seen as in a state of civil death in prison and lacked legal protection by the courts. Although the decision in *Coffin v Reichard* 143 F.2d 443 (6th Cir 1944) had extended habeas corpus to prisoners, in contrast to the hands-off approach in *Ruffin v Commonwealth of Virginia* (1871) 62 Va 21 (Gratt) 790, the courts remained hesitant in challenging prison conditions. However, from the mid-1960s to the mid-1970s the courts' hands-off approach to imprisonment was eroded. In *Monroe v Pape* 367 US 167 (1961) the court resuscitated the use of the Civil Rights Act 1871, US Code 42 section 1983, to bring civil rights actions against states for the deprivation of civil liberties, and this facilitated the growth of prisoners' rights claims. The rise of the civil rights movement was also significant, especially as many of them were incarcerated. For example, there was an increase in the number of Black Muslims in prison who were denied access to religious materials in prison, but who eventually won the right to practice their religion.[17] Prisoners also won procedural due process rights, including the right to communicate with lawyers and the right to express political beliefs and to practice political activity in a limited form. Prisoners' rights groups also received some federal and state funding in the late 1960s and achieved greater access to the outside world, through lifting of restrictions on their mail. Today they rely principally on individual donations and support from philanthropic foundations.

The political context outside the prison also needs to be considered, as the 1960s was marked by political turmoil, conflict, dissent and anti-war demonstrations, urban riots and student protests, as well as an increase in the crime rate. There was a loss of confidence in the government and an increase in a sense of entitlement. These changes affected prisons and contributed to the attack on rehabilitationist policies, including the use of indeterminate sentences. Prison rebellion was seen as part of the demand for change. The prisoner was increasingly viewed as a citizen with rights rather than as a passive recipient to be helped by rehabilitative policies. Prisoner-citizens could use the courts to enforce rights and prisoners were allowed to work together to express their interests through prisoner councils and political groups and even, in some cases, the recognition of prison gangs. As Useem and Kimball note: 'This "citizenship model" was rooted in the cultural and political swing towards entitlements and reinforced by court decisions…' (1991: 17). They cite as an example of the application of the citizenship model, the Prisoner Council at Washington State Penitentiary, which achieved a number of reforms including the right to form special interest groups and changes in dress and hair codes.

As many civil rights and anti-war activists, as well as middle-class drug users, were in prison during the period from the mid-1960s to the mid-1970s period, they came into contact with ordinary prisoners. Some political groups, for example, the Black Muslims, sought to recruit prisoners. Advocacy groups for prisoners developed in the late 1960s. For example, the People's Law Office in Illinois gathered together radical lawyers who represented the Black Panthers with other groups and also later helped with the defence at Attica and with class actions in Illinois' state and federal prisons. Yet despite the development of prisoners' rights in this period and the expansion of legitimate opportunities to challenge conditions through the courts, there was also a rise in the number of prison riots in the US from five in 1967 to forty-eight in 1972.

The most notorious riot of the post-war period was at Attica Correctional Facility in New York State in September 1971, which led to the greatest loss of life recorded in the history of US prison riots. It started when a group of inmates took over a tunnel and then prevented access to other areas of the prison. Some prisoners were reluctant to participate and protected officers. The prison administration's response to the initial incident was slow and poorly organised, although they were able to retake parts of the prison. But there remained about 1,300 inmates in D yard, who soon created their own microcosm of civil society with clear rules, for example not to fight or use drugs, and a formal democratic and social structure, based on established political principles. This 'society' was highly organised, distributing food and bedding and even running a postal system. Hostages were safer here and protected by Black Muslim guards. Many of the radical activists and Black Panthers were living in the New York area, so when they were sentenced for their political activities, they were sent to Attica. But inmates involved in riots at other prisons had also been transferred to Attica in 1970.

The prisoners' leaders appropriated typewriters to write their demands, which included an amnesty for rioters, the transportation of inmates to a non-imperialist country, and a federal injunction to prevent reprisals against rioters. The leaders included five black and two white prisoners, a political activist and the jail-house lawyer. Initially the Corrections Commissioner, Russell Oswald, negotiated with the prisoners, but was unable to reach agreement. Negotiations broke down when an officer who was injured in the riot died because of his injuries. There were also conflicts and divisions among the prisoners, with some prisoners taken hostage and threatened. Three prisoners were killed by other prisoners.

On 13 September, the prison was recaptured with an armed and brutal assault which led to thirty-nine fatalities, including ten hostages. So the hostages killed during the retaking of the prison were killed by the police rather than by the prisoners. The police used tear gas and opened fire, wounding ninety. Useem and Kimball (1991) see the reason for this violent assault as political, as the riot was seen by the authorities not just as an uprising over prison reform, but as an attack on authority per se, with revolutionaries seeking political objectives and trying to exploit public sympathy.

After the riot, the McKay Commission set up to investigate the causes, took evidence from officers and over 1,600 prisoners, the governor and staff from the Department of Corrections. The Report highlighted the poor conditions in the prison, the overcrowding, minimum recreational facilities, poor food and health care and the lack of good quality work (New York State Special Commission on Attica 1972). While the Commissioner of Correctional Services, Oswald was a liberal, it was hard for him to implement reform in practice. Prisoners were resentful over their living conditions, as well as the interference with their correspondence. At the time, the majority of the prisoners were black and Latino and many black prisoners identified with civil rights and black power movements outside the prison, rather than the internal criminal subculture. Some prisoners had been trying to bring actions against the prison authorities but had been met with resistance. Black Muslims felt the prison administration was hostile to them and prisoners interested in politics came into conflict with the prison as their mail was censored, to control access to political materials, and political organisations were prohibited. While the courts at that time were seeking to strengthen and enforce the due process rights of prisoners on this issue, in practice prison staff often resisted implementing these changes.

Some prisoners were in touch with prisoners at other institutions to formulate demands for reform. There were also new links developing at the time between the Black Panthers and Black Muslims who had previously been mutually antagonistic. A month earlier, in August 1971, George Jackson had been shot by prison guards at Soledad prison in California which further increased tensions. There had also been a strike over low wages in a prison workshop. So the riot did not occur out of the blue, but occurred in a context where there had a been a prior history of protest. Those prisoners aware of their due process rights were dissatisfied and resentful when they perceived those rights had been violated. In the aftermath of the riot, there were attacks on prisoners by officers; but while initially some charges were brought against the perpetrators, an amnesty was later granted. Despite the loss of life, there were some improvements in conditions in New York's prisons following the riot, particularly in procedural rights, such as restrictions on mail, but inmates also had more time unlocked.

Thompson (2016), in *Blood in the Water,* chronicles both the conditions in the prison in the period immediately before the riot, which she describes as The

Tinderbox, as well as during the riot and its aftermath. She had access to a range of transcripts and other documents and interviews, including with former hostages and families of the victims. As well as highlighting the treatment of inmates before and during the riot, Thompson also notes the reprisals against prisoners after the riot, when officers meted out punishment on the inmates, although the hostages had been killed by friendly fire. She is also critical of the state for its delays in reaching a financial settlement with the widows of the officers who had been killed. Thompson sees the introduction in 1973 of harsh mandatory minimum sentences for drug offences as a response to Attica, and this change set the scene for the subsequent expansion of the prison population.

The Attica riot was followed by a riot at Joliet in Illinois in 1975. Over half of the Joliet prisoners were members of one of the four main street gangs and many of the prisoners were from Chicago. Within the prison, the gangs controlled certain areas and were able to intimidate the officers. Prisoners not in the gangs ran the risk of physical and sexual assault by gang members. Prison policies had originally been accommodating to gangs, but in 1975 the prison administration tried to end gang control over the prison. When they sought to transfer three prisoners, they resisted and others joined in, resulting in seventy officers being taken hostage. The prisoners demanded cancellation of the transfer, but they were then tear-gassed and a clerk was attacked. They also demanded that the press should be allowed into the prison to film the riot, that there should be no reprisals and that the agreement should be recorded and played over the Joliet radio station. The administration agreed, played the tape and the riot ended, although the gang culture persisted within the prison.

The riot in the Penitentiary of New Mexico in 1980 near Santa Fe was extremely violent – the worst riot in the history of US prisons – and anarchic, as thirty-three inmates were killed and many were tortured, one was decapitated and another burnt alive by other inmates. In addition, prison guards were attacked and parts of the prison were destroyed with damage estimated at $20 million. Many of the rioters were drunk, or high on drugs taken from the pharmacy and intent on taking revenge on informers, and other targets. In contrast to Attica and Joliet, the inmates at New Mexico did not have links with revolutionary groups outside or inside the prison and the riot was chaotic and disorganised. There was a very small group of prisoners who had been involved in a class action against the state, but they were unable to exert control over violent prisoners, although they did play a role in negotiations. Also, unlike Joliet, the prison did not harbour criminal gangs, or gangs based on ethnic identity. Prior to the riot, the prison management was disorganised, there was a high staff turnover and tension among staff, so the administration was ill-equipped to deal with the riot. As Useem and Kimball point out 'the prison was methodically taken over, wing by wing, block by block' yet without any concerted opposition for several hours, by which time the prisoners were in control (1991: 101). The regime had also deteriorated with more overcrowding and harsher treatment by the guards and poor security. The riot began when guards were taken hostage by prisoners having a 'hooch party' with home-made alcohol, which in itself indicates the lack of security at the prison, just as the riot at Ford Prison in the UK was preceded by the consumption of alcohol. However, unlike Ford, the rioters at New Mexico used blow torches to gain access to the protective custody wing and to torture their victims, who included suspected informers, a child sex offender and a prisoner who was mentally disturbed and whose screaming at night had disturbed other prisoners. The riot lasted thirty-six hours, during which time many prisoners tried to escape, because they were fearful of the escalating violence.

After twelve hours negotiations began, with a small group of inmates demanding less crowded conditions and more due process rights. The riot ended after thirty-six hours, when an armed assault team was sent in. The rioters did not resist and a large number of prisoners escaped from the riot as they were fearful for their own safety. So it fizzled out because of the prisoners' exhaustion, low morale and disorganisation, rather than because of the response from the prison administration. Useem and Kimball note that there were some improvements in conditions after the riot. The disorder had attracted attention from policy makers and reform groups.

Colvin (1982, 1992) assisted with the investigation of the New Mexico riot. The inquiry included 299 interviews with prisoners, officers and officials. He notes that prior to the riot, during the 1970s, the prison had been quite calm, although the prisoners had conducted a sympathy strike in support of Attica in 1971, but this was non-violent, in marked contrast to the 1980 disorder. The prison had also been rebuilt in 1956 after the original prison had been destroyed in a riot.

Unlike Attica, as Colvin points out, there was, no effective leadership at New Mexico. While the Attica riot was marked by solidarity, political consciousness and a high level of organisation, in New Mexico 'political apathy and infighting had replaced the politicisation and solidarity of a decade earlier' (Colvin 1982: 449). But in the mid to late 1970s, the levels of violence increased at the prison and there were more attempted and successful escapes. But the level of security had not changed. There was dissatisfaction over food before and during the period of the 1980 riot. There had been periods of overcrowding earlier, although this had not led to rioting. However, there had been an increase in the prison's population just before the riot, but the types of offender admitted to the prison in terms of their histories of violence had not changed. Colvin argues that the increasing violence needs to be explained rather by changes to the control structure. In the early 1970s prisoners had been used to controlling and policing the prison by having responsibilities for selecting inmates to programmes and illegal drug use was tolerated and controlled by another group of inmates. There were also voluntary informants. But the changes from 1975 resulted in a disruption to relations between prisoners and staff. There was a clampdown on drugs, inmates were taken out of administrative roles in the programmes and there was increased security, including more searches and restrictions on movements. These changes led to conflict and protests and a work strike over the changes which was ended by force. Instead of voluntary informants, some prisoners were coerced into being 'snitches', and threatened with being revealed as a snitch if they did not comply, which added to prisoners' mutual suspicion. There was greater use of disciplinary segregation and removal of incentives. The leaders of the work strike, who had filed a class action law suit against the State of New Mexico, were put on segregation. So the impact of these changes effectively reduced the possibility of political cohesion among inmates. It also meant inmates sought power instead through increasing violence and competed over the extent of violence which they could inflict. These disruptive inmates were at the forefront of the violence in the riot. There was also a high staff turnover of prison administrators. A new warden in 1979 had released prisoners from segregation back into the general population, but had included in this transfer many of these violent inmates. When the court responded favourably to the 1977 class action, the recommendations were not implemented and the delays and failure made it hard for the prisoners who had brought the suit to exercise control over others. There were further restrictions following an escape of eleven inmates in December 1979. So while there had been some signs that trouble was brewing, these were not acted upon.

On the day of the riot the architecture of the prison was also significant: a glass panel had replaced iron bars which was easily broken, allowing rioters access to the whole prison. Those prisoners who had been involved in the class action did try to organise the rioters into a coherent collective protest issuing demands, but were unable to persuade the violent rioters to release hostages until the riot was nearly at an end. In his account one prisoner, Mark Rolland (1997), describes how other prisoners tried to protect the hostages.

There were also five riots in three prisons over a five-day period in Michigan in 1981, involving property damage and arson. At that time, conditions were poor, prisons were overcrowded, parole conditions had been tightened and promised improvements in conditions were not implemented. The initial trigger was action by the officers, who took over the prison for two hours, because they were dissatisfied at their treatment by the state. The impact of the decision in *Wolff v McDonnell* 418 US 539 (1974) meant that prisoners had to be given a hearing before disciplinary measures could be imposed for prison rule infringements. Officers resented these limits on their powers and the lack of support from the administration, but there were fears among inmates that they would be subjected to more lockdowns as a result of this action.

There were incidents of disorder among inmates, but instead of making political demands they just enjoyed looting food. There was no gang culture or 'snitch' culture at the State Prison of Southern Michigan. Some prisoners had formed a Prisoner Progress Association in the early 1970s, which brought class action law suits and contact had been made with political figures outside, but by the time of the riot in 1981, inmates were either unaware of the group or dismissive of it. The officers' association threatened to strike, but in the end reached an agreement to review the disciplinary policy. After the riot, the courts ordered a number of improvements, but there were insufficient funds to implement them and small-scale riots and attacks on prisoners and officers continued at the prison.

There was also a riot in West Virginia Penitentiary, at Moundsville on New Year's Day 1986, when new more restrictive rules were imposed following an escape which led to the murder of a state trooper. In the early 1980s conditions had been criticised by the courts, both physical conditions and facilities and the failure to satisfy prisoners' right to rehabilitation, which the Supreme Court of Appeals for West Virginia had recognised earlier in *Cooper v Gwinn* 298 S.E.2d 781 (1981). The necessary reforms were deemed too expensive and many were not implemented. A new warden, was appointed in 1985, who imposed restrictions on visits during the Christmas period and cuts in the amount of property prisoners were permitted. In response, the prisoners took hostages, rioted and took over the prison. Hostages were protected and generally well treated, although three prisoners were killed by other prisoners because of older grudges. The negotiating committee met in the prison library and formulated demands, which included a meeting with the governor and no reprisals. But they soon relinquished control of the prison and released the hostages. After the riot, the court ruled conditions were inadequate and demanded improvements, but there was no increase in funding for the state prisons and some prisoners were put on segregation. A recurring theme, therefore, is the failure to implement changes demanded or recommended by the court, because of a lack of funding. In 1986 there were also riots in Arizona State Prison and in Atlanta, Georgia in 1987.

The incidence of riots fell following the period of instability of the 1970s and 1980s, despite increases in incarceration. But while there has been a fall in the frequency and intensity of riots, they have not disappeared altogether and disorder has occurred in a range of establishments, with different levels of security and prisoner profiles, in new and older prisons, and in public and private sector institutions. While international attention has focused on the plight of those detained at Guantánamo – which raises issues regarding the use of torture, extraordinary rendition and unfair trials – far less attention has been given to the conditions experienced by ordinary prisoners in state and federal prisons to which prisoners have responded with violence in some cases. There was a major riot in Southern Ohio Correctional Facility in 1993 which lasted eleven days, during which time prisoners took officers hostage. By the time order was restored nine prisoners and one officer had been murdered (Lynd 2004). There was also a riot at Pelican Bay State Prison in California in 2000. Disorder has persisted in American prisons since then, with riots at Reeves County Detention Center in 2008 and 2009. Also in 2009, there was disorder at Northpoint Training Center in Kentucky and the Californian Institute for Men and hunger strikes at Pelican Bay State Prison in 2011 and 2013. There was a riot in 2015 at a private prison in Texas, Willacy County Correctional Center, which holds undocumented migrants, where inmates set fire to the prison in protest over poor conditions. There were also riots at Holman Correctional Facility in Alabama and Holmes Correctional Institution in Florida, in 2016, where the prison was understaffed and prisoners were spending more time in their cells, and a further incident of disorder at Pelican Bay in 2017.

So while there has been a decline in the number of prison riots and their levels of violence, compared to the 1970s and 1980s, this does necessarily mean prisoners are more compliant because they are more satisfied with their conditions, or that the conditions are now acceptable. Rather it reflects the more rigorous surveillance and control of inmates, using new technologies, as well as the use of segregation and the separation of disruptive prisoners. Responses to imprisonment, like those in the UK, may be individualised rather than collective. Moreover, there has been improved staff training to deal with rioters. The organisational response is now faster and better organised, through the use of rapid response groups, the Correctional Emergency Response Teams. Mock riots are used as part of the training process, with the focus on containment of incidents in the early stages, to prevent a fully fledged riot developing. The courts have also become more willing to intervene, as we have seen, and prisoners' rights litigation has developed since that period, to ameliorate the harshness of prison conditions and to respect prisoners' dignity. The number of claims expanded between 1987 and 1995. However, the increased use of prisoners' rights litigation has led to new legislation which has made it more difficult for prisoners to bring rights claims. The Prison Litigation Reform Act 1995, which was designed to stop frivolous or vexatious claims by prisoners and to curtail litigation, makes it harder to bring claims under USC 1983. Under the 1995 Act, prisoners must exhaust all internal remedies before bringing an action, whereas prior to the Act, this was a matter for the court's discretion. A more serious obstacle was a new requirement that prisoners pay court filing fees, although it is possible to do so by instalments. The Act also disallows claims for mental or emotional injury, unless physical injury can also be shown. It also stipulates that if an action is struck out by the court for frivolity or malice three times, then in any future claims, payment must be paid in advance in full and can only be brought if the prisoner is at risk of serious physical injury.

Research by the Bureau of Justice on the impact of the Act found that it appeared to have resulted in a fall in the number of civil rights petitions filed by State and Federal prison inmates: 'They filed 41,679 petitions during 1995 compared to 25,504 during 2000. Between 1995 and 2000 the rate at which Federal and State prison inmates filed civil rights petitions decreased from 37 to 19 per 1,000 inmates' (Scalia 2002). This fall in applications following enactment of the PLRA has occurred despite an increase in the incarcerated population. Furthermore, as Schlanger (2003) reports from her study of the impact of the Act, the success rate of claims has also fallen since the PLRA, even though it was designed to deter frivolous claims, which suggests that tougher standards are being applied.

We have also noted that where the courts have recognised prisoners' entitlements to a minimal standard of living and demanded change, expectations may be raised on the part of prisoners. However, local budgets may make it impossible to implement improvements quickly or fully which may itself also engender conflict. This seems to be an element in several of the riots in the US, but is also found in other jurisdictions. In her study of Russian prisons, Piacentini notes that in 1991 when the first post-Soviet penal code was being drafted, revised expectations were raised too quickly and there were riots in a number of penal colonies before the riot police regained control (Piacentini 2014: 48).

Gender and prison riots

Prison resistance, including rioting, is a gendered phenomenon. Prison riots are primarily associated with male prisoners and occur mostly in men's prisons. Perhaps this is not surprising as violence and sexual assaults are more common in men's prisons, with the risk of physical assault especially high in Young Offender Institutions. Men's prisons contain a higher proportion of violent offenders. Moreover, the opportunity to attack other prisoners is a recurring theme in major prison riots. The targeting of sex offenders in riots may be seen as a way male prisoners assert a hegemonic masculinity (Bosworth and Carrabine 2001). For example, in Kingston Penitentiary, a maximum security prison in Ontario, there was a riot in 1971, which lasted four days, in which a group of prisoners tortured prisoners on the sex offenders wing, resulting in the deaths of two vulnerable prisoners, despite the efforts of some prisoners to limit the violence (Desroches 1974). Once a riot starts, whatever the original cause, some may take advantage of the opportunity to settle old scores or target unpopular prisoners. The subsequent investigation highlighted problems of overcrowding, staff shortages, prisoners spending too much time locked up, a lack of activities and a failure to deal with prisoners' complaints. It is also important, as Ugelvik (2014) notes, when focusing on gender to consider how men negotiate and perform masculinity to reassert themselves as a successful male subject. So for younger males this may include fighting, while older men may reassert their roles as patriarchal fathers although absent from the family. In some cases, older prisoners may adopt a paternalistic role in relation to female prison officers (Easton 2018). However, men received little attention from gender studies until the mid-1990s, in, for example, the work of Newburn and Stanko (1994).

Conditions are generally better in women's prisons in England and Wales than men's, according to the Prison Inspectorate, although there are some variations between establishments (HMCIP 2016: 53) Most of the prisons reviewed by the Inspectorate achieved results that were good or reasonably good on the 'healthy prison' criteria, although Holloway did not meet expectations on purposeful activity and it closed in the summer of 2016. These judgments are made using the Prison Inspectorate's *Expectations*, or criteria for assessment of the treatment of women in prison, published in 2014 (HMIP 2014). The *Expectations* are based on the United Nation's 2010 Rules for the Treatment of Women Prisoners, known as the Bangkok Rules, but also draw on the European Prison Rules and the UN Standard Minimum Rules for Prisoners, revised in 2015.

However the fact that women, in some respects, are seen as receiving superior treatment has itself stimulated claims of discrimination and litigation. Such a claim was an element in the *McFeeley* case where it was argued that the treatment of women raised discrimination issues under Article 14 in relation to Articles 3, 8, 9, 10 and 11, because, *inter alia,* women in Armagh were allowed to wear their own clothes, but the court found reasonable justification for the differential treatment of women prisoners.

In women's prisons there has been less violence and fewer drug problems and the use of the new psychoactive substances is not so widespread. Generally in women's prisons, drugs issues are more likely to arise in relation to the misuse of prescribed drugs. The Prison Inspectorate found that there were better relations between staff and prisoners than in men's prisons and women were more likely to have extended family visits. However, the treatment of women in immigration detention centres has raised concern, with instances of physical and sexual abuse by SERCO staff at Yarl's Wood (HMCIP 2016, see also Bosworth 2014).

Women prisoners are more vulnerable in terms of mental health, displaying high levels of self-harm. While men also engage in self-harm, women prisoners are five times more likely to self-harm than male prisoners (HMCIP 2017: 9). While the incidence of suicide is lower for women than for male prisoners, there was an increase in self-inflicted deaths for women in 2015–16 (PPO 2016: 32). In 2016–17 there were eleven self-inflicted deaths of women prisoners (PPO 2017: 35). Until the 1990s, women were marginalised in studies of imprisonment, including studies of prison disorder and resistance. Research on disorder has tended to focus on male prisoners, as they have dominated prison riots and major incidents of disorder, rather than on less dramatic or spectacular examples of resistance. Studies of women prisoners have focused on their vulnerability rather than their threats to the prison order, or their dangerousness. However, Bosworth has argued that women need to be considered as agents rather than victims: 'The meaning of "agency" needs to be recast to include symbolic and small-scale acts of resistance instead of simple, instrumental ability to "get things done"' (1999: 161). Bosworth conducted fieldwork in three institutions HMP/YOI Drake Hall, HMP Remand Centre at Pucklechurch and the Women's Annexe at HMP Winchester, which has now closed, and found that women resist in a variety of ways. Women reassert themselves as agents, despite the constraints of imprisonment. Identities in prison – collective and individual – are not fixed and are constituted by a variety of social relations: 'Despite their seeming passivity and the notorious absence of women from large-scale disturbances in female prisons, women constantly engage in strategies to reduce the pains of imprisonment' (1999: 7). In responding to the pains of imprisonment, women may self-harm, but may also seek an alternative identity through education, or use a traditional female identity, to reassert themselves as good mothers, or focus on their appearance. So prisoners are not just passive, but express their agency in constructing identities.

Bosworth and Carrabine (2001) stress that a wide range of acts can be seen as strategies of resistance, apart from full-scale riots. Based on their fieldwork, respectively in women's prisons and Strangeways, they stress that the strategies of resistance selected by prisoners 'reflect their race, gender and sexuality' and more attention needs to be given to these dimensions of power relations (2001: 502). They see the driving force of resistance as subjective identity: 'prisoners draw on ideas and practices of race, gender and sexuality in their performance of self to create alternative meanings and to resist the instrumentally superior nature of the institution's power' (at 513). The common identity of black prisoners may be a source of solidarity. Lesbian and gay relationships may also be seen as way of challenging stereotypical notions of gender, as well as a response to the pains of imprisonment.

Although the emphasis in feminist criminology in the 1990s had been on the ways women were regulated by discourses of femininity and on the over-medication of women prisoners if they were seen as disruptive, there was less interest in how women themselves negotiate gendered power discourses in prison. Bosworth and Carrabine cite one example of a prisoner who refused to take her diazepam. The authors are critical of the assumption that those who do not resist in overt ways accept the legitimacy of the regime. Women may be wary of engaging in conflicts if this affects parole decisions or access to children, or because they are fearful of violence, rather than because of normative compliance.

While women may internalise their response to imprisonment or resist in less dramatic ways, of course this does not mean that women do not riot as well and they are certainly not 'shrinking violets' in addressing their grievances. Women's involvement in prison riots has a long history, although this has been overshadowed by the major riots in men's prisons, notably Attica (Law 2009). At the first women's prison in New York State in 1835, there was a riot over the austere conditions and staff were attacked. In 1974, there was a riot at Bedford Hills women's prison in New York state, known as the August rebellion. Here a prisoner had brought a legal challenge to being segregated without warning or without a hearing, but when she was then put into segregation without a hearing and assaulted, she resisted and this led to a riot in which women which took over the prison. There was also a riot at a women's prison in North Carolina in 1975. Here women demonstrated over their conditions and when a prison officer responded with violence, the women fought back and the disturbance ended only when extra officers from other prisons were sent in to restore order. Law also gives an example of women resisting by refusing medication, refusing prison food and organising their own Christmas dinner, and setting fire to their mattresses in protest at their conditions in Arizona state prisons in 2009. These conditions had included the use of un-shaded outdoor cages in intense heat which resulted in the death of a prisoner, Marcia Powell, at Arizona State Prison Complex – Perryville. Women have also engaged in prisoners' rights litigation. A key case in the rights litigation of the 1970s was *Glover v Johnson* 478 F Supp 1075 (E.D. Mich 1979), where women prisoners in Michigan used the equal protection clause of the Fourteenth Amendment to challenge the failure to provide educational facilities at women's prisons while offering such programmes in men's prisons. The court decided in the women's favour and ordered the prison administration to provide comparable educational facilities and a course on legal skills to facilitate women's access to the courts. Women then took advantage of these courses to develop their skills, which they then used to bring further law suits against the Michigan Department of Corrections. In 1996, 500 women who had been assaulted by officers brought an action in *Neal v MDOC,* Case No. 96-6986-Cz. This litigation was only finally settled in their favour in 2009 when they were awarded substantial financial compensation. Further litigation has been initiated on behalf of women prisoners in Michigan regarding the strip-searching of women in

Salem v MDOC, Case No. 13-14567 (1 May 2015). In *Cooper v Gwinn* 298 S.E.2d 781 (W.Va. 1981) prisoners at the West Virginia State Prison for Women demanded better educational and rehabilitative programmes and the court acknowledged that the failure to make this provision violated their constitutional rights and issued a writ of mandamus.

There have also been riots at women's prisons in Canada. At the Prison for Women in Kingston in 1994, there were four days of violence and arson and an officer was taken hostage. The riot was triggered by women responding to an allegedly racist comment by an officer. But the response to the riot, which was recorded, did lead to public condemnation, as the all-male emergency response team which was sent in conducted body searches. The Arbour Report on the riot was critical of the regime and the degrading treatment of women in the response to the riot and the prison closed in 2000 (Arbour 1996). Closer to home, women at Armagh prison took the prison governor hostage in 1974.

Women have also participated in strikes, demonstrations and occupations, such as the one at North Carolina in 1975. More recently, there have been reports of women withholding labour in California and Virginia as part of the national wave of strikes in the US in September 2016, although support for the strike in women's prisons was more limited than in men's prisons. Women may be more reluctant to engage in collective actions because of the ramifications for their release and specifically have concerns over being reunited with their children. Women prisoners may also be fearful of the consequences within prison, for example, being segregated.[18]

So women may resist their conditions of confinement in a variety of ways. For example, in prisons in England and Wales, the rate of proven adjudications per 100 women was higher for women (148 per 100) than for men (118 per 100) in 2015 and while the rates for both men and women have increased since 2011, the rise was sharper for women (NOMS 2016: 23). While most legal challenges have been brought by men, this is not surprising. Men constitute the majority of prisoners in the UK and US, including prisoners serving long sentences, who are more likely to have the time and resources and incentives to litigate. Nonetheless, women have brought legal actions on a number of issues including access to Mother and Baby Units,[19] and the Books for Prisoners Case,[20] where restrictions on the number of books prisoners could receive and keep in the cells following changes in the IEP scheme, were successfully challenged. Prison education can assist in developing the skills needed to bring a challenge, although the prison population also includes women with higher level qualifications. The litigant in the Books for Prisoners case, Barbara Gordon-Jones, has a PhD in English Literature.

Explaining prison riots

Obviously there will be specific local and internal factors which contribute to prison riots, but general themes have been identified including poor conditions, understaffing and under-resourcing, a crisis of legitimacy when prisoners are treated unfairly, or their conditions are changed suddenly and that change is poorly managed, and failures of the organisation, for example, a slow and uncoordinated response to signs of tension which allows full-scale disorder to develop. In the past, in some prisons, power has been maintained through sharing power with key prisoners. In the maximum security prison studied by Sykes, order had been maintained by power sharing with prisoners, but when the prison administration tried to enforce prison rules in 1952 prisoners responded by rioting (Sykes 1958). Similarly, in the New Mexico penitentiary, changes introduced by a new administration which weakened the power of prisoners, contributed to the riot there in 1982 (Colvin 1992).

Useem and Kimball's analysis of riots in the United States in the period 1971–1986, focused on the issues of administrative disorganisation, legitimation crises and deprivation. If the prison is well managed even conditions which fall below standard may be accepted. 'Prison riots', they argue, 'change with time and place. They are shaped by the political events and issues of the day, the prevailing ideas about imprisonment, and the political struggles in and around prisons' (1991: 9). They analysed the major riots in men's prisons in the 1970s at Attica and Joliet and in the 1980s in New Mexico, West Virginia and Michigan. They consider possible explanations, including deprivation, resource mobilisation and the breakdown of normal control mechanisms and use the term 'riot' to refer to the situation 'when the authorities lose control of a significant number of prisoners, in a significant area of the prison, for a significant amount of time' (1991: 4). However, the behaviour of prisoners may vary from looting to violence against fellow prisoners or officers. They note that while riots may be perceived as chaotic irrational events, from prisoners' standpoints they may be seen as rational and organised.

They identify five stages in the process, beginning with the pre-riot stage, during which prisoners and state forces develop material and cognitive resources which determine the course of the riot. This is followed by the initiation stage, 'the action by prisoners which first crosses the line into open rebellion' and the state's response (1991: 5). If the riot is not then crushed, the next stage begins of expansion, in which prisoners seek to take control of 'as many human, material and spatial resources as possible against the resistance or non-resistance of the state' (ibid). There then follows a state of siege in which prisoners control some territory within the prison, while the state reorganises its forces to recapture it, but there may also be bargaining between the parties. The final stage is recapture or termination.

The disorganisation of the state was a key factor in the riots they studied as there was weak administration and poor security, of which prisoners were aware. By good administration, they mean the ability to maintain prison conditions to a reasonable standard, rather than the imposition of strong discipline. Conditions were perceived by prisoners to fall below the acceptable constitutional standards prescribed by the courts and therefore were not seen as legitimate. The courts and regulatory bodies had exerted pressure on the prisons to improve conditions, but the prisons had insufficient funds to meet those demands.

A similar approach is taken by Boin and Rattray (2004) to explain the Strangeways Riot in 1990, namely, a focus on administrative breakdown and a failure to contain disturbances or to deal with changes such as cuts in prison budgets or changes in the regime, leading to a loss of legitimacy. Poor conditions per se cannot account for riots as they have occurred in prisons with good conditions or undergoing improvement. Boin and Rattray argue that 'Riots are an effect, not a cause. That is prisoners do not riot in furtherance of a "cause" in a political sense – riots are an effect of the interaction between structural and cultural pathogens' (2004: 60).

However, while the contextual preconditions are clearly important, a political cause should not be excluded. There may often be a specific grievance which triggers the riot, which directly addresses the limits of the state's treatment of the prisoner and the power of the prison. Moreover, the act of rioting can be construed as a political act, as a rejection of the authority of the prison administration. It can also be seen as political in the sense that many riots may also involve formulating goals, holding meetings, making decisions on the basis of prisoners' contributions, so prisoners are performing politics. Even if some prisoners are simply enjoying the excitement or using it to loot, for other inmates, it may constitute a political act.

Carrabine (2005) is not persuaded that riots are inevitably caused by administrative disorganisation, legitimation crises and deprivation. He locates the issue in the context of the problem of order. The assumption that in the context of very poor conditions, a minor incident can spark off a riot is difficult to sustain, he says, as the most common response to deprivation is to do nothing. Poor conditions may lead to conflict, boredom, alienation, a lack of outside contact, and a fear of violence and assaults, rather than to rioting. He is also unconvinced by the 'legitimacy' argument, as many prisons with legitimacy deficits do not erupt in riots. Given that most prisons hold alienated prisoners and staff who feel powerless, he says, we should find more disruption in the system. We need to understand why riots do not happen more often and to understand the interplay between agency, institutional history and social structure. So Carrabine says that we should see the everyday resistance of prisoners as lying on a continuum; so if a riot happens it should not be seen as an aberration. He also cautions against seeing a sharp divide between normal prisons and pathological prisons, as prisons may drift in and out of periods of heightened conflict.

Carrabine refers to Durkheim's concept of fatalism to explain why incidents of disorder do not arise more often, even when a regime lacks legitimacy. He argues that prisons generate diverse forms of social order, including a fatalistic order, when power structures are seen as inevitable, so it seems that nothing can be done to change them. In that case, some prisoners may simply wish to do their time until release, although the response may change over time, as we saw earlier. Carrabine studied Strangeways during the period from 1965 to April 1990, which included the spring before the riot. There had been periods of unrest before the riot, but conditions had deteriorated immediately preceding the riot.

However, Rubin (2015, 2017) argues that recent prison research has focused on agency and resistance and underplayed the role of structure in shaping the behaviour of prisoners, although structure can also enable agency. Referring to her research on Eastern State Penitentiary in Philadelphia from 1829–1875, she seeks to show how prisoners' friction and resistance are enabled, constructed and shaped by structure. By structure, she means forces external to prisoners, including prison personnel, the architecture and the daily routines, as well as ideologies of power. Rubin distinguishes what she calls 'friction' from resistance. Friction refers to reactive behaviours 'that occur when people find themselves in highly controlled environments', which is distinguished from resistance, that is, 'consciously disruptive, intentionally political actions' (2015: 24). Although, there is, she notes, a tendency to romanticise prisoners' resistance as challenging authority and reasserting their humanity and to see resistance as a result of strong agency, many prisoners do not resist. This romantic view also treats structure only as a target of resistance, rather than as shaping resistance. However, Crewe's (2009) work which shows the impact of drugs on prison culture, Kruttschnitt and Gartner's (2005) study of women's prisons which examines how different penal and institutional cultures shape adaptation styles and Bosworth and Carrabine's (2001) analysis of resistance as culturally and socio-economically constructed, have given more attention to structure. In Rubin's own research, there were many instances of friction at Eastern State Penitentiary, including passing letters and tapping on pipes, and engaging in illicit relationships, rather than politically motivated resistance and the term resistance, she argues, is over-used. In some cases she found prison guards helped prisoners infringe prison rules. The architecture of the prison may also be relevant; for example, at Eastern State Penitentiary the plumbing system enabled prisoners to communicate. Some actions, such as workplace sabotage, are clearly political, as an expression of protest, others may see a riot as way of exacting revenge on others, while others wish to improve prison conditions. Moreover, for collective action to be possible prisoners have to be able to contact each other and to be in close physical proximity.

Haslam and Reicher (2012) approach prisoner resistance from the standpoint of social psychology, drawing on experimental studies as well as historical events. However, they note that most studies of prisoners by social psychologists have focused on oppression and conformity, rather than resistance. Most famously the Stanford Prison Experiment focused on abuse and domination, when students assigned to the role of guards meted out vicious punishments on student 'prisoners' (Haney, Banks and Zimbardo 1973). But Haslam and Reicher argue that we can also find examples of resistance, which they define as 'the process and act of challenging one's subordinated position in a given social system', in the most oppressive circumstances (2012: 155). The Stanford Experiment focused on group pressure in which people conform to those pressures, resulting in oppressive behaviour, but even in that experiment, there was some rebellion although it was crushed and some guards were reluctant to be oppressive. Moreover, evidence from the later BBC Prison Study showed that where there are extreme inequalities, people can challenge and subvert the authority of their guards (Reicher and Haslam 2006). In the BBC study, the experimenters did not tell the guards how to behave and also introduced and then eliminated the possibility of being promoted to a guard. They also introduced a trade unionist to the group who was expected to question the regime and promote a sense of possible alternatives. Some prisoners tried to get promotion when this was possible, but when the rule changed, they began to see themselves as a group with a shared social identity and used collective strategies to challenge the regime, also mocking and challenging the guards and occupying the guards' quarters, while the guards themselves were disunited.

Social identity theory assumes that people can define and act as individuals in terms of personal identity, or as members of social groups (social identity) and when a given social identity is salient, people strive to see their group as different from and superior to other groups. If they are in a subordinate position but think they can improve their position by themselves, they focus on individual mobility, but if they think such movement is impossible, they are more likely to see themselves as group members with a shared social identity. If they view inequality as illegitimate and unstable, they are also more likely to work together to resist domination. Haslam and Reicher argue that 'resistance is always possible, even in the most unequal and the most repressive of situations' (2012: 173). They claim that 'however quiescent people might seem, the possibility of resistance is ever present' (Haslam and Reicher 2012: 155). Social identity can be a source of social power and a means of challenging subordination.

Three repressive regimes are examined from this standpoint: the Maze in Northern Ireland, Robben Island in South Africa and the most extreme context of Sobibor Extermination Camp in Poland, where resistance flourished. In the Maze prison in the 1970s, there were protests over the refusal of the government to recognise the status of IRA prisoners as political prisoners. Protests included going on the blanket, a no-wash protest, speaking in Gaelic and hunger strikes, and later there was a major escape of thirty-eight prisoners in 1983. As we shall see, while these prisoners did not achieve political status – the aim of the resistance – some concessions were won. What happened inside prison affected the political process outside. International criticism, following the death of Bobby Sands, increased pressure on the UK government to reach a political solution. Ultimately, many paramilitary prisoners were released under the Good Friday Agreement. The situation in the Maze will be considered in more detail in Chapter 6. Robben Island in South Africa held political prisoners from 1959 to 1996, as well as ordinary prisoners. The political prisoners were kept apart from the general prison population and a shared social identity developed within this group. The political prisoners, like the Republicans, were aiming to achieve political change outside and used their resistance to change society, as well as conditions inside the prison (Buntman and Huang 2003, Buntman 2003). There was a highly developed structure with prisoners running their own 'university' with classes.

There were also examples of resistance in the Nazi extermination camps including Auschwitz and Sobibor, where resistance included faking illness, obtaining extra food and swapping names with those already dead to avoid being killed. But there was also collective action in planning escapes and an uprising in Sobibor in 1943, when inmates raided an arms store and used the arms to kill the guards and to escape. Fifty prisoners survived the escape including the leader, Alexander

Pechersky, who joined the partisans. His arrival at the camp was important because he had served in the Red Army and had experience of military organisation, and was able to mobilise active resistance. Whether such a shared identity emerges will depend on a common experience of subordination at the hands of prison officials. So housing political prisoners together helps this process. The longer prisoners are together the more likely a shared identity will develop and this was a problem in the camps as many prisoners were killed so soon after arrival. Prisoners also need to see existing inequalities as insecure and to see a possibility of change. Political prisoners may start by questioning the legitimacy of the regime and conceive of an alternative as they recognise that they are likely to be killed. For this reason the Nazi regime initially tried to perpetuate the fiction that deportees were being relocated rather than exterminated. In Sobibor, where death was likely, there was little to lose in seeking to resist or to escape.

Leadership is important as groups need to organise effectively, although the leaders are often killed. If the leaders have organisational skills such as Pechersky's military training, or Mandela's legal knowledge, or Bobby Sand's literary skills, this will also be a significant factor in mobilising support inside (Sands 1993, 1996). But the groups also need to try muster support outside, so in Sobibor escape was crucial to making clear to the outside world what was happening.

Segregation and resistance

However, while as we have seen, resistance is also evident in modern prison settings, disruptive prisoners may also be neutralised by segregating them. In England and Wales, prisoners on segregation may be locked up for as long as twenty-two hours per day, with adverse effects on their health (HMCIP 2016: 25).[21] Prisoners can be removed from association under PR 45 (and YOI R 49) and segregated for reasons of good order or discipline – which applies to the majority of prisoners on segregation or for their own protection. Under PR 46 they can be held in a Close Supervision Centre (CSC) or in a designated cell within a segregation unit. A prisoner may also be awarded cellular confinement (PR 55(e)) or removed from the wing for offences against prison discipline.[22] A prisoner who is awaiting an adjudication hearing may also be kept apart from others pending the inquiry (R 53(4)). Prisoners on a no-wash protest will also be segregated under PR 45. Where necessary prisoners may be held in more austere special accommodation with the furniture removed and replaced by cardboard fittings. Reasons for segregation may include security breaches and risks to staff, other prisoners or property. The procedures and policy for the management of segregation units are found in PSO 1700. Prisoners should be segregated for the shortest possible time consistent with the original reason for separation. CSCs are also used to deal with prisoners who display violent and/or disruptive behaviour. Under the Mandela Rules, solitary confinement should be used as a last resort and for as short a time as possible.

Solitary confinement is usually understood as confinement for twenty-two hours or more without meaningful human contact. The European Prison Rules also stipulate that it should be used as a punishment only in exceptional cases and for a specified time which should be as short as possible (EPR 60(5)). In the *Bourgass*[23] case, Bourgass was convicted for his involvement in the 2002 ricin plot and had been segregated several times in Whitemoor, because of concerns over his influence on other prisoners which threatened good order and security. The Court of Appeal saw this treatment as justified and dismissed the appeal. The court stressed that the association with others was a privilege rather than a right. The prison had taken an administrative decision to curtail it in the interests of good order and security. The case went to the Supreme Court in *R (on the application of Bourgass and another) v Secretary of State for Justice UKSC* [2015] 54, where the court held that the segregation, in this case beyond seventy-two hours, was not authorised by the Secretary of State and was therefore unlawful (at para 127). The Supreme Court also stressed that unless there are risks to others or to prison security, the prisoner should be told the reasons for segregation. Without that information, prisoners are unable to challenge the segregation decision. Following *Bourgass*, a revised policy was put out for consultation. New legislation came into effect in September 2015 which introduced additional safeguards for prisoners in prison and young offender institutions.[24] Removal from association for more than seventy-two hours, up to fourteen days, may be authorised by the governor. But the governor must obtain leave from the Secretary of State to sanction removal, where the period in total amounts to more than forty-two days. The policy was under review in 2017.

Control and restraints procedures may also be used on disruptive prisoners which, if used inappropriately, may be unsafe, an issue highlighted by the Prisons Inspectorate and the Prisons Ombudsman. These procedures set out in Prison Service Order 1600 31/8/2005 were amended and updated in 2015 by Prison Service Instruction 30/2015. Control and restraint techniques should be used as a last resort to bring a violent or refractory prisoner under control and applied for as short a time as is possible. Prisoners may also be held in a separate wing because of a particular characteristic, for example, protected witnesses, vulnerable prisoners and older prisoners, or because of extremism where there are concerns other prisoners may be radicalised (see Chapter 5). A special purpose-built unit to hold the most dangerous extremist inmate was set up in HMP Frankland in 2017, with two more units to follow at HMP Woodhill and Full Sutton.

Shalev and Edgar (2016) reviewed the conditions in segregation units and close supervision centres in England and Wales, in a major study published by the Prison Reform Trust. The authors sent a survey to all prisons and visited fifteen prisons, including local, training and high security prisons, one YOI and two women's prisons, fourteen segregation units and four Close Supervision Centres (CSCs) which are intended to deal with most disruptive or dangerous prisoners. They interviewed prisoners, prison officers and managers. In the period of their research, January to March 2014, nearly 10 per cent of the prison population spent at least one night in segregation, while CSCs held on average fifty prisoners with an average stay of forty months. Shalev and Edgar found the practice of continued segregation was widespread (Shalev and Edgar 2016: 25). 9 per cent of the segregated prison population were held for over eighty-four days, 20 per cent from fourteen to forty-two days, and 71 per cent for under fourteen days. 95 per cent of segregated prisoners were men. In the period January to March 2014, black and black British prisoners made up 12 per cent of the prison population, but 15.5 per cent of the segregated population. They were also more likely to be segregated for more than eighty-four days (ibid: 47). However, the majority of prisoners in CSCs were White British. Some prisoners deliberately engineered their segregation by behaving disruptively, to obtain a transfer, to 'ship out' to another prison, but also, in some cases, to avoid repaying debts to other prisoners, to avoid cell sharing and drugs and violence on the wing and to draw attention to their demands. The authors give the example of a prisoner going onto the netting for this reason. Prisoners also had better access to health care staff when on segregation.

The researchers found that segregated prisoners could spend as much as 23.5 hours alone in their cell. CSC prisoners could spend more time in association, but still no more than one hour a day (ibid: 52). Although relations between staff and prisoners in the segregation units were good, with a greater focus on care and treating the prisoner decently, the regimes were marked by inactivity and social isolation and the provision of exercise did not meet international standards – usually lasting at most thirty minutes, when the European Prison Rules and the UN Standard Minimum Rules require a minimum of sixty minutes' exercise in the open air if the weather permits (EPR 27.1). It was also clear that the officers thought that the majority on segregation and in CSCs had mental health needs and ideally should not have been segregated, but were waiting for a place at a psychiatric hospital. Many CSC prisoners did not understand why they were being held there, or what they needed to do to be allowed to leave the centre. However, the authors also found examples of good practice, but argue more activities should be provided and the period spent on segregation should be reduced to lessen the harmful impact of isolation.

The adverse effects of segregation on the mental health of prisoners are well known.[25] In Shalev and Edgar's study, a substantial proportion of prisoners on segregation or in a CSC reported problems, including anxiety, insomnia and depression. Prisoners at risk of suicide or self-harm should not be held in a segregation unit, unless there are exceptional circumstances or a risk of harm to themselves or others, and no alternative location is deemed appropriate. However, the authors found prisoners on segregation on an open ACCT (Assessment, Care in Custody and Team-work). Prisoners on segregation also did not have access to Listeners, who provide support to vulnerable prisoners (see Chapter 3). The Prison Service Instruction 64/2011 on *Safer Custody* and the Prison Service Order 1700 on *Segregation* recommends avoidance of the use of segregation for prisoners on ACCT where possible and it should be used in exceptional circumstances, where other options have been considered and exhausted. The Ombudsman has noted that between January 2007 and March 2014, twenty-eight prisoners took their lives while they were held in segregation units, of whom nine were on ACCTs at the time of their death (PPO 2015: 6). Not surprisingly many of those already suffering from mental health problems will find that segregation worsens their condition.

Segregation has also been increasingly used since the 1970s, in the US, as a means of managing disruptive prisoners and to weaken the power of prison gangs. The separation of gang members has been a driving factor in the development of supermax prisons which represent an extreme form of segregation. Here prisoners may be held in individual cells for over twenty-two hours a day and carry out daily activities and routines separate from other prisoners. Supermax prisons have heightened security, based on the deployment of advanced technological means of surveillance and control and their isolation. Prisoners are fed in their cells, take exercise alone and rarely leave their cells. There are also special individual education cells for prisoners to participate in online education programmes. These prisons have been used to hold prisoners perceived to be dangerous and as a means of undermining gang control in prisons (Shalev 2009). An example of a supermax prison is the Pelican Bay Security Housing Unit (SHU) in California which, until recently, could hold 1,170 prisoners. These prisons are also usually located far from urban areas.

Once assigned to the Unit, the inmate no longer associates with other prisoners and may see them only in passing, for example, as he walks through the unit to go to the shower. Exercise is also taken individually. The cells are windowless with skylights in the corridors. Studies of prisoners in these conditions have found, not surprisingly, high levels of stress and anxiety because of the prolonged isolation (see Haney 2003, Smith 2006 and Shalev 2009).

Because the environment is so highly controlled with high levels of security, and given the isolation of prisoners, prisoner solidarity is inevitably weakened. It is clearly very difficult to engage in any collective resistance and even individual resistance is limited. As Shalev observes: 'Staging collective action to increase their bargaining power with prison authorities under such circumstances is almost impossible, because, as one officer put it, "it takes more than one to have a disturbance"' (Shalev 2009: 163). Inmates are allowed out of their cells only one at a time and escorted by two officers and they are fully restrained with handcuffs, so any resistance is very difficult. However, she found occasional acts of resistance to rules, for example, prisoners may illicitly send messages or items to each other using string through their cell doors, may refuse to return their food trays at the end of day, or in more extreme cases resort to 'gassing', the throwing of bodily fluids at officers. In such cases there is usually a quick reaction from officers, with the use of CS gas, and restraints. While the use of some of the more extreme measures was successfully challenged in the Pelican Bay case *Madrid v Gomez*, 889 F.Supp 1146 (1995) disruptive behaviour will be met with a strong response. The Court did see some sanctions as excessive, for example, being held naked or partially dressed in small outdoor cages in bad weather and the use of leg irons.

Shalev questions whether supermax prisons have achieved their various objectives. For example, they have not led to a fall in violence in the prison estate, a point also made in *Madrid v Gomez*. Neither have they reduced gang activity, as others may move in to fill places in gangs if the leaders are segregated. One purported justification was that removing difficult prisoners would allow others to follow educational programmes in peace, but in fact California, where Pelican Bay is located, spends relatively little on such programmes. Another rationale is public protection, but this could be achieved with a strong external perimeter. Moreover, the supermax imposes high economic costs because the regime demands high levels of staffing and results in high social costs, as prisoners released following isolation may lose social skills and will find it harder to reintegrate, so this may ultimately contribute to increased recidivism.

However, while these regimes have stifled collective action, including riots and demonstrations, the Pelican Bay prisoners have engaged in litigation, casting a spotlight on conditions in supermax prisons. There are clearly human rights issues as the conditions arguably constitute cruel, inhuman and degrading treatment or punishment and therefore breach Article 7 of the International Covenant on Civil and Political Rights. In *Madrid v Gomez* in 1995, the Pelican Bay prisoners brought a civil rights class action under U.S.C. 1983, challenging their conditions, highlighting problems in a wide range of areas, including assaults, insufficient training opportunities, inadequate medical care, access to lawyers and solitary confinement in the SHU. The District Court verified many of the prisoners' claims and was especially critical of the prison administration's failure to deal with prisoners' medical needs adequately. It ordered the prison to develop a remedial plan to address the problems. But while the court was critical of the conditions, it would not say that security housing units per se are unconstitutional: 'They do not, however violate exacting Eighth Amendment standards, except for the specific population subgroups identified in this opinion' (at 1280). The specific groups were the mentally ill and those at high risk of mental illness. Further litigation on costs was unsuccessful in the Court of Appeals for the Ninth Circuit in *Madrid v Gomez* 190 F.3d 990 (1999).

Since then there has been continued resistance and protests at the SHU at Pelican Bay. In 2011, prisoners organised a hunger strike which lasted three weeks in protest against their conditions of solitary confinement. It was supported by other prisoners at other establishments in California. At one point 6,000 prisoners in California were refusing meals. The Pelican Bay strike ended when the prisoners were assured that they would be given wall calendars, outdoor clothing and educational opportunities. The California Department of Corrections also agreed to review policies on gang validation. A law suit was also filed against the state over prolonged isolation and their conditions and criteria for gang validation in 2012 in *Ashker v Governor of California* Case No. 4:09-cv-5796 CW. The case was settled in 2015 with an agreement to end indeterminate solitary confinement. The state can now no longer give indeterminate sentences, time on the unit must be subject to regular reviews, and inmates' behaviour rather than gang member status will be used as the basis of admission. These changes are expected to reduce the numbers held in isolation and the period of time spent there. Nearly half of the cells on the unit were converted to general use in 2017.

Conclusion

As we have seen in the UK and the US, prisons remain volatile and unsafe environ-ments. Despite periods of calm, they have remained unstable with sporadic instances of violence. In the UK prisoners have been subject to greater controls and surveil-lance, through the use of CCTV and body cameras as well as controlled by the incentives and disincentives of the IEP scheme. The availability of synthetic drugs has also offered prisoners an individual means of mental escape, but also contributed to violence and to an increase in mental health problems. Despite the fragmenting effects of modern methods of surveillance and control, protests have continued. As the prison population has increased, tensions have persisted and prison violence has reached record levels and the situation has been likened to a powder keg.

While riots damage the prison infrastructure, and may lead to injury and increase public hostility to prisoners, they may also generate change and focus public attention on prison conditions. The year of riots in 1990 was effective in bringing about change in prisons in England and Wales, and already the disorder of 2016 has stimulated debate on the changes needed to prison regimes and led to increases in prison staff. In the US the dramatic riots in Attica and New Mexico did achieve some changes.

Whether prison protests and riots should be seen as political acts is debateable. As we have seen, in some cases rioting is alcohol inspired or an opportunity for looting rather than a political act. But in a broader sense, prisoners' resistance and rebellion may be seen as an attempt to retain some power over their lives, challenge unpopular changes to prison life, and protest over their conditions and in some cases to achieve regime change. The politicisation of prisoners during the Attica riot additionally reflected the political changes outside the prison. Of course as well as riots and disorder, prisoners may respond through internalising anger and despair at their conditions through self-harm, drug use and suicide.

It is also clear from the experience of the riots that a lack of political structure which allows prisoners to express grievances or demands for change can exacerbate the discontent. In New Mexico the depoliticisation of prisoners by dismantling of structures which gave prisoners a voice, had adverse effects. So political structures such as prisoner councils and the development of engagement and political awareness through education and the development of active citizenship can offer a better prospect of stability. In this respect the political life of the prisoner should be seen as a positive rather than a negative development. In some of the riots pris-oner representatives had played a positive role in seeking to constrain violence and formulating demands and engaging in negotiations with the prison administration.

But rioting, of course, is not the only means or a desirable means to achieve change. We have also seen a recent revival of prisoners' unions in Europe which may offer a more reflective and overtly political challenge, as well as prisoners' strikes in the US. Litigation to protect and recognise prisoners' rights can also be seen as a political challenge and may be more effective than violent disorder. In the UK, some of the same due process rights as those as demanded at Attica were achieved without violence in the *Silver*[26] case in Strasbourg, through European Convention jurisprudence. The fight for voting rights, for example, addresses directly the heart of the political rights of the citizen in a democracy and will be considered further in Chapters 3 and 4. But prisoners' litigation on the more immediate conditions of prison life, access to the courts, and on contact with the outside world, can be seen as an expression of political consciousness, in seeking to change their situation and to challenge the exercise of power in prison.

The relationship between riots and rights is complex and the protection of rights may be achieved without disorder, but direct action has highlighted problems and brought prison life to the attention of the public. However, while we have seen an expansion of rights in a range of areas, including procedural justice, the potential has been limited by restrictions on litigation in the US in the Prisoners Litigation Reform Act 1995 and in the statutory changes in the UK, made by the Legal Aid, Sentencing and Punishment of Offenders Act 2012 (LASPO) and the subsequent changes in the Criminal Legal Aid (General) (Amendment) Regulations 2013 SI 2013 No. 2790. However, following a recent challenge by the Howard League and the Prisoners' Advisory Service, the Court of Appeal has ruled that cuts to legal aid for prisoners were unfair and therefore unlawful.[27] This challenge began in 2013 and the government has since made concessions in relation to applications to Mother and Baby Units and licence conditions, as well as segregation cases and resettlement cases regarding a prisoner's accommodation or care following release, which engaged Article 8, and in these areas, exceptional case funding will be made available. The Court of Appeal also considered the remaining areas of pre-tariff reviews by the Parole Board, Category A reviews and decisions on moving a prisoner to a Close Supervision Centre where legal aid was denied and the Court ruled that denial of legal aid did reach the threshold requirement for unfairness, as these were complex and significant matters. However, the Court was not persuaded that unfairness was reached in the other two areas considered, Offending Behaviour Programmes and disciplinary proceedings, resulting in additional days of imprisonment. Moreover, even where the courts recognise the need for change, the failure to implement change in prisons because of financial or organisational constraints, for example, may itself, as we have seen, generate further unrest.

Notes

1 *Campbell and Fell v UK* (1984) 7 EHRR 165.
2 The interference with correspondence issue raised in *McFeeley* was later addressed in *Silver and others v UK* App No. 5947/7 (25 March 1983) which decided that interference with correspondence did breach Article 8.
3 *National Socialist Party of America v Village of Skokie* 432 US 43 (1977).
4 www.insidetime.org/
5 Reported in the Netherlands Info Service News Bulletin, 31 July 2013.
6 Philip Oltermann 'Inmates set up world's first union for prisoners', *The Guardian*, 30 May 2014.
7 www.equaltimes.org/prison-workers-in-germany-are#.WACb-NQrKt9; www.global-labour-university.org/fileadmin/GLU_Column/papers/no_224_Nowak.pdf

8 See Blankenship (2005) for discussion of the case for expansion of prisoner unions in the US.

9 See Cummins (1994) for a history of California's radical prison movement.

10 See Scraton et al. (1991) for analysis of the Peterhead riot.

11 For further discussion of disciplinary transfers in the period before the riots, see King and McDermott (1990).

12 www.publications.parliament.uk/pa/cm201516/cmhansrd/cm160127/debtext/160127-0003.htm#16012749000003.

13 Broadcast 13 February 2017, *Behind Bars: Prison Undercover.*

14 http://unlockedgrads.org.uk/what-is-unlocked/, accessed 29 December 2017.

15 PSI 04/2017 *Body Worn Video Cameras.*

16 See *Madrid v Gomez* 190 F.3d. 990 (9th Cir. 1999).

17 See *Cooper v Pate* 378 US 546 (1964).

18 The fear of solitary confinement may even mean that women are reluctant to report sexual abuse (Swavola et al. 2016: 16). In the US there is a requirement following the 2003 Prison Rape Elimination Act to screen all prisoners for the risk of victimisation on admission and transfer, and where there is a sexually abusive incident and if there is deemed to be a risk, a prisoner may be isolated.

19 *R (CD) v Secretary of State for the Home Department* [2003] EWHC 155 (Admin).

20 *R (on the application of Barbara Gordon-Jones) v Secretary of State for Justice and The Governor of HMP Send* [2014] EWHC 3997 (Admin).

21 Moreover, even prisoners not on segregation may be locked in their cells for long periods, although they may be sharing cells. The Prison Inspectorate found that in local prisons 31 per cent of offenders reported being locked in their cells for twenty-two hours or more a day, with figures higher for young adults. (HMIP 2017: 3). But this was not as a result of their behaviour but rather reflected levels of staffing and overcrowding.

22 Cellular confinement cannot be given to young offenders.

23 *R (on the application of King) v Secretary of State for Justice; R on the application of Bourgass and another v Secretary of State for Justice* [2012] EWCA Civ 316.

24 The Prison and Young Offender Institution (Amendment) Rules 2015 (UK SI 2015/1638).

25 See, for example, Haney (2003) and Smith (2006).

26 *Silver v UK* App No. 5947/7 (25 March 1983).

27 In *R (Howard League for Penal Reform and the Prisoners' Advice Service) v The Secretary of State for Justice and the Governor of HMP Send* [2017] EWCA Civ 244.

3

THE QUEST FOR CITIZENSHIP
IN PRISON

Introduction

This chapter will examine the efforts of prisoners to become citizens while in prison. As we shall see, there are a number of means of pursuing citizenship, including volunteering, peer support and participating in prisoner councils (also referred to as 'prison councils'), as well as engagement in campaigns for voting rights and other rights in prison. Discussions of prisoners and citizenship have focused principally on voting rights – the quest for formal citizenship rights – but there are other means of expressing or performing active citizenship. In this context the role of peer mentors and volunteers is becoming increasingly important. Assisting older prisoners is also becoming a significant element of peer support, with the ageing prison population, and will be considered below. Peer support is well established outside prisons in community and neighbourhood programmes, for example, but it has also become more important inside prisons, and is a significant resource at a time of budgetary constraints, but also can help mentors as well as recipients (Perrin and Blagden 2016). Prisoners may also seek to acquire citizenship status as representatives on prisoner councils, as well as taking part in the prisoners' unions, as referred to in Chapter 2. Another dimension of citizenship is participation in education, which is receiving greater attention in penal policy, and has been given fresh impetus with the publication of the Coates Report (Coates 2016).

The struggle for enfranchisement still remains an important element of the quest for citizenship and campaigns on voting rights will be discussed in this chapter, with reference to the UK and the US, before going on to consider in more detail, in Chapter 4, the purported justifications for felon disenfranchisement. As we shall see, the exclusion of prisoners from the formal rights of citizenship reflects the view that prisoners do not deserve citizenship, but this is short-sighted, as this exclusion undermines rehabilitation. Promoting citizenship, by giving prisoners a say in their communities through the ballot box, encourages self-reliance and responsibility, while facilitating active citizenship can improve prison life and is consistent with the current focus on rehabilitation. The role of volunteering and education, as well as the campaign for voting rights, will be considered in discussing the development of the prisoner as a *zoon politikon*. These manifestations of citizenship will now be explored in more detail.

Volunteering and active citizenship

Active citizenship was stressed by the Labour Government in the period 2000–2003, with specific reference to the contexts of health and to engagement with communities, but the focus was on life outside rather than inside prison, so prisoners were not included in this vision (Blunkett 2003). Indeed, it has been argued that the prison has been invisible within democratic theory (see Harcourt 2014). Prisoners' contributions to the wider community have received little attention, compared to the attention given to formal rehabilitation programmes. Prison reformers have stressed that there are a number of ways prisoners can engage as active citizens, including working for charities both in the wider community where permitted, and also within the precincts of the prison, or assisting other prisoners, or, more formally, by participating in prisoner representative groups, such as prisoner councils.

The active citizenship schemes currently found in prisons in England and Wales include literacy programmes, such as the Toe by Toe reading scheme run by the Shannon Trust and the Listener schemes, found in most prisons, where prisoners are trained by the Samaritans to offer a listening service to distressed fellow prisoners. There are also peer advisor programmes run by the St Giles Trust, programmes offering assistance with translation for foreign national prisoners and community support schemes which help others outside. For example, prisoners may work in charity workshops, or repair goods for charities. In some cases prisoners may be released on temporary licence to work unpaid in the community and for the community. Citizens Advice in Oxford, for example, has engaged prisoners from the local prison to answer queries from public, following appropriate training, and this has also been followed in other prisons.

Restorative justice can be seen as a form of active citizenship, for example, in victim awareness courses. Prisoners may also mentor young offenders from the community. User Voice is a charity led by former prisoners which encourages offenders to contribute to services across the criminal justice system. Its stated aim is to promote dialogue between service users and service providers, to promote rehabilitation and a more effective system and to promote active citizenship. Within prisons it recruits and trains representatives for prisoner councils. Furthermore, User Voice provides support for those leaving custody. There are also arts and media projects in prisons, as well as radio stations and prison newspapers. For example Pimlico Opera runs music and drama projects inside prison which the public may be invited to attend. Fine Cell Work teaches prisoners sewing and quilting. Insiders gives information and support to newly arrived prisoners.

Active citizenship is defined by Edgar et al. (2011) as understanding and exercising rights and responsibilities within a community, which suggests political literacy, social and moral responsibility and community involvement. Applying this to the prison context they say: 'Prisoners are active citizens when they exercise responsibility by making positive contributions to prison life or the wider community' (2011: 10). Any risks to safety and security in giving prisoners these roles can usually be managed to facilitate their involvement.

The Prison Reform Trust Report, *Barred Citizens,* examined opportunities for prisoners to exercise responsibility and the involvement of prisoners in volunteering and active citizenship and found that the main means of involvement in decision making were prisoner councils and wing forums (Levenson and Finola 2002). This was followed by a later report by Solomon and Edgar on prisoner councils in 2004, *Having their Say: The Work of Prisoner Councils.* In 2011 a further PRT study, *Time Well Spent: A Practical Guide to Active Citizenship and Volunteering in Prison,* looked at a range of activities conducting fieldwork in twelve establishments and a survey of all prisoners (PRT 2011).

While key policy documents, including *Breaking the Cycle* and *Transforming Rehabilitation,* have stressed the importance of developing voluntary and community sectors, as well as the private sector, they have not acknowledged prisoners' actual and potential contributions through their own voluntary work (Ministry of Justice 2010, 2013). Successive governments have focused primarily on the working prison, but could provide more purposeful activities by expanding citizenship opportunities. The use of volunteers from outside prison to work inside prison with offenders is well established and has provided a key link for prisoners with the outside world, but the potential of prisoners as volunteers has recently received more attention and support, as volunteering is seen as an expression of a desire to contribute to communities (see Abrams et al. 2016).

Edgar et al. (2011) studied volunteering in its various forms in prison and interviewed prisoners and staff involved in active citizen schemes available in most prisons. Prisoners may act as volunteers for outside groups, helping those in the wider community, as well as improving life within the prison environment. They identify a number of areas where citizenship can be developed in prison, for example, prisoners supplying braille units, working in workshops refurbishing old wheelchairs and bicycles for developing countries, and providing opportunities for individuals with disabilities to come into the prison to work with prisoners in prison gyms. They note that the range of possibilities has expanded considerably in the last twenty years and attribute this to a range of factors, including the publication of Stephen Pryor's *The Responsible Prisoner,* published in 2001, which argued that prison regimes should not take away more responsibility than is necessary to keep people in custody, and to the 2002 Decency Agenda which focused, *inter alia,* on time being actively filled. Peer mentoring is used increasingly in a wide range of contexts in prison, although the Prison Inspectorate has noted the importance of appropriate selection, supervision and training to prevent exploitation or abuse of vulnerable prisoners (see HMCIP 2015: 43).

A review of the Listeners scheme was conducted by Jaffe (2012) whose survey included men's and women's prisons, adult and young offender establishments. She found that that most prisoners were aware of the scheme and the support it offered, having learnt of it through publicity in the prison and from prison staff. Prisoners recognised the service was confidential and saw Listeners as trustworthy. Jaffe found that 'positive perceptions of Listeners were more common than negative perceptions among the prisoner survey sample' (Jaffe 2012: 29). Two-thirds of prisoners in the survey said that they would recommend Listeners to others. However, prisoners who spoke English as their first language were more positive than those for whom English was not their first language.

Although the major source of support for prisoners was their peers, prisoners were more likely to seek support from Listeners for emotional or mental health problems. Remand and first time prisoners were more likely to indicate a willingness to seek help from Listeners and prisoners are more likely to access Listeners during the first few days in prison. Contact is more common during the evening or night. The study also found significant interest among prisoners in becoming Listeners, particularly among male and Asian prisoners (2012: 4).

Those who were already Listeners thought that their training had been very helpful and that it had improved their communication skills, which benefited their relationships with staff, family and friends, as well as callers, and that it had boosted their self-confidence. They also felt better able to cope with their own problems since becoming a Listener. Some Listeners had decided to pursue a future career in counselling or social work because of their experience as a Listener. Most of the staff respondents were positive about the scheme and thought it helped save them time in dealing with distressed prisoners. With current high levels of self-harm and suicide, the scheme is particularly valuable.

Prisoners receive full training before and during their time as Listeners. The Samaritans had been working in prison before the scheme was established, training staff in suicide awareness (Samaritans 2011). But the suicide of a fifteen-year-old boy, Philip Knight, on remand in HMP Swansea in 1991, encouraged them to shift to a peer befriending scheme. This began in Swansea in 1991 and by 2012 there were 120 schemes in prisons in England and Wales. By 2010, Listeners had taken over 90,000 calls (ibid). At the same time the Prison Service has developed its approach to deal with suicide and self-harm and worked with the Samaritans to develop policies to reduce them. Jaffe interviewed fourteen Listeners and asked about their motivation: 'Many Listeners described an altruistic concern for other prisoners' (Jaffe 2012: 65). Some had experienced depression themselves in the past, or among their friends or family. On the wing, Listeners were respected as doing something useful. They found the role satisfying because it made them feel valued and respected by other prisoners and staff, and said that taking on this task had improved their behaviour. Jaffe recommends that more research should be undertaken on whether there are long-term benefits for prisoners in adopting the Listener role. The role is demanding as they may be approached by other prisoners on the wing and cannot switch off from it, which would be easier to do outside.

While prison itself can be seen as form of social exclusion and negation of citizenship – in areas such as disenfranchisement – volunteering offers a means of strengthening social bonds, promoting social inclusion and focusing on the needs of others. It undermines isolation and is essentially communitarian rather than individualistic. Moreover, while the routines of prison life generally do not allow prisoners to take responsibility, participation in these citizenship activities does offer benefits in encouraging the prisoner to take responsibility, improving self-esteem and accruing social capital by developing skills, such as working with others, which will be useful on release and may contribute to desistance. Taking responsibility for the duties inherent in the role and being trusted by the prison officers and other prisoners can give a sense of belonging and of giving something back to the prison community and the wider society. It may also help demonstrate to the Parole Board a change in behaviour and attitudes, which will be especially useful if the offender has been unable to obtain a place on or to complete a relevant offending behaviour programme. In Edgar et al.'s (2011) study, a prisoner peer support worker took on the role initially for an instrumental reason, to improve his chance of parole, but once he started the work, he saw it as a genuine opportunity to change his life. Engaging in mentoring and other voluntary activities means that prisoners acquire social capital.

Furthermore, there are advantages to the prison management as peer support may free overworked staff and contribute to good order in defusing conflicts. While the current climate is challenging with resource cuts, developing active citizenship schemes is not necessarily expensive and prisoners are an untapped resource which could be utilised more and this use can be cost-effective. Listeners may help avert crises, while Prisoner Councils contribute to the smooth running of the prison. A prison governor interviewed by Edgar et al. said 'Citizenship can be promoted in very practical terms: less self harm, less disruption, better social order, better compliance with offending behaviour work' (Edgar et al. 2011: 57). It also contributes to resettlement as it promotes a sense of belonging. Promoting responsible prisoners can in addition enhance dynamic security, as these prisoners may be able to use their influence on the wing to deal with problems and prevent issues escalating. Peer support may be particularly effective in a prison context, where prisoners may be sceptical regarding assistance from staff or professionals and be concerned over confidentiality and male prisoners may find it harder than women prisoners to discuss their personal problems with others.

The potential impact on desistance is significant, as desistance research suggests that engaging with the wider society can be beneficial in developing a new sense of self as a law-abiding citizen. For example, Uggen et al. (2004) and Burnett (2004) have stressed the ways in which desistance involves a change of self-image, as the offender develops new roles, in relation to work, family and community and can be seen as a process of civic reintegration. Edgar et al. acknowledge that the evidence in their study is not enough to prove conclusively that active citizenship contributes to desistance, but the prisoners interviewed did believe their experiences of volunteering had changed their life and way of thinking. Some said that their experience of peer support would help them in future to avoid committing offences. Prisoners interviewed found it meant that they could use their time inside more usefully and learning skills they could apply outside. So active citizenship encourages offenders to see themselves differently. Maruna's (2001) study of reformed ex-offenders also found that those most likely to reintegrate successfully were significantly more oriented towards the needs of others. However, prisoners who want to take on caring roles on their release, may find it difficult to obtain the necessary Disclosure and Barring Service certificates. Edgar et al. recommend that governments acknowledge the contribution of volunteering and active citizenship to rehabilitation and discuss ways of further promoting it, by introducing quality standards for active citizenship, ensuring safety, security and equality of access, involving officers more in volunteering and active citizenship and ensuring that prison policies do not inhibit the exercise of responsibility, as well as engaging with the local community and commissioning research to look at the contribution of outcomes of active citizenship to desistance. Prisons should avoid transferring prisoners who are in training as volunteers, or at least arrange for prisoners to shadow volunteers, to ensure a smooth transition. Buddy schemes and assistance for other prisoners could be further developed, with rewards for those who become prisoner helpers and proper training given. The Prison Service, they argue, should expand the opportunities for active citizenship involving the voluntary sector, for example, in relation to helping those with learning disabilities, caring for older prisoners, as well as in training and education, in the arts and the media. The Parole Board, and those involved in assessing prisoners, should take account of these contributions as active citizens.

However, the current climate for charities working with prisoners, especially smaller charities is particularly challenging, given their lack of public funding and the problems they face in accessing independent sources of funding, especially given the current focus on payment by results, following the *Transforming Rehabilitation* agenda. These problems were highlighted in a recent report, *Beyond Bars*, by New Philanthropy Capital (Wyld and Noble 2017).

It is also important to involve officers in the schemes, especially if they are anxious that some of their work is being taken over by prisoners. Good risk management by staff is also important, whether prisoners are working outside or inside prison, if there is a risk of prisoners facilitating an attempt to abscond, fomenting conflicts, exploiting a position of trust to gain illegitimate benefits, intimidating other prisoners, betraying a confidence, or failing to pass on information about activities which undermine security.

Another way citizenship skills may be acquired is through participation in prison clubs. Inderbitzin et al. (2016) discuss the experience of prisoners who were elected leaders in the Lifers' Unlimited Club at the men's maximum security Oregon State Penitentiary. These prisoners represented the interests of members in discussions with prison administrators and other prison clubs and worked with staff to organise events and panels and to cooperate with outside community organisations to raise and distribute funds. As the authors note:

> Participation in such prisoner-led clubs reinforces principles of democracy by showing incarcerated individuals that their votes and voices can be made to count and that they can make a difference in their own daily lives and

the lives of others. Leaders in these prisoner-run clubs are often the "good citizens" of the prison, recognized as such by both their fellow prisoners and prison staff, and they consistently make efforts to give back to the larger community by participating in fundraisers and contributing to organizations that work with children and at risk youth on the outside.

(Ibid: 56)

For many inmates, their experience of citizenship is acquired only within prison and prior to that they may be alienated from the democratic process. A further example of altruistic work is the use of volunteers in prison-centred hospices in the US. Prisoners are screened and trained to work with dying prisoners in custodial settings in, for example, the hospices at Angola Prison in Louisiana and the Dixon Correctional Center in Illinois (Cichowlas and Chan 2010). Work for the community may be recognised with qualifications or awards. Another example is the Paws for Progress Dog Training Rehabilitation Scheme at Polmont Young Offenders Institution in Scotland, which began in 2010. This scheme enables young offenders to help with the training and rehabilitation of dogs for re-homing. In doing so they may acquire an Association of Pet Dog Trainers Good Companion Award. In the US there are numerous dog training prison-based programmes which are well established, as well as programmes involving the training of horses, and general livestock management (Strimple 2013). Some of these programmes raise funds for the prison, but they also give inmates vocational skills and improve their self-esteem. Until recently there have been few rigorous studies of their value. However, van Wormer et al. (2017) assessed the outcomes of a state wide prison-based dog handler programme offered in most of the prisons in Washington State. Their research which, examined data relating to 1,001 prisoners, comparing those on and off the programmes, found that there were significant improvements in three of the four areas tested, namely serious infractions, violent infractions and grievances filed. So membership of the programme was associated with lower involvement in serious infractions and with fewer violent infractions, and dog handler participants also filed fewer grievances. In relation to the fourth area, of sanctions imposed, there was a reduction, but it was not statistically significant. The authors refer to these benefits as intermediate outcomes, as they do not directly relate to recidivism, but clearly contribute to the safety of the prison. However, skills acquired, including working with others, may improve job prospects on release, which will have implications for reoffending. There may also be less tangible skills, such as the development of empathy in working with animals and improved self-esteem.

Assisting the elderly

In the context of the rapid increase in the number of older prisoners, the support of younger prisoners may play a crucial role. The over sixties are the fastest growing group within the prison population in England and Wales and the numbers have tripled since 2001. In June 2017, the over fifties constituted 15.5 per cent of the prison population with 13,376 prisoners aged fifty and above. There were 8,564 prisoners aged fifty to fifty-nine, 3,213 aged sixty to sixty-nine and 1,599 aged seventy and over (Ministry of Justice 2017: 11). This rise reflects the wider penal expansion, with an increase in sentence length, as well as a greater willingness to prosecute and punish older offenders. A significant factor has been a rise in the number of prisoners sentenced for historic sex offences. Moreover, the latest Prison Population Projections for 2017–22 suggest that: 'The populations of over 50, 60 and 70 year olds in prison are all projected to increase, both in absolute terms and as a proportion of the total population' (Ministry of Justice 2017: 11). The Report notes that this is 'driven by increases in sexual offence proceedings since 2012. This effect is compounded in the interim by the longer sentences offenders are receiving, resulting in an increase in the number turning 50, 60 or 70 whilst in custody. Further growth relates to projected growth in recalls and an ageing lifer population' (ibid). This does mean that any current prison building programmes should be designed to accommodate the limited mobility of many older prisoners.

Older prisoners are more likely to suffer from ill-health and disabilities associated with ill-health and to require social care which mean high demands are made on the prison (House of Commons Justice Committee 2013). Until recently, their needs have been overlooked and there is still no national strategy for this group of prisoners. In some prisons older prisoners, including those with cognitive impairments, may receive assistance from younger prisoners through a buddy system, so these helpers perform a range of tasks, including collecting meals and newspapers. They are not permitted to undertake personal care because of privacy and safety issues. Buddy schemes and help for older prisoners could be further developed, with appropriate rewards for those who assist as well as proper training. If the work is fully accredited, it may enable prisoners to acquire an NVQ in social care and boost their employability.

It may also help older prisoners to integrate with the wider prison community and promote better relations between the two age groups, as many older prisoners are fearful of assault and bullying by younger prisoners. But it is not just younger prisoners who help. Within an older persons' wing, as Fry (2005) notes, older prisoners may develop their own citizenship skills, by offering support to each other and learn to tolerate others less fortunate than themselves.

As well as formal associations to represent prisoners, there may also be specific forums for older prisoners to provide help and support. These groups may engage visiting speakers to discuss writing wills, rights in relation to end of life care and other relevant issues (NACRO 2009b). Furthermore, they give prisoners a platform to raise concerns over their peers if they become withdrawn, which could be helpful in identifying prisoners with early stage dementia who could then receive a full health assessment (Moll 2013: 24). The number of older prisoners requiring peer support is likely to increase with the ageing of the prison population, particularly with the probable increase in the number of older patients with dementia, which will increase pressure on prisons (Fazel et al. 2002). At present the prevalence of dementia among older prisoners is unknown. However, Moll (2013) estimates that on the basis of rates in the community, combined with accelerated ageing in prison, dementia could affect 5 per cent of prisoners over fifty. Cases may be missed, in the early stages, because the depressive symptoms will manifest themselves in quieter behaviour, rather than more visible florid symptoms. Older prisoners are also less likely to engage in self-harm or to challenge prison discipline and to thereby bring themselves to the attention of prison officers. Moll argues for greater staff awareness and training in dementia awareness, although he notes that the Alzheimer's Society does offer courses in Exeter and Dartmoor. The organisation RECOOP (Resettlement and Care for Older Ex-Offenders and Prisoners) also offers support to prisoners and some prison establishments run memory cafes.

Education and citizenship

Education in prison is a further means of developing citizenship skills, but education also reflects the shared values of citizenship and recognises prisoners as citizens. Participating in courses and following national curricula gives the prisoner a valuable link to the wider society. Education is also a key element of rehabilitation, promoting the social inclusion of the prisoner, both on release and while in custody. A striking example of the potential of education in strengthening citizenship values would be the case of Anders Breivik, convicted of the murder of eight people in Oslo and sixty-nine people at Utoya Summer Camp. Breivik was accepted by Oslo University to study for a political science degree. While many opposed his admission, the University took the view that he should be allowed to apply for a place if he met the admission requirements and would follow the course through online materials. He began the course, but stopped to pursue an appeal against his conditions of confinement in 2016, arguing also that his conditions made it difficult for him to pursue his studies. He has also threatened to go on hunger strike in protest at his conditions. Clearly studying the principles of political obligation, the nature and terms of the social contract, and the rights and duties of all citizens would be particularly beneficial in such a case, and obviously beneficial to society if acceptance of those values and principles reduced the risk of future crimes.

Education has become increasingly important in penal policy. The Coates Report, published in 2016, reviewed the role of education in prison, its role and effectiveness, and considered ways of strengthening it and encouraging prisoners' participation in education (Coates 2016). The then education minister, Michael Gove, had also stressed the importance of education and even indicated that education could be a passport to early release if courses were successfully completed. It is accepted that education is a key contribution to the rehabilitation process. While the focus in recent years has been on basic skills, there is a wide range of educational capacity in prison with some offenders capable of progressing and benefiting from higher education. However, the problem has been in maintaining access to higher level courses given recent changes, for example, the requirement to take out student loans for higher education and a six-year rule which means that longer serving prisoners must be within six years of release, or their tariff date, before being allowed to apply for a degree-level course (PSI 32/2012). Moreover, because of the changes in funding and the six-year rule, very few prisoners now complete higher level courses and the numbers are declining.

Prisoners' right to education is protected by a range of international human rights instruments, including the UN Universal Declaration of Human Rights, the International Covenant on Economic, Social and Cultural Rights and the European Prison Rules. Article 26 of the UN Universal Declaration of Human Rights states that 'everyone has the right to education. This right is also protected by Article 13 of the International Covenant on Economic, Social and Cultural Rights which stipulates that 'The States Parties to the present Covenant recognise the right of everyone to education. They agree that education shall be directed to the full development of the human personality and the sense of its dignity, and shall strengthen the respect for human rights and fundamental freedoms...'. The Covenant also imposes obligations on states parties to guarantee that the right will be exercised without discrimination. Article 2 of Protocol No. 1 to the European Convention also protects the right to education: 'No person shall be denied the right to education.' However, the UK and many other states have made reservations to this Protocol. The UK has accepted the principle only in so far as it is compatible with the promotion of efficient instruction and training and avoidance of unreasonable public expenditure' (Schedule 3, Part II of the Human Rights Act 1998). In addition, the UN Minimum Standard Rules for Prisoners, recently revised and now known as the Mandela Rules, state that 'provision shall be made for the further education of all prisoners capable of profiting thereby, including religious instruction in the countries where that is possible... So far as is practicable, the education of prisoners shall be integrated with the educational system of the country so that after their release they may continue their education without difficulty' (R 104).

The European Prison Rules also state that 'Every prison shall seek to provide all prisoners with access to education programmes which are as comprehensive as possible and which meet their individual needs while taking into account their aspirations' (EPR 28.1). The Rules stress that education should not be given less status than work and that prisoners should not be disadvantaged by participation in education (EPR 28.4). In the UK, Prison Rule 32 states that every prisoner able to profit from the educational facilities at a prison should be encouraged to do so. Educational classes should be available for all prisoners and provision should be made for those with special educational needs. So it is clear that prisoners do have a right to education and it is one they frequently exercise, as large numbers of prisoners are engaged in courses. Coates (2016) observes that, in 2014–15, 101,600 adult prisoners were taking part in prison education with 81,800 on courses below level 2, 19,300 at level 2 and 100 on level 3. As well as following courses within prison, prisoners may be released on temporary licence to attend courses outside, although the numbers who do so are relatively low. Prisons are also required under the Prison Rules to provide a library in every prison and for every prisoner to be allowed to have library books and to exchange books. Library facilities are also a requirement of the Mandela Rules (para 40).

It is also easier to gain public support for education than for other prisoners' rights campaigns such as voting. There is less hostility from governments or the public towards prison education, as the value of education is clearer. Education is also a crucial right precisely because it offers a means of realising other rights, by empowering individuals especially those from economically or socially deprived backgrounds. To pursue a prisoners' rights claim requires a certain level of literacy and most prisoners' rights cases have been brought by longer serving prisoners and by those with literacy and other skills. Education is particularly important at a time of cuts in legal aid for prisoners introduced by the Legal Aid, Sentencing and Punishment of Offenders Act 2012 (LASPO) and subsequent further changes, although the government has made some concessions and the High Court has challenged some of these cuts as unlawful.[1]

However, the right to education may be limited by the availability of appropriate courses. Currently, some courses have waiting lists which means that some prisoners may find themselves repeating courses. The Strasbourg Court has made clear that realising the right to education will depend on the educational system of the particular states and states are not required to establish at their expense, or to subsidise, education of any particular type or at any particular level.[2] Not all courses are academic or vocational. Participation in offending behaviour courses, which focus on changing behaviour, may also be a necessary element of proving the reduced risk of the prisoner in future parole applications. The failure to provide sufficient courses has been criticised by the domestic courts and the Strasbourg Court.[3] Where there are insufficient courses, participation in active citizenship will give prisoners a means of arguing that their behaviour and attitudes have changed.

Education also provides opportunities to demonstrate active citizenship through the use of prisoners as peer mentors. Learning to read, for example, is a major milestone for prisoners with literacy problems, and literacy also opens the door to taking other courses and enhances job opportunities within prison and on release. The Shannon Trust, which was established in 1995, has collaborated with Toe by Toe to produce a Reading Plan suitable for use inside prison and using prisoners as peer mentors on a one-to-one basis. The Trust gives free copies of the manual to all prisons which have adopted the scheme and it has been used successfully for many years. Each year learners and mentors are surveyed to discuss the impact of the Reading Plan. Learners report improvements in learning and communication skills and self-confidence and say that learning to read has made prison life easier and that they want to engage in more learning in the future. Mentors also record improvements in self-confidence, organisational skills and teamwork and say that they have been encouraged to undertake more learning themselves and feel that engaging in the scheme is a good use of their time in prison.[4]

Coates also found excellent examples of peer mentoring in her review of prison education (Coates 2016). Training and rewards for mentors might also encourage more prisoners to take part, although it might be argued that this will undermine the altruistic value of the activity which is an essential element of citizenship. Prisoners may also give informal support to other prisoners outside the formal literacy schemes, and may help others acquire or improve their language skills. Using prisoners in literacy and other schemes can cut the costs of education.

In addition, education can contribute to rehabilitation. If education improves access to employment on release, then the risk of reoffending may be cut. But as well as imparting transferable practical skills, education can also sharpen rationality, improving the ability to make decisions, particularly when making choices on whether crime is worthwhile. We also know that the further the offender travels through education, then the greater the chances of a change in self-image, to identify with an alternative image to that of 'offender'. If education gives the opportunity for reasonably paid employment, then this will also reduce demand for benefits. But if it also reduces reoffending, then clearly social advantages will accrue as well.

A number of studies, including those of Steurer et al. (2001), Wilson et al. (2000) and Davis et al. (2013), have demonstrated that costs invested in education may generate benefits in excess of those costs. Steurer et al. (2001) studied over 3,000 inmates released in 1997 and 1998 from prisons in three states and found that those who had participated in prison educational programmes had lower re-offending rates than non-participants. They also found that for every dollar spent on education society reaped a return of more than two dollars in reduced costs of future imprisonment. Wilson et al.'s meta-analysis of thirty-three independent experimental and quasi-experimental evaluations of recidivism for education, vocation and work programmes, found that participants in those programmes had higher rates of employment and lower recidivism rates than non-participants (Wilson et al. 2000: 361). A later meta-analysis of research on the effect of inmates' participation in prison education found that participants had a 43 per cent lower rate of reoffending than those who did not, as well as better job prospects (Davis et al. 2013). A UK study by the Ministry of Justice Datalab found statistically significant differences in one-year reoffending rates for offenders receiving grants from the Prisoners' Education Trust (PET) for distance learning and for materials, compared to those who were refused grants (Ministry of Justice 2015). Intervention by the Prisoners' Education Trust led to a reduction in reoffending rates of between 6 and 8 per cent (ibid: 4).

Prisoners value education as it offers a way of using time inside constructively, acquiring new skills, offers a chance to exercise responsibility within an otherwise authoritarian and infantilising prison environment and provides a means of improving self-esteem. It may make life in prison more bearable and also provides a means of keeping in touch with the outside world. Contacts with teaching staff are especially valued. In a study of prison learners by the Prisoners' Education Trust, many respondents praised the teaching staff and learning support staff for their assistance (Taylor 2014). Crewe (2009) also found in his study of a Category C prison that prisoners were positive about and supportive of education staff and protective of them. Prisoners reported that they got on better with education staff than other staff.

Education is now accepted by the government as a key element in rehabilitation and resettlement. However, in practice, education competes with other prison activities including work, but also with court visits and other prison routines. If prisoners can earn more in work, then they may be less inclined to follow courses. Therefore Coates and others advocate that prisoners should receive the same, if not more, for education as other activities and governors should design incentives to encourage participation in education and educational progression. The Coates Report argued for further support for education and the government said it would accept her recommendations. But obviously unless further resources are available, the changes proposed by Coates will be difficult to implement effectively.

The Prisoners' Education Trust study in 2014 found that 80 per cent of the prisoners surveyed had prior educational qualifications (Taylor 2014: 2). A further problem is providing sufficient higher level courses, and progression to higher level courses is a major problem for many prison learners. If insufficient courses at higher levels are available, prisoners may be deterred from further study, or unable to continue with their studies. Limited access to IT resources, often due to security concerns, may also make it difficult to pursue some courses. The prison system's intranet, Virtual Campus, which gives prisoners access to community education and training courses and employment opportunities, is under-used. Respondents in the PET study of prison learners said that access to the Virtual Campus was poor and some prisoners had never even heard of it (Taylor 2014: 3). The Prison Inspectorate also found it was rarely fully operational and in one prison was not available even to Open University students (HMCIP 2015: 61). Prison learners are a diverse group, with different educational needs, and include prisoners with a range of levels of prior educational attainment, as well as foreign national prisoners, and older prisoners, with distinct resettlement requirements. The commissioning of private providers, with contracts being awarded on the criteria of course completion and level of attainment, may discourage provision of a wide range of courses and the current focus on payment by results will favour courses which move prisoners more rapidly into employment. The quality and quantity of education and training is variable, as noted by the Prison Inspectorate in its reports. The Chief Operating Officer of Ofsted, Matthew Coffey, has also reported a decline in the quality of course provision in prisons and highlighted problems facing prison educators.[5] He noted that 'Only 27 of the 78 prisons we have graded for learning and skills and work since 2009 were judged to be good for overall effectiveness or leadership and management at their latest inspection. That's just 35%. None was outstanding. Eleven were inadequate – that's nearly 15%. Too much education and training is simply not good enough' (ibid: 5). Issues highlighted included poor attendance and punctuality, poor-quality teaching, vocational qualifications which are too low, and weak careers information and advice.

One dimension of education which could be further developed is to provide citizenship courses and this would be particularly useful if prisoners were given the vote. A citizenship and law course was offered by the Centre of Criminal Justice and Human Rights at University College Cork to prisoners at Cork Prison in 2009. It covered a range of topics, including the European Convention and Criminal Justice and the Irish Legal System.

The Inside-Out Prison Exchange Programme which began at Temple University in Philadelphia in 1997, promotes courses in prisons, on crime and justice and matters of social concern. It takes students into prison to discuss key issues with offenders and the project is intended to be transformative.[6] These types of programmes are found in thirty-seven states in the US as well as in Australia and the UK. For example, a criminology module has been taught at HMP Durham under the Inside-Out Prison Exchange programme. Learning Together, based at Cambridge University, brings prisoners and students working together on courses inside prison and supports other universities seeking to develop their own programmes at prisons in their area. Over the past few years it has run courses on criminology and literary criticism at HMP Grendon, and Philosophy/Theology at HMP Whitemoor (Armstrong and Ludlow 2016). A Learning Together course involving students at York University is being run at Full Sutton prison.

Prisoner councils and prisoner forums

The disorder and riots of the 1980s and 1990s demonstrated the limits of maintaining prison order primarily on a coercive basis. The impact of the riots and subsequent Woolf Report, with its focus on fairness, justice and legitimacy, stimulated more input from prisoners on key issues affecting prison life. The focus on justice had started earlier with the revival of a due process approach in the 1980s, in response to concerns over rehabilitative models and indeterminate sentencing. In modern prisons, the focus now is on dynamic security, relying on good relationships between prisoners and staff, so that prison staff become aware of any problems or grievances before they escalate into conflict. Dynamic security is also a requirement of the European Prison Rules (EPR 51.2). This form of security is more effective than relying only on physical barriers or surveillance. In this context, prisoner representative groups, also called councils or forums, provide a means of defusing conflicts and managing change, and they give individuals the opportunity to develop citizenship skills and provide experience of contributing to a political process. Following the publication of the Woolf Report, the use of prisoner councils flourished and they have expanded further since 2000. They may contribute to the politicisation of prisoners, in the broad sense of engaging with a democratic process, if elections are involved and in acting as representatives of an interest group seeking to influence outcomes. Although the European Prison Rules do not refer explicitly to prisoner councils, EPR 50 states that: 'Subject to the needs of good order, safety and security, prisoners shall be allowed to discuss matters relating to the general conditions of imprisonment and shall be encouraged to communicate with the prison authorities about these matters'. Prisoner councils are found throughout European prisons but, as Bishop (2006) notes, their precise form may vary.

Solomon and Edgar (2004) conducted the first detailed study of prisoner representation in England and Wales. They visited seven prisons, including HMP Grendon and a private prison and interviewed staff and prisoners. They also sent the same questionnaire to other prisons with prisoner councils. They define a prisoner council as 'any structure that exists for consulting prisoners on a wide range of issues as opposed to having a specific remit, such as suicide prevention or equality and diversity' (Solomon and Edgar: 2004: 1). They may represent the whole body of prisoners at a prison, or a section of them. They found that these groups provided a useful channel for feedback, and improved communication and relationships between prisoners and staff. However, some staff were concerned that prisoners would not be mature enough to take on responsibility, or would use their position on the council to further their own interests.

Solomon and Edgar see the councils as a means of involvement in a democratic process, which is important given prisoners' exclusion from voting in general and local elections. Most of the councils in their study recruited prisoner representatives by election, although the processes were informal and did not involve candidates offering manifestoes. Rather, prisoners who expressed an interest in standing, were nominated by another prisoner, and if no objections were raised, they took their place on the council. In some cases elections were combined with staff recommendations.

At the council meetings, there was often a formal agenda. Prisoner representatives would canvass other prisoners on their wing to see what subjects they wished to raise at council meetings. In most of the councils in their study, the agenda was flexible and open to suggestions from prisoners, rather than simply driven by management. The most popular subjects were food, stock and prices in the canteen, followed by clothing and visits. Issues of discipline, complaints, diversity and drug treatment were often excluded from council discussions. Solomon and Edgar found that only a minority of councils were democratic, in the sense of taking decisions by a majority vote, and served as a means of discussion of issues, rather than as decision-making bodies. But they were still useful as they gave prisoners an opportunity to communicate their views, and prisoner representatives claimed their views did have an impact in achieving improvements and, in some cases, changes to policies. Prisoners also thought the councils had improved relations between staff and prisoners. Prisoners may prefer to raise issues via their representatives, rather than using the formal complaints procedures and the councils gave prisoners a voice.

From a management perspective, the councils offered a useful way of informing prisoners on any changes in policy and finding out their views. This clearly offers a better way of managing conflicts between management and prisoners than disorder or riots. While there was a resurgence of disorder in 2016, despite the existence of councils, there has been a period of relative stability since 1991, and the current crisis, as we have seen, is linked to other factors, such as overcrowding, understaffing and synthetic drugs. One governor in the 2004 study said that councils prevented prisoners from thinking there is no other option than to disrupt the prison. The councils can deal with tensions as they arise and act as a safety valve. Other governors agreed that they contributed to the smooth running of the prison, lifted prisoner morale, helped to manage change and reduced tensions, as grievances could be addressed in a timely fashion. The failure to establish the legitimacy of changes, as we saw in Chapter 2, was an important element in many of the riots in the UK and the US.

The representatives themselves also developed a sense of responsibility in protecting the interests of other inmates. The authors conclude that 'involvement in councils is a way of promoting active citizenship. Taking responsibility and having a say play a critical role in the rehabilitation of prisoners, in preparing them to return to society. Prisoners continue to be citizens despite their incarceration, but to enable them to act as citizens they need to have a real voice through councils' (ibid: 34). Solomon and Edgar advocate giving councils in England and Wales a similar legislative basis to those bodies in Canada which have a statutory basis under the Corrections and Conditional Release Act 1993 and which can contribute to decision making on most areas other than security matters.

The Prison Service Order 4480 (03/07/2002) *Prisoners' Representative Associations*, gives advice to governors and controllers on how to respond to prisoners who wish to set up or participate in prisoner representative associations in both public and private prisons. The operation of these associations is a matter for local discretion. Governors should take account of local conditions and the implications for good order and discipline. It is made clear that associations only have standing at the local level and not at a national or area level. While these associations are not new, as there have long been committees for communicating with prisoners, this Order clarifies the situation in relation to Article 11 of the European Convention, following the implementation of the Human Rights Act (para 4).

Article 11 protects the freedom of peaceful assembly and association with others. So it would apply to prisoners wanting to form or join representative bodies of other prisoners. But, as noted earlier, Article 11 is a qualified right and can be limited in the interests of national security, to prevent disorder or crime and to pro-tect the rights and freedom of others, provided any interference is proportionate and necessary in a democratic society. So in the context of imprisonment, the need for good order will be strongly weighed in the balance. The PSO makes clear that the associations and their members have no rights beyond those enjoyed by indi-vidual prisoners, no national standing, and that there is no obligation on the part of the prison to provide the association with facilities at public expense. However, '(T)he Prison Service encourages prisoners to take responsibility for their actions and to help both themselves and fellow prisoners' (para 3). This PSO also notes that an association may attract those wishing to subvert its actions for their own purposes, so must be monitored, and that the views expressed by members may not be representative of all prisoners. So it mostly focuses on negative aspects, but it does at least acknowledge the Article 11 right, which is added to the arsenal of prisoners' rights. Participation in prisoner councils can be seen as an important element of active citizenship, even if they do not have formal decision–making powers, unlike councils in some other states, such as Denmark and Canada. So councils provide a way of dealing with grievances and conflicts which might otherwise be resolved through physical conflicts or self-destructive behaviour. It is important that all prisoners have equal opportunities to develop citizenship skills. Councils may also offer an opportunity for prisoners with disabilities to participate, provided that assistance is given with presenting ideas and accessing documents. There have been some attempts to engage prisoners in decision making, for example, in the case of the humane therapeutic regime at Barlinnie Prison, which specialised in creative arts and relied on prisoners contributing to the small prison community (Nellis 2010). The Special Unit at Barlinnie opened in 1973 and closed twenty years later, despite successful outcomes with some very challenging prisoners.

Since the Solomon and Edgar study, there have been some interesting developments. One prisoner council model used in the UK is User Voice which was set up by an ex-offender, Mark Johnson, in 2009. It seeks to 'build structures that enable productive collaboration between service users and service providers',[7] to improve the criminal justice system and ultimately to reduce offending. It now has charitable status and employs ex-offenders. It is an independent organisation and charity which is contracted by prisons to develop, organise and maintain the prisoner council. It organises the election to the council, encourages prisoners and staff to take part, and supports the council in its work when in operation. It employs ex-offenders who can be role models for prisoners. It aims to give prisoners a voice and to focus on issues which affect the whole community and to promote a dialogue between prisoners and staff. Prisoners vote for parties, rather than individuals in council elections. So, for example, at the council election in Maidstone prison in March 2017, 64.4 per cent of prisoners and staff voted for four parties standing for seats on the council, including the Foreign National Labour Party, the Resettlement Party, the Residential Party and the victorious Equalities and Justice Party.

Schmidt (2013) conducted a participant observation study over three months in Birmingham, Aylesbury and Maidstone prisons. She reports that some staff were initially worried that the council would give prisoners too much power in the running of the prison, or threaten the status of staff, but once the council was up and running these concerns were assuaged. If the basic issues prisoners raised were resolved, this improved relationships between staff and prisoners, which were marked by greater mutual respect and empathy and prisoners became more aware of constraints on staff.

Contact with the employees, who were ex-offenders, also showed to prisoners the prospects of life outside, to help them focus on the future. Using ex-offenders also gave the council itself legitimacy. Focusing on achieving improvements to the prison community encouraged collective responsibilities and social inclusion. The council's focus is on the prison rather than the prisoner and on shared goals and collaborative efforts. It introduces prisoners to a democratic process which may affect how they see their role in the community outside and may contribute to desistance, if it offers the alternative identity of a responsible citizen, who participates in community life by volunteering and voting.

The status of prisoners on the council meant a new identity for prisoners as individuals who could contribute positively to the community and improve their sense of self-worth. As Schmidt notes 'Participating in the council enabled them to construct new roles that they saw as productive, helpful and beneficial to others' (Schmidt 2013: 13). Prisoners also matured and felt that they had to set a good example to other prisoners. So, when given more responsibility, they behaved more responsibly. The success of the council will obviously depend on the level of commitment of prison governors and staff, and its legitimacy may depend on positive changes arising from council deliberations, 'A User Voice council has significant implications for prison life and reversing potentially damaging penal practices of identity stripping through "civic death" and forced helplessness' (ibid: 17).

The campaign for the right to vote

A further dimension of the quest for citizenship in prison is the campaign for sentenced prisoners to regain the right to vote. Currently, convicted prisoners are not permitted to vote in the UK, during their period of incarceration, under section 3 of the Representation of the People Act 1969, as amended in 1983 and 2000. The purported justifications for the ban are considered in more detail in Chapter 4. However, the campaign in the UK has been active now for over sixteen years. It has mobilised large number of prisoners and a recent UK case on the issue in the European Court of Human Rights, *McHugh and others v UK* App No. 51979/ 08 (10 February 2015) involved over one thousand applicants.

The campaign began in 2001, when three prisoners brought a case to the High Court challenging their denial of voting rights. The Court declined to rule that the government was acting unlawfully, so one of the three prisoners, Hirst, continued with the action and brought a Convention challenge in the Strasbourg Court. In *Hirst v UK No. 2* App No. 74025/01 (6 October 2005), the European Court of Human Rights ruled that the blanket ban constituted a breach of Article 3 of Protocol 1 of the Convention, which provides that states should hold free elections at reasonable intervals by secret ballot, under conditions which ensure the free expression of the opinion of the people in the choice of the legislature. A blanket ban which took no account of the gravity of the offence or the differences between prisoners was an arbitrary and indiscriminate measure. However, the UK government has still not amended the law, despite two Consultation papers and a major inquiry by a Joint Committee, which considered a Draft Bill, heard evidence and published its Report, which recommended restoring the vote to some prisoners, namely those serving less than twelve months. We have also had confirmation by the Electoral Commission that arrangements could be made for sentenced prisoners to vote, without adversely affecting the integrity of the voting process (Electoral Commission 2009). Remand prisoners are currently allowed to vote, so there are appropriate procedures already in place. The former Prime Minister, David Cameron, made it very clear that he would oppose a restoration of the vote. Yet the Republic of Ireland has amended its law in response to the decision in *Hirst* and, worldwide, the move has been towards restoring the vote to prisoners. The Strasbourg Court has continued to criticise the blanket ban on prisoners' voting, while approving disenfranchisement in some very limited cases in other states.

In response to successive governments' failures to implement change, prisoners have continued to campaign for the right to vote. Because of the time taken to bring a case, most of the prisoners involved are longer serving prisoners on whom the ban has the most detrimental effect. In 2007 the legality of the May 2007 elections in Scotland and Northern Ireland was unsuccessfully challenged in the domestic courts on the grounds of incompatibility with the Convention.[8] But the courts did criticise the delays in amending the law. In 2009, in *Chester*,[9] the High Court declined to issue an additional declaration of incompatibility, as one had already been issued, or to exert pressure on the government to implement change, because the matter was then under review by the government. At that time, the government had issued a second Consultation Paper inviting views on the appropriate threshold in terms of sentence length for restoring the vote, although as we now know, that Consultation did not result in change. In 2010 the issue was considered again by the Strasbourg Court, in *Greens and MT v UK* App Nos. 60041/08 and 60054/08 (23 November 2010), when the Court made clear that a declaration of incompatibility was just satisfaction and that damages were not appropriate. The Court also said it would discontinue hearing repetitive applications pending compliance with the Court's judgment. A challenge to the denial of the vote in UK European and Scottish elections was unsuccessful in the domestic courts in *Chester and McGeogh*[10] in 2013, when the UK Supreme Court dismissed the appeal and declined to issue a further declaration of incompatibility or award damages. By then the Strasbourg Court, in *Scoppola v Italy (No. 3)* App No. 126/05 (22 May 2012), had approved bans on prisoners serving longer sentences elsewhere in Europe, and the Court also noted that under any of the options being considered by the UK, Chester and McGeogh would not be allowed to vote as they were serving life sentences. A further challenge to denial of the vote in the Scottish Referendum was brought in 2014 in *Moohan and Gillon v The Lord Advocate* [2014] CSIH 56 in the domestic courts, but this did not succeed, as the Court ruled that the Convention jurisprudence referred only to national and local elections, but not to referendums. However, a challenge to the denial of the vote to prisoners in the European Parliamentary elections in 2009, heard in 2014, did succeed in Strasbourg, in *Firth and others v UK* App Nos. 47784/09 and 47806/09 (12 August 2014). Here the Court acknowledged that there was a violation of Article 3 of Protocol No. 1, but said that this finding was sufficient just satisfaction for any non-pecuniary damage experienced by the applicants.

The Strasbourg Court reconsidered the issue a year later in *McHugh and others v UK* App No. 51987/08 (10 February 2015). The Court reaffirmed the breach by denial of the right to vote in Parliamentary elections in 2009, the 2010 General Election and the 2011 elections to the Scottish Parliament and the Welsh and Northern Ireland Assemblies. The case was brought by 1,015 applicants incarcerated at the time of the 2009, 2010 and 2011 elections. However, it declined to award compensation or legal costs, for the reasons given in *Firth*, namely that in the opinion of the Court, it did not consider legal assistance necessary to bring the case, as it was straightforward to bring an application citing Article 3 of Protocol 1, so costs were not reasonably incurred. It had made clear earlier in *Greens and MT v UK* App Nos. 60041/09 and 6005/08 (23 November 2010) that it was unlikely to award costs in future.

We can see from the continuing litigation and jurisprudence that the quest for citizenship through the democratic process has persisted, albeit with failures, as well as successes. However, during the period since *Hirst*, we have seen a hardening of opinion of the UK government against granting the vote, as well as a more fundamental rejection of the rights jurisprudence which has framed the successful assertion of prisoners' rights. We have also seen that the Strasbourg Court is more willing to defer to governments on matters of criminal justice policy.

Yet the voting issue remains a significant one in terms of the quest for citizenship. The vote has substantial symbolic and practical significance. It is the key emblem of citizenship status and if granted, affirms prisoners' status as individuals with dignity. In practical terms, the right to vote would give prisoners a stake in the political process and an opportunity to influence the outcome of an election. While prisoners are normally excluded and marginalised, having a vote would give them the opportunity to raise issues in relation to imprisonment and possibly influence policies which affect all prisoners. Historically, the fight for suffrage has been a key element of improving the position of groups without power in society, including the working class in the nineteenth century and women, who did not receive the vote until the early twentieth century. Moreover, the numbers affected by the bar are substantial. At the time *Hirst* was heard it affected about 48,000 sentenced prisoners and clearly numbers have grown since then.

Furthermore, as with the other examples of active citizenship considered above, it could also be argued that the act of voting itself would have social advantages in promoting a sense of civic responsibility, by considering what is best for the community rather than one's own narrow interest. The notion that participation in the public life promotes virtue has a long history and has underpinned the Aristotelian notion of citizenship. The *zoon politikon* looks beyond his or her immediate interests to consider wider concerns. There are also implications for rehabilitation, as the available research suggests that there is an association between voting and law-abiding behaviour. Uggen and Manza (2013), for example, found differences between voters and non-voters in self-reported criminal behaviour, arrest and incarceration. While a correlation does not establish a causal link, nonetheless it is likely that reflecting on the democratic process and election issues and seeing oneself as having a stake in society, may assist the change in self-image crucial to desistance and ultimately promote reintegration.

In the US, there have also been strong campaigns for restoration of the vote for felons. The rules on felon disenfranchisement are more severe than the UK, in so far as the disqualification, in some states, persists on release and, in some cases, for life. However, there are considerable variations between states. In some states the ban applies only to certain offences. On release, ex-offenders may be worried about voting in case they are committing an electoral offence, as there have been prosecutions and convictions for perjury, wrongful registration, and electoral fraud, so many potential voters may not register to vote, or actually vote, even if they are legally able to do so. The problem of the political impact of disenfranchisement has been exacerbated by the substantial expansion of imprisonment since the mid-1970s. In 1976, 1.2 million citizens were disenfranchised because of a criminal conviction, but this had increased to 6.1 million by 2016 (Uggen et al. 2016:4).

The demand for voting rights has been pursued by a range of groups, including the American Civil Liberties Union and other civil rights groups, the Sentencing Project, the Brennan Centre for Justice and the NAACP, as well as the American Bar Association and the American Probation and Parole Association. The focus has principally been on achieving racial justice, as there is a pronounced racial disparity in the impact of felon disenfranchisement laws, given the disproportionate number of black Americans who are incarcerated. A recent study found that black Americans were incarcerated in state prisons at five times the rates for whites and in five states, Minnesota, New Jersey, Vermont, Wisconsin and Iowa, the rate was ten times that of white Americans (Nellis 2016). For Latinos, the imprisonment rate was 1.4 times that of whites. In twelve states, over half the prison population was black. If we examine the imprisonment rate, that is, the number of prisoners from that group per 100,000 of residents, the figures for state prisons across the country were 1,408 per 100,000 for blacks, 275 for whites and 378 for Latinos. The reasons for these patterns, highlighted by Nellis, include policies and practices which drive disparity, bias and stereotyping in decision making, as well as structural disadvantages experienced by black communities, which are associated with high rates of offending. Moreover despite a fall in the prison population in some states, there has been a rise in the number of life-sentenced prisoners. As Nellis points out: 'Today one in nine people in prison is serving a life sentence while many other countries' use of life sentences is quite rare. Nearly half of lifers are black and one in six is Hispanic' (2016: 13).

As these patterns indicate, felon disenfranchisement laws have a disparate impact on black Americans, this has implications for the integrity of the electoral process. Recent analyses suggest that black Americans of voting age are four times more likely to lose their vote than the rest of the adult population and 5.8 million black Americans are excluded from voting because of a felony conviction (Chung 2016). One in every thirteen black Americans has lost the vote because of felon disenfranchisement laws, compared to one in fifty-six non-black voters. Many of these disenfranchised voters are actually outside prison, and are on probation, or on parole. Furthermore, twelve states deny the vote on release from prison, even if the person is no longer on probation or parole. In only two states, Maine and Vermont, is the vote of those with convictions unrestricted even for serving prisoners.

Since the 1950s, constitutional challenges to felon disenfranchisement have been brought in the courts. In *Richardson v Ramirez* 418 US 124 (1974) a challenge to California's felon disenfranchisement policies, brought under the Fourteenth Amendment, was rejected by the Supreme Court, which held that section 2 of the Amendment did allow for denial of voting rights for participation in rebellion or other crime. Where specific restrictions have a disparate impact on black Americans, there has been some success in bringing challenges, but not in relation to felon disenfranchisement per se. Moreover, it has been necessary to show discriminatory intent (*Hunter v Underwood* 471 US 222 (1985)). But in *Farrakhan v Gregoire* in 2010, the Ninth Circuit Court of Appeals initially held that the felon disenfranchisement law in Washington State was discriminatory as black Americans, Latinos and Native Americans were more likely to be detained.[11] The Court initially struck down the scheme because it violated section 2 of the Voting Rights Act 1965, in the light of statistical evidence on differential incarceration rates. However, at a hearing later that year by the same court, it reversed its earlier decision, to the disappointment of those campaigning for change, who saw this as a lost opportunity as well as a mis-interpretation of section 2 of the Act.[12]

The campaigns in the US have focused principally on restoring the right on release, rather than during incarceration, and this may be seen as a more urgent issue and, strategically, as one which is more likely to receive public support. Some states have modified their rules, repealing the lifetime ban in some cases. The Governor of Virginia, Terry McAuliffe, ordered the restoration of voting rights for 200,000 convicted felons by executive order, exercising his power of clemency. The Order applied to those who had completed their sentence, probation or parole. However, this was successfully challenged in the Virginia Supreme Court in July 2016.[13] The Court – in a split decision (4:3) – ruled that no previous governor had issued a clemency order to a group of unnamed felons, without considering their crimes, and that no power to grant a blanket pardon existed. The text of the Constitution prohibited en masse restorations. Clemency cannot be given without regard to the nature of the crimes and individual circumstances relevant to a request from the indi-vidual concerned. The court ruled that the governor's power to restore those rights had to be exercised on a case-by-case basis. He then approved restoration of voting rights for 13,000 respondents, using a replica of his signature under the seal of the Commonwealth. An application to find the governor in contempt of court failed. Virginia is a swing state and many of those affected would have been black Americans, the majority of whom are also Democrat voters. In the 2016 election, for example, exit polls indicate that 88 per cent of black voters did vote for Hillary Clinton.[14]

A class action complaint for declaratory and injunctive relief was also filed in September 2016, challenging the felon disenfranchisement law in Alabama, arguing that it violates section 2 of the VRA.[15] The provision in the Alabama law is similar to the intentionally discriminatory and vague 'moral turpitude' provision the Supreme Court struck down in *Hunter v Underwood* 471 US 222 (1985). Even if the court does not strike down the law, it may require changes in how it is applied and its extent after release for those convicted of lesser offences. In Florida there is a campaign to restore voting rights for most individuals on completion of prison, probation or parole, excluding those convicted of murder or felony sex crimes. The Voting Restoration Amendment proposed by Floridians for a Fair Democracy needs to garner a sufficient number of votes in order to be balloted in November 2018.

The rationale for rejecting demands for voting rights will be considered in more detail in Chapter 4, but regardless of the varying levels of success, the above campaigns demonstrate the demands for prisoners to be recognised as citizens and awareness of their role as participants in a democratic state, and are a key example of the prisoner as a *zoon politikon*.

Conclusion

As we have seen, investment in active citizenship whether through education or volunteering may be cost effective, as the financial costs are not excessively onerous and may save money by promoting responsibility and the improved self-perceptions of prisoners may give longer term benefits in terms of employability. Volunteering may make prison life more tolerable and promote a new sense of self-worth which may be a key element of desistance. The pursuit of active citizenship in prison may be an important element of the politicisation of prisoners as the various avenues we have discussed offer offenders ways of engaging with the prison community and the wider community, in looking beyond self-interest and taking account of the interests, needs and rights of others, inside prison or outside. While the decision-making powers of prisoner councils are limited, participants may develop skills of presentation and representation and achieve some small changes which improve prison life. As well as giving prisoners a voice, prisoner councils improve the legitimacy of prison regimes and give prisoners experience of rudimentary political practice, which may ultimately contribute to their reintegration into society. Prisoner councils may also give a sense of power-sharing even if their powers are limited. In the New Mexico riot, for example, referred to in Chapter 2, the removal of the council was a precipitating factor in the riot. The campaign for voting rights has also stimulated prisoners' interests in current affairs and given them experience of negotiating the legal system. These paths to change are less dramatic than the riots considered earlier, but may still be important elements of the politicisation of prisoners as citizens.

Notes

1 R *(Howard League for Penal Reform and the Prisoners' Advice Service) v The Secretary of State for Justice and the Governor of HMP Send* [2017] EWCA Civ 244.
2 *Belgian Linguistic Case No. 1* (1968) 1 EHRR 252. See also *Velyo Velev v Bulgaria* App No 16032/07 (27 May 2014).
3 *Secretary of State for Justice v James (formerly Walker and another)* [2009] UKHL 11, *James, Wells and Lee v UK* [2012].
4 www.shannontrust.org.uk/
5 www.gov.uk/government/speeches/ofsted-further-education-and-skills-annual-lecture-2013-seizing-the-moment.
6 See Weil Davies and Sherr Roswell (eds) (2013).
7 www.uservoice.org/
8 See *Smith v Scott* [2007] CSIH19 XA 33/04, DB [2007] CSOH 73, *Toner and Walsh* [2007] NIQB 18.
9 R *(Chester) v Secretary of State for Justice* 2009 EWHC 2923 (Admin).

10 R (on the application of *Chester*) *v Secretary of State for Justice; McGeoch v The Lord President of the Council* [2013] UKSC 63.

11 *Farrakhan v Gregoire & State of Washington*, 590 F.3d 989 (9th Cir. 2010).

12 *Farrakhan v Gregoire & State of Washington*, 590 F.3d 989 (9th Cir. 2010).

13 *William J. Howell et al. v Terence R. McAuliffe et al.* (Record No 16784) 22 July 2016.

14 https://ropercenter.cornell.edu/polls/us-elections/how-groups-voted/groups-voted-2016/

15 *Thompson v Alabama*, No. 2:16-cv-783, 2016 WL 5405634 (M.D. Ala.) (26 September 2016).

4

LOSING CITIZENSHIP IN PRISON

Introduction

This chapter will discuss imprisonment as the negation of citizenship in relation to the loss of the right to vote. While the UK position on the voting rights of prisoners is less draconian than many other states, sentenced prisoners are currently still not permitted to vote. Despite a successful challenge to the UK's denial of prisoners' voting rights in the Strasbourg Court in 2005 and the recommendations of a Joint Parliamentary Committee in 2013 for limited change, the vote has still not been restored. In fact the UK government has announced that it would rather withdraw from the Convention than comply. The most it is prepared to concede is to allow prisoners released on temporary licence to vote. This chapter will consider whether condemning prisoners to civil death is appropriate in modern democratic societies. The issue of prisoners' right to vote in recent years has focused more attention on prisons and received much more attention than other aspects of imprisonment. It is also interesting because it raises questions regarding the purpose of punishment and the social exclusion of prisoners and the meaning of citizenship, as well as the role of public opinion in penal policy and the disparate impact of the ban on specific groups.

At the same time, there has been a worldwide trend towards re-enfranchisement; many states have restored the vote, or at least narrowed the exclusions from voting for serving prisoners. This trend seems to have accelerated since the late 1990s, as a number of states have amended their laws to allow for prisoner voting. For example, in 2010, the Interim Independent Constitutional Dispute Resolution Court in Kenya, allowed prisoners to vote in a referendum on a new constitution. This was the first time prisoners had been permitted to vote. In 2014, the High Court in Benin ruled that prisoners have a right to vote in all elections in Nigeria. Even in the US, where there are well-established felon disenfranchisement laws, there has been a movement towards re-enfranchisement in some states. Prisoners have been allowed to vote in South Africa since 1999 and in Australia the ban is limited to those serving over three years. In Israel, all prisoners who are Israeli citizens may vote, regardless of the length of the sentence, including the offender who assassinated the prime minister, Yitzhak Rabin, in 1995. In some European states for example, Spain, Sweden, Denmark and Portugal, all prisoners are permitted to vote. In other states, for example, France, Germany, Italy and the Netherlands, prisoners serving shorter sentences may vote. Some European states changed their law after *Hirst*, including the Republic of Ireland and Cyprus, but not the UK.

This liberalisation of the law reflects the increasing cosmopolitanism of legal reasoning across a range of diverse jurisdictions. In recent years, there has been a cross-fertilisation of constitutional ideas and principles as they 'migrate' between constitutional courts. A number of key judgments, including the cases of *August and another v Electoral Commission and others* CCT 8/99 [1999] ZACC 3 and *Ministry of Home Affairs v NICRO and others* CCT 03/04 [2004] ZACC 10 in the South African Constitutional Court, *Sauvé v Canada (No. 2)* [2002] 3 SCR 519 in Canada, *Roach v Electoral Commissioner* [2007] HC 43 in Australia and *Hirst v UK (No. 2)* App No. 74025/01 (6 October 2005) in the Strasbourg Court in 2005, make cross-references to the reasoning in these landmark cases. The South African Constitutional Court is also a major influence on the developing jurisprudence of other African states on a range of human rights and equality issues. So the courts have been increasingly aware of changes and jurisprudence in other jurisdictions.

The shift in favour of felon re-enfranchisement also reflects the increasing recognition of prisoners as citizens and the developing jurisprudence and penal law on prisoners' rights. Another important factor in reform is the role of activist groups. In the Republic of Ireland a penal reform group, the Irish Penal Reform Trust, was campaigning before the *Hirst* decision, but that case gave fresh impetus to it and there was support from some of the main political parties, which has been lacking in the UK (Hamilton and Lines 2009). So it seems a concerted campaign to effect change is needed. Whether change prevails clearly depends on the wider political, historical and social context, as well as the constitutional framework of individual states. In the UK, non-governmental organisations, such as the Prison Reform Trust, have supported prisoner voting, but they have primarily focused on other key issues, including segregation and prison violence, where the impact on prisoners' lives may seem more immediate and pressing than the voting question.

At the same time, disenfranchisement has persisted in many states, including the US and the UK. Of the forty-seven Council of Europe states, the UK is one of only five states, that have a total ban.[1] The civil death of prisoners has also been a significant issue in the US, where it has been accompanied by penal austerity and penal expansion. However, there are variations between different states, just as there are differences within Europe. In the US, local political traditions are very important in shaping penal policy (Barker 2009, Garland 2010). It has been suggested by Uggen et al. (2009) that re-enfranchisement is more likely in states with low incarceration rates, which suggests a less punitive society, as well as in states with more advanced social and economic development, but in fact recent developments indicate that prisoner enfranchisement is permitted across a wide range of states.

Imprisonment and social death

Imprisonment – both physically and symbolically – constitutes a form of social exclusion, or even social death, as the inmate is physically separated from society, stripped of income and status and political power. Forfeiture for felons, which included loss of the vote, has a long history and was found in Roman law and in Ancient Greece. With the loss of voting rights, the prisoner experiences civil death, in addition to the numerous humiliations, deprivations and status degradations which accompany imprisonment. Denial of the formal rights of citizenship, most significantly the right to vote, reinforces the exclusion of the prisoner from the community. But social inclusion is a key element of citizenship, as Marshall stressed, and for Marshall, the concept of citizenship incorporates civil, political and social rights (1950).

In the debate over prisoners' rights, governments have construed the denial of citizenship through disenfranchisement as self-inflicted, as prisoners by breaching the social contract, have forfeited the right to participate in the government of the country.[2] On entering prison, sentenced prisoners forfeit the right to vote and while today prisoners' rights are generally much better protected and acknowledged than in the past, this particular omission is striking. Of course, until the late nineteenth century, the social death of prisoners was more extreme, with prisoners losing their property rights on conviction, as well as civil rights. However, the Forfeiture Act 1870 Act abolished most forms of forfeiture.

While we can find increasing recognition of prisoners' rights in the UK, US and Europe, the most striking symbol of civil death in the UK is the ban on voting which was preserved in the 1870 Forfeiture Act and more recently in the Representation of the People Act 1969, as amended in 1983 and 2000. In contrast to the prohibitions in UK domestic law, the right to vote is strongly protected in international human rights law as a fundamental civil and political right. So Article 25 of the International Covenant on Civil and Political Right stipulates that 'All citizens have the right to vote and to be elected.' Article 21(1) of the Universal Declaration of Human Rights provides that 'Everyone has the right to take part in the government of his country, directly or through freely chosen representatives.'

Article 3 of Protocol No. 1 to the European Convention provides that states are obliged to hold free elections under conditions which will ensure the free expression of the people in the choice of legislature. So while this provision does not explicitly refer to the right to vote, it is clear from Convention jurisprudence, that the right to vote, as well as the right to stand for election, is protected by Article 3 of Protocol 1 which the UK has ratified. The European Prison Rules also stipulate that: 'Prison authorities shall ensure that prisoners are able to participate in elections, referenda and in other aspects of public life in so far as their right to do so is not restricted by national law' (EPR 24(1)). Voting is not mentioned in the

Mandela Rules, which concentrate primarily on prison conditions and prisoners' treatment, but Rule 1 does state that 'All prisoners shall be treated with the respect due to their inherent dignity and value as human beings' which would seem to be inconsistent with a state of civil death'.[3]

While the loss of the right to vote has a long history, the current debate on restoring the right was triggered by the European Court of Human Right's judgment in *Hirst v UK* in 2005, which found the UK's blanket ban incompatible with Article 3 of Protocol No. 1 to the Convention. Yet despite a strong case being made for re-enfranchisement and the worldwide move towards re-enfranchisement, including, close to home, the restoration of the vote to prisoners in the Republic of Ireland, there has been no significant change in the UK on this issue. In fact resistance to change has hardened in recent years, as the expansion of prisoners' rights has been caught up in the wider debate and attack on human rights. In contrast in the Irish Republic, prisoners were given the right to vote by post in the Electoral (Amendment) Act 2006, passed after the *Hirst* judgment. Prior to the Act, prisoners had been allowed to vote but were not given a postal vote, so they could only exercise their right if they happened to be on temporary release, or working outside the prison on the day of the election.

The development of the law on prisoner disenfranchisement

In the Middle Ages persons guilty of treason or felony were subject to 'attainder', the loss of all their civil rights. They were not allowed to own or transfer property and their property was confiscated by the Crown. Property ownership was a precondition of voting for ordinary citizens and this persisted until the 1918 Representation of the People Act abolished most property qualifications for men, as well as giving the vote to property-holding women over thirty.[4] So for most of the nineteenth century, those convicted of serious offences were not able to vote. Those convicted of lesser offences, misdemeanours, did not lose their property, so were not subject to that bar, but in practice they could not vote because they could not obtain release to do so. In *re Jones* [1835] 111 ER 169 a prisoner did try to get out of prison to vote, but this was rejected by the Court. The Forfeiture Act 1870 abolished the confiscation of a felon's property, but section 2 of the Act prevented any felon sentenced for more than twelve months from voting, or standing from election. There was still no prohibition on those serving under twelve months from voting, but still they were unable to vote, because they were unable to visit a polling station. Postal ballots were not made available to 'civilians' until the 1948 Representation of the People Act. They had previously been limited to those in the armed forces. It was reported in *The Times* that some prisoners did in fact vote using postal votes in the February 1950 General Election.[5] The distinction between felonies and misdemeanours was subsequently abolished by the Criminal Law Act 1967 (s 1). Consequently the disqualifications in the 1870 Act only applied to those convicted of treason. So in the period 1967–69, there was no statutory limit on the right to vote for prisoners. In practice, the qualifying address for postal votes was the offender's home address, but as the electoral register was published annually, this meant the prisoner could only vote until the new electoral register was published, so they had a maximum of one year to vote, because by the time of the next register they would not be at their home address.

However, the Representation of the People Act 1969 explicitly prohibited prisoners from voting, following the recommendations of the Speakers' Conference on Electoral Law which met in 1965–68. In its Report, published in 1968, it recommended convicted prisoners be denied the right to vote. The prohibition in the 1969 Act was then replaced by section 3(1) of the Representation of the People Act 1983, which states that 'A convicted prisoner during the time that he is detained in a penal institution in pursuance of his sentence... is legally incapable of voting at any parliamentary or local government election'. The ban applies only to convicted and not to remand prisoners and it means that the sentenced prisoner is eligible to vote on his release, in contrast, for example, to the situation in some states of the US. There are also exceptions for sentenced prisoners, who are incarcerated for contempt of court and non-payment of fines, who may vote (ss 3(2)(a) and 3(2)(c)).

However, there had been no Parliamentary debate on this issue during the passing of the 1983 Act which suggests that it was not seen as particularly important. Although remand prisoners were allowed to vote, in practice it was difficult for them to do so because of the problems of designating their place of residence. This was remedied by the Representation of the People Act 2000 which facilitates the formal right they already have by allowing remand prisoners to be regarded as resident at the place to which they are detained, for entry on to the electoral register (RPA 2000, s 7A). This concession to remand prisoners reflected the view that disenfranchisement was part of the punishment of convicted prisoners and this view has persisted despite increasing recognition of prisoners' rights in other areas (Easton 2011).

The exception for remand prisoners is a significant concession, but given that remand prisoners constituted only 11 per cent of the prison population in England and Wales in 2017, the numbers affected are not that great. The number of remand prisoners has declined since 2012 and fell by 6 per cent between 31 March 2016 and 31 March 2017 (Ministry of Justice 2017b). There were 8,842 men on remand on 21 March 2017 and 577 women (ibid: 2). However, this still means that large numbers of convicted prisoners are affected by the voting ban.

Moreover, the prison population has increased since *Hirst* was decided in 2005. At that time it was thought that 48,000 sentenced prisoners were disenfranchised by the RPA, but the numbers would be higher now. While the prison population includes foreign nationals who would not have voting rights, the number of British prisoners affected still remains high. Because the UK's incarceration rate is the highest in Western Europe, the impact of a blanket ban will have considerable reach, just as in the US, mass incarceration has increased the level of felon disenfranchisement.

Hirst v UK and its aftermath

The voting ban was unsuccessfully challenged by John Hirst and two other prisoners in the High Court in 2001 (*Hirst v Attorney-General, Pearson and Martinez v Secretary of State for the Home Department* (2001) EWHC Admin 239). The court thought that the UK's position lay in the middle of the spectrum of approaches in democratic societies and that the UK's position on the spectrum was a matter for Parliament, rather than the court. However, Hirst then took his case to Strasbourg where the Court in *Hirst v UK* made very clear that a blanket ban on voting infringed Article 3 of Protocol No. 1 of the Convention. In the view of the court the ban was not proportionate, as proportionality requires a 'discernible and sufficient link between the sanction and the conduct and circumstances of the individual concerned' (para 71). It stressed that any restriction should be limited to those who had committed major crimes. An infringement on a right must be in support of a legitimate aim and the means used should be proportionate to the aim and should not infringe the right more than is necessary. The UK measure did not meet its aims and there was no link between the denial of the vote and the prevention of crime or respect for the rule of law. Furthermore, it was disproportionate because it was not linked to the seriousness of the offence or the length of the sentence. It was also an arbitrary punishment, as whether the punishment took effect in a particular case depended on the external factor of the timing of the election. Excluding prisoners from the democratic process also made it harder for prisoners to have any influence on penal policy or other matters.

The Strasbourg Court acknowledged that Article 3 of Protocol 1 was not absolute, that there is scope for implied limitations, and that states must be allowed a margin of appreciation as there are different ways of organising elections. But there is no room for an automatic disqualification, especially one which is based on what might offend public opinion. Both before and after the *Hirst* decision, the Court has upheld the removal of the vote in some limited circumstances in other jurisdictions, but it has not approved a blanket ban.[6] The Court in *Hirst* did acknowledge that withholding voting rights to prevent crime and to enhance civic responsibility and the rule of law may be legitimate aims. But the means by which they were pursued in the UK – an automatic restriction on all sentenced prisoners – fell outside the margin of appreciation. The ban took no account of the gravity of the offence, the length of the sentence or the particular circumstances. The Court was also critical of the failure to consider the ban fully in Parliament. However, a dissenting judge noted that the Speaker's Conference had considered the matter, the UK did allow some prisoners to vote – namely remand prisoners – and that the matter should be left to Parliament to decide.

The UK government had defended its ban on the ground that it was intended to prevent crime, to enhance civic responsibility and to impose an additional punishment. Although the Court accepted these were legitimate aims, they were not rationally linked to the loss of the vote because they applied to all regardless of the offence. The Court has consistently taken the view that if the vote is removed, it must be limited to those serving longer sentences for more serious crimes.

Despite repeated criticism from the Strasbourg Court affirming the incompatibility of the blanket ban with the Convention, it remains in place. However, the issue of 'lack of discussion' has now been addressed, as two Consultation Papers have been published. There was also a Parliamentary debate on the issue in 2011, where it was clear that the majority of MPs were against restoring the vote. The matter was also considered at length by a Joint Parliamentary Committee in 2012–13.

Prisoners have continued to bring actions challenging their loss of voting rights, as we saw in Chapter 3. The Strasbourg Court has also re-visited the issue of legitimate limits on voting in dealing with cases from other jurisdictions. In *Scoppola v Italy* (No. 3) App No. 126/05 (22 May 2012) the Court upheld a prohibition on voting for a five-year period by prisoners serving sentences of three to five years, and a lifetime ban for those serving five years or more. However, those who were permanently deprived of the right to vote were permitted to apply for restoration three years after the end of their sentence and the Court said that this showed that the Italian system was not excessively rigid (para 109). In Italy the ban was not automatic or indiscriminate because the legislation took into account the gravity of the offence and the conduct of the offender, in contrast to the UK's position criticised in *Hirst*. A blanket ban is disproportionate and incompatible with Article 3 of Protocol No 1. However, the court has changed its position on the role of the judiciary. In *Scoppola* it said that the decision on who should retain the vote did not need to be made by a judge, in contrast to its earlier view in *Frodl v Austria* App No 20201/04 (8 April 2010) where the Court was critical of the fact that a ban had been imposed without judicial consideration.

In 2013, the Strasbourg Court reactivated the cases against the UK which had been frozen – which it then heard in *Firth and others v United Kingdom* App Nos. 47784/09 and 47806/09 (12 August 2014), although at that point the Joint Committee was considering ways of restoring the vote. In *Firth* the court did recognise the steps the UK had taken to address the situation, with the publication of the Draft Bill and the Joint Committee's report[7], but as the law was law still unchanged in the UK, it was still in breach of Article 3 of Protocol 1.

In 2010, the Coalition Government had indicated that the vote might be restored to prisoners serving shorter sentences to meet its international human rights obligations and also because of fears that there might be financial costs in paying compensation to the large numbers of prisoners affected, but did not initiate any changes. However, the Strasbourg Court subsequently made clear in *Greens and MT v UK* in 2010 and *Firth and others v UK* in 2014 that declaring a violation is just satisfaction and that damages would not be awarded.

The fact that the court will not award costs or damages in relation to repetitive applications was obviously strongly welcomed by the Ministry of Justice. In *Greens* the Court used a pilot judgment procedure as they had received over 2,000 applications on the same issue. Under this procedure the Court will reach a decision on a leading case and the remaining cases are expected to be sent back to the domestic courts to deal with, in light of the pilot judgment. Moreover, in *McHugh and others v UK* in 2015, it also declined to award costs unless they have been reasonably and necessarily incurred which was not the case here.[8] So, this financial threat has receded. The court also declined to hear future repetitive applications, while waiting for the UK to comply with the *Hirst* judgment. The domestic courts have also declined to make further declarations of incompatibility.[9]

Some voting rights cases have been deemed inadmissible by the Strasbourg Court, for example, *McLean and Cole v UK* App Nos. 12626/13 and 2522/13 (11 June 2013). This application, which covered a range of elections, was ruled inadmissible because it was filed too late in relation to past elections and too prematurely for forthcoming elections. It also included local government elections and the referendum on alternative voting which were not covered by the Convention. The Court noted that local authorities have administrative rather than legislative powers. A similar approach was taken in *Dunn and others v UK* App Nos. 566/10 (30 May 2014), because the case concerned forthcoming elections and it was unclear whether the 131 applicants would be detained at the time of the election.

However, while the law remains unchanged, there has been much discussion of the voting question. The first Consultation Paper in the UK, which was published in December 2006, had invited views on the issue as a matter of principle and on a range of possibilities, namely linking the ban to sentence length, or giving discretion to sentencers, or simply removing the vote for those convicted of electoral offences. Each of these methods have been used in other jurisdictions. At that time the UK government seemed to accept that some change was inevitable to meet the Court's demands, to restore the vote to some groups of prisoners. However, it was clear that it would not contemplate removal of the ban for all prisoners. A large number (47 per cent) of respondents to the Consultation favoured removing the ban for all prisoners, while a quarter wanted continued disenfranchisement. There was also a mixed response on whether to involve sentencers in deciding the issue, as this would create an extra burden on them. It would also add to the length of the trial and could lead to arbitrary results, with differences in voting rights between those who have committed similar offences. Even if guidelines were available, there would still be scope for interpretation. It would also be a retrograde step, given the efforts being made to improve the coherence and consistency of sentencing.[10]

The Second Consultation Paper published in 2009 invited views on where to set the threshold for voting, although the (Labour) Government made it very clear that at most it would restore the vote to those serving lesser sentences, while those convicted of more serious offences would continue to be subject to a ban. The paper also revisited the issue of judicial discretion and the disenfranchisement of those convicted of electoral fraud and those serving indeterminate sentences. The four options put forward were allowing prisoners to vote automatically if serving less than one year, less than two years, less than four years, and finally, allowing prisoners serving between two and four years to apply for the right to vote subject to judicial permission. The Consultation Paper made clear that the disenfranchisement was an additional punishment, but reinstatement of the prisoner's right to vote would 'mark his re-entry into society, and is aimed at enhancing his sense of civil responsibility and respect for the rule of law' (Ministry of Justice 2009: 23).

Had the vote been restored then to prisoners serving under four years in 2009, it was estimated that 28,800 prisoners would have benefited from the change.

The response to the 2009 paper was not published before the 2010 election, but it soon became clear that the incoming government did not favour change, with the then Prime Minister, David Cameron, famously saying it made him 'physically ill even to contemplate having to give the vote to anyone who is in prison. Frankly, when people commit a crime and go to prison, they should lose their rights, including the right to vote.'[11] However, in December 2010, the government did state that it would restore the vote in Parliamentary and European Parliament elections to prisoners serving less than four years, unless the judge when sentencing considered this inappropriate.[12] But this was not pursued. Instead, in office, Cameron made it clear that he did not want any change and that they would not be given the vote under his government.[13] This was supported by the Labour Party.[14] However there were dissenting voices. At the time of the Parliamentary vote in 2011, there were disagreements between members of the Cabinet. The then Justice Secretary Ken Clarke, in an interview on BBC radio, said that the government should do the minimum necessary to comply with the court's judgment and warned that the government would be unpopular if it wasted public money on compensating prisoners for a right they probably would not bother to exercise if it were granted.[15] Labour's John Prescott, in an interview with the BBC, said Britain had no choice but to comply,[16] and in 2014 he supported the return of the vote to some prisoners.[17] It has also been reported that Jeremy Corbyn supports change.[18]

The issue has also been raised of voting in European elections. In *Millbank and others v UK* App Nos. 44473/14 et al. (30 June 2016) the Strasbourg Court conjoined applications for twenty-two prisoners and found a breach of Article 3, because they were unable to vote in the European elections in 2014 and Westminster elections in 2015. The issue was also considered in relation to EU law by the European Court of Justice in *Thierry Delvigne v Commune de Lesparre-Médoc and Préfet de la Gironde* Case C-6501/13 in 2015, where the court ruled that the disenfranchisement for an indefinite period of a French prisoner, serving a twelve-year sentence for murder, met the requirement for proportionality.[19] Delvigne argued that the ban was incompatible with his rights under Article 39 of the (EU) Charter of Fundamental Rights and Freedoms. The Court thought the ban reflected the nature and gravity of the offence and the duration of the penalty. It was also possible under French law to apply for reinstatement of this civic right. The Court made it clear that the Charter did not prohibit disenfranchisement for those convicted of serious crimes. The opinion delivered by the Advocate General of the Court in *Delvigne* stated that:

> Article 39 of the Charter of Fundamental Rights of the European Union does not preclude national legislation such as that at issue in the case in the main proceedings, provided always that it does not prescribe general, indefinite and automatic deprivation of the right to vote, without a sufficiently accessible possibility of review, the latter particularly being a matter which it is for the national court to establish.[20]

The *Delvigne* case is also of interest because the Court construed Article 39(2) as including the right to vote in elections to the European Parliament, in contrast to the Supreme Court's view in *Chester and McGeoch*[21] that EU law and the Charter did not create a right to vote for individuals, but only obligations on the part of the state. Their Lordships also acknowledged the principles in *Hirst,* but said there was no point in making a further declaration of incompatibility and noted that prisoner disenfranchisement was being considered by the Joint Committee. However, in any case, Chester and McGeoch were unlikely to regain the vote under the options being considered by the Joint Parliamentary Committee, given the seriousness of their offences, namely murder. Their Lordships were also critical of Strasbourg for inconsistencies but affirmed the need to comply with the Convention (at para 86).

The survival of and support for the ban through Labour, Coalition and Conservative Governments, shows the difficulties of challenging disenfranchisement. Change has been avoided by successive governments who are wary of public reactions if prisoner enfranchisement is implemented. In the Parliamentary debate on the issue in 2011, a large majority (234 to 22) supported a motion endorsing the status quo and stated that decisions on such matters should be a matter for Parliament, for democratically elected lawmakers.[22] The Parliamentary campaign was led by the Conservative MP David Davis and supported by Labour's Jack Straw. But effectively this is saying that it is a matter for the electorate to decide who should be permitted to vote. The lobby opposed to change has also received a boost from the broader attack on human rights in recent years. The campaign for prisoners' votes has suffered greatly from being linked to this debate, which has diverted attention away from the fundamental issues of civic death and social exclusion.

The Joint Committee's Report on the Draft Prisoner Voting Bill

Nonetheless, a Joint Committee was formed to consider the issue further in 2012. The Committee published a Draft Bill on Prisoner Voting in November 2012, which included three options: to disenfranchise sentenced prisoners serving over six months, secondly, to disqualify those sentenced to over four years, and thirdly to retain the status quo, with a ban on all convicted prisoners.

The Committee then took oral and written evidence in 2012–13 from a wide range of interested groups and individuals, including those involved in prison reform, constitutional experts and penologists, NOMS and the Prison Governors Association, the Attorney General, the Secretary of State for Justice and a representative from the Council of Europe. The Committee also visited HMP High Down and HMP Downview to discuss the issue with prisoners.

The Committee published its Report in 2013 and the majority of members endorsed some limited change (Joint Committee 2013). It said the most persuasive option was allowing those serving twelve months or less to retain their right to vote (2013: para 236). Only three members of the Committee dissented from this. So this suggests that the most we are likely to achieve is very small groups of prisoners being permitted to vote if the Committee's proposals are accepted. While the twelve-month provision is not as generous as many campaigners would wish, it is at least a step in the right direction and once the provision is on the statute book and it is clear that no adverse consequence follow from it, then there may be a possibility of extending it further.

The Report stressed the importance of the UK's compliance with its obligations under international law. Non-compliance would undermine the standing of the UK 'and would also give succour to those states in the Council of Europe who have a poor record of protecting human rights and could regard the UK's actions as setting a precedent for them to follow' (Joint Committee 2013: 3). Giving the vote to a few thousand prisoners would be far outweighed by the importance of respecting the rule of law and the desirability of remaining part of the Convention system. The Committee was not convinced by the penological arguments used to justify loss of the vote, but it accepted that those convicted of the most serious crimes should continue to lose the right. Restoring votes to those convicted of the most heinous crimes, it thought, would not be acceptable to Parliament or the electorate.

It considered denying the vote to specific offences which undermine the state, such as terrorism offences, but thought that there would be problems of parity between offenders who had committed different crimes. Using length of sentence as a threshold would link the punishment to the seriousness of the crime and proportionality requires that the punishment fit the crime and sentence length is the best measure. Of course, there will always be arguments over where to set the threshold and it might appear arbitrary wherever it is drawn. A four-year sentence threshold would indicate seriousness, but neither Parliament nor the public, the Committee thought, would accept this. Using six months might be seen as too weak. However, twelve months would reflect the law in the Forfeiture Act 1870 where there was a loss of the vote for prisoners convicted for a felony, that is, attracting a sentence of more than twelve months. It would take the UK back to the situation when the Convention was signed, when twelve months was the threshold. This would mean that offenders convicted in the magistrates' court would not lose the vote, but those sentenced in the Crown Court would be unable to vote. The twelve-month threshold thus had the merit of re-instating the pre-1967 position. It also corresponds with the existing right to sit in the House of Commons or to stand for election. Section 1 of the RPA 1981 stipulates that it is not possible to stand for Parliament if the offender is sentenced to over one year in custody. Although this provision was ostensibly designed to address a loophole in the law, it was widely seen as a response to the election of the Republican prisoner, Bobby Sands, to the Westminster Parliament.[23]

The Committee did not rule out the possibility that prisoners serving longer sentences could regain their vote towards the end of their sentence. Prisoners would be allowed to apply six months before their scheduled release date to be registered to vote. It might also be possible for prisoners to earn back the right to vote and they could reapply when eligible to apply for parole, for example, earning the vote through good conduct, or completing a citizenship course, or other educational programme (para 219). Re-enfranchisement could be linked to a programme of civic education. This would then bring the focus onto the individual prisoner and meet the test of proportionality required by the Strasbourg Court and also act as an incentive to prisoners to engage with their social responsibilities. However, this would impose extra costs and the prisoners who the Committee met were not happy at the prospect of having to earn the vote. Clearly a civic right is not normally dependent on the behaviour of the right-holder. Earning the right to vote through the completion of citizenship courses, for example, would impose costs and administrative burdens and the public might resent the fact that prisoners receive citizenship education denied them. However, the Committee concluded that it was not feasible to leave the decision to a judge to determine on an individual basis.

The Committee recognised the issue of Parliamentary sovereignty which had exercised MPs, but thought that sovereignty rested in the power to withdraw from the Convention, rather than simply picking and choosing which obligations to follow, or which decisions to implement. One Strasbourg judge, Niels Muižnieks, in a letter to the chair of the Committee, had said that the UK should leave the Council of Europe if it refused to comply with the judgment. The Committee accepted that the UK is under a binding obligation to comply with *Hirst*, so Parliament should comply with it or renounce the Convention, of which it had been a prime mover. But the Committee thought it would not be worth doing so for a relatively minor issue.

It acknowledged that the ban is difficult to justify on the major theories of punishment and that the case for depriving prisoners of the vote as part of punishment is weak. The Committee thought the government had failed to advance a plausible case in terms of penal policy; for example, it had not established a deterrent effect of disenfranchisement on offending. It also questioned whether the ban was a proportionate means to achieve the legitimate aim of enhancing civic responsibility. Moreover, the Committee recognised that there might be some benefits from engaging prisoners in the democratic process, as voting could be used to generate discussion on other aspects of citizenship. It also noted that prisoners who took part in prisoner council elections were more interested in voting after release (para 144). While some respondents had focused on the contribution of voting to rehabilitation, the Committee did not consider this a sufficiently strong argument in favour of change.

The Committee therefore recommended that the government introduce a bill in the 2014–15 Parliament containing two options for consideration, one representing compliance with the Strasbourg Court's judgment and the other representing non-compliance. The compliance option recommended that all prisoners serving twelve months or less be entitled to vote in all UK, Parliamentary, local and European elections, in the constituency where they registered before sentencing. It was intended that the prisoner would vote by post or proxy, but not in person. If there is no identified prior residence, prisoners should register by means of a declaration of local connection. This would address the potential problem of bloc voting where results could be distorted by prisoners voting for a specific candidate, if a constituency was relatively small in size, but included a substantial number of prisoners. The Committee also proposed that prisoners should be allowed to apply six months before their scheduled release date to be registered to vote in the constituency into which they are due to be released (para 239). The majority of the Committee favoured compliance, but a minority favoured non-compliance arguing that the Strasbourg Court's jurisprudence on prisoner voting was incoherent.

Chris Grayling, the then Lord Chancellor, announced the publication of the Draft Bill in November 2012. When he introduced the Bill, he said he recognised the importance of upholding the rule of law, but also recognised that Parliament was sovereign.[24] He acknowledged the Report in a letter to the Chair of the Committee on 25 February 2014, but no detailed response was given.

Despite the continuing pressure from Strasbourg, the blanket ban remained in place for the 2015 and 2017 General Elections. The failure to change the law in response to the Strasbourg Court's judgment in *Hirst* was criticised by the Joint Committee on Human Rights in its Seventh Report, where it emphasised that 'States are under a binding legal obligation to implement [judgments], an obligation voluntarily assumed by the UK when it agreed to Article 46(1) of the European Convention on Human Rights. Compliance with the judgments of the Court concerning prisoner voting is therefore a matter of compliance with the rule of law' (Human Rights Joint Committee 2015: para 3.22). The Committee thought it 'highly likely that, if Parliament were to legislate to give effect to the recommendation of the Joint Committee on the Draft Prisoner Voting Bill, the Committee of Ministers would accept that the UK had done enough to implement the outstanding judgments against the UK, and the Court in any future challenge would also uphold the new law as being a proportionate interference with prisoners' right to vote' (at para 3.20). The Committee also noted that failure to comply would weaken the UK's credibility in criticising other states for their human rights failures (para 3.23).

The number affected by the various options proposed in the Draft Bill and the Report would have been relatively small. On 30 June 2013, 65,963 prisoners were excluded from voting. If prisoners serving less than four years had been given the vote, this would enfranchise 24,000 prisoners. The second option, of allowing prisoners sentenced to six months or less would give the vote to just over 4,000 prisoners. The one-year threshold would have allowed 7,000 prisoners to vote.

In December 2015, the then Justice Secretary, Michael Gove, indicated that he hoped to give a substantive response to the Joint Committee's report after the government had published its consultation document, but this has yet to appear.[25] Dominic Raab has reported that he went to the Committee of Ministers in September 2015 'to explain why the domestic climate, including the views of Parliament, make it unlikely – or unrealistic – that the ban will be lifted in the foreseeable future'.[26] He told them that the UK government 'will keep engaging constructively with the Committee of Ministers but I do not sense an appetite on either side for a tectonic clash over this, so I do not think that this will be necessary' (ibid). Neither the May 2015, nor the June 2017 Queen's Speech included any reference to possible changes to the law. However, the then Secretary of State for Justice, David Liddington, announced to Parliament in November 2017 that administrative changes would be made to give the vote to offenders who are released on temporary licence, for example, to attend employment, and temporary release, of course, is subject to a risk assessment.[27] They would vote outside the prison. This change is expected to enfranchise up to 100 offenders. So the prisoner would have to meet the requirements to register at his home address and would not be able to vote or register at the prison address, but would vote in the community. Because the measure is deemed purely administrative, no change in the law would be required and it would be simply a matter of changing the Prison Service guidance. In addition, it is proposed that judges will make clear to offenders when sentencing that they will lose the right to vote. Prisoners in custody would continue to be denied the vote. This proposed concession is intended to meet the Court's objection to a blanket ban and comply with the UK's international legal obligations. But the proposal clearly constitutes a minimal change well short of the Committee's proposals, and is a disappointing outcome to over a decade of reviews and litigation. In presenting the proposed change, the Justice Secretary stressed that other members of the Council of Europe maintain bars on prisoners voting and that the rulings of the Court since *Hirst* have acknowledged the legitimacy of denying the vote for prisoners convicted of serious crimes.

The clash with Strasbourg

The failure to restore the vote since *Hirst* has been heavily criticised by the Court and the Committee of Ministers on several occasions. Moreover, the issue has become enmeshed in the general critique of the European Convention in recent years and in the continuing clashes between the UK government and the Strasbourg Court on a range of criminal justice issues, including hearsay evidence and the deportation of foreign national prisoners. There have also been clashes between the domestic courts and the Strasbourg Court on these issues. Senior judges in the domestic courts have been more willing to challenge the Strasbourg Court and have argued that many of the problems addressed by Strasbourg are better dealt with in the context of domestic law.[28] In *Kennedy v The Charity Commission* (2014) UKSC 20, the Supreme Court vigorously asserted the importance of the common law, making the point that the common law did not end with the Human Rights Act. It was also stressed in this case that the court was not bound by Strasbourg's decisions, but rather those decisions were simply to be taken into account (at para 211). However, the Strasbourg Court has also modified its position on issues such as whether admission of a hearsay statement, as the sole or decisive evidence against the accused, will automatically breach Article 6(1) of the Convention.[29]

   The Committee of Ministers of the Council of Europe at its meeting on 25 September 2014, noted with concern and disappointment that the UK authorities did not introduce a bill to Parliament on prisoner voting at the start of its 2014 to 2015 session, as recommended by the competent Parliamentary committee. It urged the UK authorities to introduce such a bill as soon as possible and to inform them as soon as this has been done. It decided to resume consideration of these cases at their forthcoming meeting in September 2015. It then published its decision calling on the UK government to introduce a bill to Parliament to respond to *Hirst*, as well as to *Greens, Firth* and *McHugh*.[30] It recorded its concern over the delay in introducing the bill and said that it in the absence of change it would prepare a draft resolution. The 2015 Report of the Committee on Legal Affairs and Human Rights of the Council of Europe welcomed the Draft Bill and the Committee's Report and consideration of the issue, but was critical of the fact that the recommended changes had still not been implemented (para 235, Doc 13864). In December 2016, the government assured the Committee of Ministers that it would provide proposals for change by the time of the Committee's next meeting in December 2017. But as noted above the proposals are extremely limited.

However, it is not just the UK which been criticised by the Strasbourg Court on the matter of prisoner disenfranchisement. Turkey, Russia and Bulgaria have been censured in a line of cases including *Kulinksi and Sabev v Bulgaria* App No. 63849/09 (21 July 2016), *Anchugov and Gladkov v Russia* App Nos. 11157104 and 15162/05 (4 July 2013), *Murat Vural v Turkey* App No. 9540/07 (21 October 2014) and *Söyler v Turkey* App No. 29411/07 (17 September 2013), where the court has found their automatic and indiscriminate bans on prisoners' right to vote breaches Article 3. In *Murat Vural v Turkey*, the applicant had been given a twenty-two-year prison sentence for throwing paint over statues of Ataturk, which was reduced to thirteen years on appeal. The automatic ban on voting in Mural Varal's case extended even when he was on conditional release and the Court ruled it violated Article 3, as did the automatic ban in Soylar's case which, the Court noted, applied even when the offender was serving a suspended sentence. In *Kulinksi and Sabev v Bulgaria*, the Bulgarian government stressed that the offender could vote when he left prison, but this did not invalidate the violation while in custody. In *Anchugov and Gladkov v Russia*, the Court found a breach because of the indiscriminate and automatic ban on the electoral rights of convicted prisoners, which was underpinned by Article 32(3) of the Russian Constitution. Both applicants were serving sentences of fifteen years, but the ban applied to all convicted prisoners, serving from two months to life. The Strasbourg Court thought that it was open to the Russian government to explore ways of complying with the Convention, whether through a political process or by interpreting the Constitution in harmony with the Convention. However, the Russian Constitutional Court has responded by saying that it rejects the decision in *Anchugov* and will not implement the ruling, relying on new powers asserting the supremacy of the Russian Constitution, granted in December 2015.[31] On the general question of states' compliance across the whole range of issues considered by the court, the Report of the Committee on Legal Affairs and Human Rights noted in 2015 that that there were nearly 11,000 unimplemented European Court of Human Rights judgments (Doc. 13864, para 4).

The Coalition Government had argued for reform of the Strasbourg Court, with enhanced filtering mechanisms to reduce its workload, as well as for greater freedom for states, where the issues have already been considered by the domestic courts and on matters of social policy. The Strasbourg Court has responded to these critiques and has been more willing to allow states a margin of appreciation. The Court has also taken a more conciliatory approach in response to criticisms from the domestic courts in its judgments on major criminal justice issues, including sentencing and punishment, as well as evidential questions, such as the admissibility of hearsay evidence.

Reforms to the Council of Europe were announced in the Brighton Declaration in April 2012, which added Protocols 15 and 16 to the Convention, which reaffirm the margin of appreciation for states in securing the rights and freedoms of the Convention. Protocol 16 provides for non-binding advisory opinions to be sought by states from the Grand Chamber in the context of a case before a domestic court or tribunal. These changes were intended to reduce the backlog of cases.

The attack on human rights

But far from modifying its position, the Conservative Government has hardened its approach to prisoner voting. In its manifesto for the 2015 General Election, the party listed the continued denial of prisoners' voting rights as one of its key achievements. It also made clear its dissatisfaction with Strasbourg in its paper *Protecting Human Rights in the UK*, where it criticised the encroachment of the Court into the area of domestic policy and noted its intention to seek to confine the court's role to an advisory one and to limit its intervention to the most serious breaches of rights (Conservative Party 2014). It argued that the Convention had extended beyond its original purpose and scope and gave the example of the pressure to restore prisoners' voting rights as an example of the Court overreaching its role. It also made clear that if the powers of the Court could not be limited, it would consider withdrawing altogether from the Convention. Prisoners' voting rights has become entwined with the debate on Parliamentary sovereignty. In earlier comments, Cameron denounced the Human Rights Act as giving an invitation to terrorists and would-be terrorists to come to Britain. The party also included the repeal of the Human Rights Act in its 2015 Manifesto, but did not include it in the Queen's Speech that year and said that it wanted to undertake further research on the question.

In 2015 the Tories and UKIP specifically referred to maintaining prisoner disenfranchisement in their manifestoes, but Labour and the Liberal Democrats did not refer to it. The Liberal Democrats before they entered the Coalition Government had in fact supported prisoner voting and there are some individuals within the main parties who are sympathetic to change. Nick Clegg also said in 2011 that he would be reluctant to be suspended from the Council of Europe over the prisoner voting issue. The Green Party in 2015 said that it would restore prisoners' right to vote (Green Party 2015: 76). The Scottish Nationalist Party does not support prisoner enfranchisement and a clause prohibiting prisoners from voting was included in the Scottish Independence Referendum Bill in 2014.

There were no references to prisoners' right to vote in the Conservative, Labour or Liberal Democrat manifestoes in the 2017 General Election (Labour Party 2017, Conservative Party 2017, Liberal Democrat Party 2017). However, UKIP did state that it stood by its 2015 pledge to refuse to give prisoners the vote (UKIP 2017: 41). The status of the Human Rights Act was referred to by the Conservative Party in its manifesto, where it said it would not repeal the Human Rights Act while the Brexit process was underway and that it would remain a signatory to the European Convention for the duration of the next Parliament (Conservative Party 2017: 37). However, Labour is committed to the retention of the Human Rights Act, as are the Liberal Democrats, who will oppose any attempt to dilute the HRA or withdraw from the Convention (Labour Party 2017: 80, Liberal Democrats 2017: 69).

The Strasbourg Court has been criticised by the UK government for extending Convention rights beyond those originally in the Convention, by seeing the Convention as a living instrument. Yet, as Gearty (2016) observes, the number of declarations of incompatibility in the Supreme Court has declined and since 2010 there have been far fewer instances of incompatibility than the hysteria around the Convention would suggest. Moreover, when a Commission to consider a Bill of Rights for the UK was established, the majority of members of the Commission, while supporting a UK Bill of Rights, made it clear that it should build on existing obligations under the European Convention (Commission on a Bill of Rights 2012).

It is also worth noting that the Convention influenced the development of prisoners' rights in the UK, long before the enactment of the Human Rights Act, on a range of issues, even though it was persuasive rather than binding. For example, some of the landmark prisoners' rights cases such as *Golder v UK* (1975) and *Campbell and Fell v UK* (1984) on access to the courts, under Article 6, and *Hamer v UK* App No. 7114/75 (13 December 1979), on the right to marry under Article 12, predated the Act. However, the Act has considerably accelerated the process of challenging claims which can now be heard in the domestic courts and has strengthened the status and impact of the Convention and entrenched human rights within judicial culture and penal law.

In addition, the position of the Strasbourg Court itself has changed in relation to prisoners' rights and expectations, as the Court is now more willing to challenge limits on rights which governments seek to justify in terms of cost or expediency, as, for example, in the case of *Gusev v Russia* App No. 67542/01 (15 May 2008), and this has not has not endeared it to governments. The Convention has been a key weapon for prisoners in the UK challenging their continued detention, including in relation to whole life sentences, in *Vinter and others v UK* App Nos. 66069/09, 130/10 and 3896/10 (9 July 2913) and *Hutchinson v UK* App No. 5792/08 (3 February 2015), to delays in parole reviews for lifers, in *Stafford v UK*, App No. 46295/99 (28 May 2002) and to the conduct of disciplinary proceedings in *Ezeh and Connors v UK* App Nos. 39665/98 and 40086/98 (15 July 2002). The Strasbourg Court has also become more critical of governments' appeals to public opinion when discussing issues of penal policy, or when limiting prisoners' rights. Furthermore, prisoners themselves have become more aware of their Convention rights and have demonstrated the potential of Convention jurisprudence for challenges to their conditions and continued detention.

Justifying the denial of citizenship

The chequered history of the prisoners' voting rights campaign raises the question of why the restoration of the most fundamental emblem of citizenship has been so strongly resisted. The answer, in part, seems to be a question of political strategy as governments are mindful of what they see as a lack of public support for change. The first Consultation Paper stressed that the majority of the public supported felon disenfranchisement. A poll by the *Manchester Evening News*, conducted in October 2005, found only 25 per cent in favour of giving prisoners the vote, with 75 per cent opposed to it. A Sun/Yougov poll in 2010 found that 76 per cent of respondents opposed prisoners voting and 17 per cent were in favour (cited in Behan 2014b: 171).

However, during the hearings in Strasbourg, successive UK governments have strongly defended the ban on grounds of principle, although these principled arguments are open to criticism. Their main arguments are that prisoners have lost the right to participate in the democratic process because of their crimes, so the ban is justified as an additional element of punishment. Moreover, for a custodial sentence to be imposed, the offence must meet a threshold of seriousness so there is an element of proportionality.

The argument that prisoners deserve to lose the vote, because of their moral failings, has also underpinned the ban. By committing offences prisoners implicitly deny their citizenship and forfeit their citizenship rights. Conversely, the presence of prisoners in the electoral process, it is argued, corrupts the purity of the ballot box. This argument has a long history in US jurisprudence on the issue.[32] For example, prisoners could sway the vote in favour of unsuitable candidates, thereby sullying the process. There is a perception that offenders swayed by self-interest and impulsivity will make bad electoral choices.

The defence of disenfranchisement in terms of preserving the integrity of the electoral process is also advanced by Ramsay (2013a) who argues that if we allow prisoners to vote this is faking democracy, because they cannot be part of the democratic process of collective self-determination. He stresses that democracy means collective self-government, that the people are authors of the laws they obey; but this is not possible unless citizens have the freedom to communicate and organise around political ideas which prisoners are unable to do, and democratic citizenship is more than simply choosing different candidates in an election. Allowing prisoners to vote, says Ramsay, would be 'a contribution to counterfeiting democracy, extending the outward form of democratic government as a cover for the absence of the political substance of democracy – the self-government of the people' (2013: 11). He argues that 'in a state that takes collective self-government seriously voters should not be in prison' (2013b:421). The right to vote should be accompanied by freedom of association and movement in order to facilitate self-government which prisoners lack: 'without civil liberty, voting citizens (whether prisoners or not) retain the symbol but not the substance of self-government' (Ramsay 2013b:435). They are unable to discuss or influence the preferences of others, unlike citizens outside prison, but are dependent on and subject to executive control. But against this, one could argue that there is some potential for prisoners to participate more actively in democratic life within the confines of the prison, by organising discussion of current political issues, through canvassing and distribution of materials. There is also rudimentary political activity in prison available in the election of members of prisoner councils. Moreover, encouraging participation in voting and the democratic process, while in prison, may lead to prisoners becoming more engaged in political and civic life on release. Also as a matter of principle, exclusion of groups from the process itself undermines democracy. As Ruth et al. argue 'limited access to political participation for certain classes of citizens is equivalent to social injustice and results in an illegitimate democracy' (2017: 56). They consider the issue in relation to convicted felons, the homeless and immigrants, noting that in the US voting is skewed towards wealthier citizens.

In *Hirst*, the Strasbourg Court had made clear that it could not endorse the notion of civil death which underpins the UK's blanket ban. A similar approach was taken by the Canadian Supreme Court in *Sauvé v Canada (No. 2)* [2002] 3 SCR 519 where the Court said that construing prisoners as lacking the moral virtue needed to vote undermines the constitutional commitment to recognise the worth and dignity of all citizens which is essential to the legitimacy of the democratic process (para 35). In that case, a ban in section 51(e) of the Canada Elections Act 1985 – which originated in a civil death statute, the 1791 Constitutional Act, and which prohibited prisoners serving over two years from voting was deemed unconstitutional and a regressive law inappropriate to a modern democratic society. The court thought that the ban could not be justified as a punitive measure, as it was arbitrary and disproportionate and not linked to the blameworthiness of the offender, or to the harm caused. It also had a disparate impact on indigenous Canadians who constituted a disproportionate number of prisoners, relative to their size in the population as a whole. It also undermined respect for the law and for democratic life.

Similarly in the *August*[33] case in 1999, the South African Constitutional Court stressed that voting was an emblem of dignity and personhood and universal suffrage made clear that everyone counts, regardless of their wealth or power. The South African government's challenge to the *August* decision in 2004 in *Minister of Home Affairs v NICRO*[34] failed and the Court ordered the government to set up facilities for prisoners to vote in the forthcoming election. It also drew attention to the way disenfranchisement had been used in the past to bolster white supremacy and marginalise the majority and stressed the importance of respecting the right. It was also sceptical regarding the government's claim that allowing prisoners to vote would suggest to the public that it was too soft on crime, and it said that even if the government was concerned over the public's misunderstanding of this issue, this was not a good ground to deprive prisoners of a fundamental right.

The link between voting and virtue is clearly problematic and difficult to reconcile with the universal nature of rights, which should not depend on the characteristics of those who hold them. In *Hirst* the applicant had argued that denial of the vote was 'tantamount to the elected choosing the electorate' (para 46). In *Sauvé* the court also made clear that it could not allow elected representatives to rob a section of the population of its vote.

Rights do not depend on virtue and if they are universal then, by definition, they apply to all regardless of the unworthiness of the rights-holder. War crimes tribunals, from Nuremberg to those on Rwanda and the former Yugoslavia, as well as the International Criminal Court, have all emphasised the importance of due process rights for those accused of the most heinous of crimes. Many of these due process rights relate to interrogation, for example, the right to silence and to counsel and to the pre-trial and trial stages of the criminal justice process. But defendants are usually remanded in custody during the trial and following conviction and they remain subject to appropriate international human rights standards during their time in detention. Moreover, an extra-judicial punishment or execution of the most depraved offender will meet with widespread revulsion, because it violates the principles of justice and due process integral to a modern democratic society.

In any case, if we reserve voting for the virtuous, many offenders do not receive a custodial sentence, and so are permitted to vote, although they have undermined the social contract and are still lacking in virtue. There is also the dark figure of unrecorded crime which suggests the loss of virtue is more widespread than suggested by the formal badge of a criminal conviction. Studies of self-reported crime indicate a range of criminal behaviours across a wide range of groups, yet the perpetrators may not attract the attention of law enforcement agencies. Reiman (2005: 7) cites Zaitzow and Robinson's study of 522 professional criminologists, which found 25 per cent of the sample reported committing battery, 22 per cent burglary and 19 per cent tax fraud at some point in their lives, to emphasise that 'both criminals and noncriminals are morally mixed – neither are wholly immoral or wholly moral' (ibid).

The denial of citizenship to prisoners is also difficult to justify as in other respects prisoners are expected to perform citizenship duties while in prison, for example, those with sufficient wealth or earnings will be subject to obligations to pay tax and their children are expected to attend school. However, offenders in the UK are disqualified from drawing their state pensions or social security benefits if they are undergoing imprisonment or detained in legal custody, even if they have contributed for decades.[35] Also, if they earn enough while incarcerated, they will continue to make further national insurance contributions. Similarly, when women were fighting for their right to vote in the UK and the US, they were subject to all the obligations of citizenship, including taxation, but denied any participation in the election of governments who made decisions on how to use those funds.

In prison, offenders are expected to conform to the rules of the institution as well as the wider obligations of citizens to obey the law. They may also, of course, as we saw in Chapter 3, engage in a variety of forms of voluntary active citizenship. In the US, former prisoners could be fighting in conflicts to further the state's military aims, even though they are unable to vote in those states where disenfranchisement extends to former felons on their return to the community. Disenfranchisement is often defended because the social contract has been breached by prisoners' offending, but even if a term of the contract has been breached, the offender is not completely negating the contract or denying its significance. The punishment of imprisonment is the means of negating the crime to rectify the breach and a further loss – of the right to vote – is superfluous.

While it is difficult to establish the benefits of the denial of citizenship, we can find positive advantages arising from enfranchisement in terms of promoting the reintegration of prisoners. If there are some benefits and if no risk would result from voting, it would make sense to restore the vote. There is a strand in political thought, principally associated with Aristotle, which sees participation in the life of the community, performing public duties, as promoting virtue, because the citizen looks to the community's interest, which transcends private self-interest. So the lack of virtue per se does not preclude citizenship, but performing the duties of citizenship may promote virtue, for the *zoon politikon*. This argument is also found in Mill's discussion of representative government where he argues that taking part in political life promotes civic responsibility (Mill 1861).

A key justification of disenfranchisement, as outlined by the UK government in *Hirst v UK (No. 2)* App No. 74025/01 (6 October 2005) and in *Scoppola v Italy* (No. 3) App No. 126/05 (22 May 2012), where the UK acted as a third-party intervener, is that it is an additional punishment for prisoners, one which enhances civic responsibility and promotes respect for the law. The government also stressed that it is not an excessive measure, as the right is restored as soon as the offender leaves custody, in contrast to some states in the US.

These arguments are unconvincing. It is difficult to justify disenfranchisement, as an additional punishment as loss of liberty *is* the punishment. But even if we accepted that a further punishment is appropriate, disenfranchisement is hard to justify on the established principles of punishment. It cannot be supported on the grounds of retribution as it applies to all offenders regardless of the degree of culpability, the seriousness of the offence and the harm caused. If it were linked to the offence in a coherent way, for example, to electoral offences, or to crimes committed in public office, then that might be more justifiable. Removing the vote for those committed of electoral offences, for example, was supported by the Electoral Commission (2009). There is also sufficient censure in the prison sentence without an additional element being necessary. Furthermore, it is arbitrary because the impact of the punishment will depend on the timing of the election which is completely unrelated to the original crime. More importantly from the standpoint of retributivism, it is a degrading punishment in reducing the offender to a state of civil death.

The loss of voting rights is also difficult to justify on the grounds of deterrence, as the prospect of losing the vote would seem to be less compelling than the risk of a prison sentence. Moreover, for deterrence to work awareness is necessary, yet many voters may be unaware of the relevant law, so there is little scope for perceptual deterrence. Even where there is awareness, the loss of the vote may carry far less weight than the loss of liberty or the threat of penal austerity. Proving a deterrent effect is not easy to establish even with highly visible and harsher punishments, such as execution and imprisonment.

Felon disenfranchisement also does not satisfy the rehabilitative principle of punishment. The UK government's defence of the ban was that it promotes civic responsibility but, as we have argued, the ban epitomises the social death and social exclusion of the offender. Conversely, engaging prisoners in the life of the community arguably assists their rehabilitation and reintegration and the act of voting reminds voters of the obligations and responsibilities of citizenship. As the Canadian Supreme Court stressed in *Sauvé*, there is a connection between having a voice in making the law and the obligation to obey the law. The legitimacy of the law ultimately rests on the fact that all citizens have a stake in the law through the ballot box. Conversely, denying the vote has no rational connection to the aim of promoting civil responsibility, which was the stated aim of the specific provision being contested in *Sauvé*.

A further issue is whether the ban is justified in terms of public protection and whether prisoners' enfranchisement is harmful to others, that is, whether there are any risks to the public in permitting the vote. Here the arguments focus on the impact on the integrity of the electoral process. One might argue that individuals convicted of electoral fraud or interference with the process have already demonstrated that they are a risk and may continue to pose a risk if allowed to vote. In *Hirst* the Strasbourg Court said a voting ban would be justified where the individual had undermined the democratic foundations of society by gross abuse of a public position. It has upheld voting bans in such cases in *Glimmerveen and Hagenbeek v The Netherlands*, App Nos. 8348/78, 84-06/78 (11 October 1979) and *MDU v Italy* App No. 58400/00 (23 January 2003). But the UK ban extending to all convicted offenders is obviously much broader than this.

In the current political context, where there are concerns over the integrity of postal voting and risk of personation, and questions regarding the practices of the leading parties in relation to electoral expenses, the anxiety over reintroducing prisoners into the electorate might be understandable. But the integrity of postal voting has been strengthened with new requirements. Personation is harder to achieve in prison where there are constant roll calls and identity checks, and fewer opportunities to arrange 'additional' votes at the voter's place of residence. Remand prisoners already vote without incident and it would not be difficult to extend the procedures set out in PSO 4650, to sentenced prisoners. The Electoral Commission (2009), in its response to the Second Consultation Paper, thought that it would not be problematic to allow prisoners to vote by proxy or postal votes, so prisoners do not need to leave the confines of the prison to exercise their democratic rights.

The other issue is bloc voting, that is, whether the presence of prisoners voting together in a numerically small constituency, or in a marginal seat. For example, if there were a Titan prison, or an amalgamation of smaller prisons, such as HMP Isle of Wight, in such a constituency, this might influence the outcome of an election. If the result of an election could be determined by prisoners voting en bloc, it is argued that this would distort and sully the process. There is also the concern that prisoners could elect other ex-prisoners or career criminals to Parliament. This matter was raised by the Latvian Government in its submission as a third-party intervener in *Hirst* (at para 55). But diffusing prisoners across a wider range of constituencies reduces this risk.

Behan and O'Donnell (2008) discuss this issue in relation to the election results in the Republic of Ireland. Although prisoners in the Republic of Ireland had been allowed to vote under the Electoral Act 1992, as there were no facilities in place to do so, voting depended on whether the prisoner was outside prison on the day of the election. In *Holland v Ireland* 93A DR15 (1998), the European Commission of Human Rights had ruled that there was no constitutional right to a postal vote. Although a claim demanding the right to vote succeeded in the High Court in 2000, the government appealed and the Supreme Court in *Breathnach v Ireland and another* (2001) IESC 59 denied convicted prisoners the right to vote in prison. However, the law was changed by the 2006 Electoral (Amendment) Act to comply with *Hirst* and to meet the Republic's international human rights obligations.

Behan and O'Donnell note that the impact of the prisoner vote will be less significant if there are relatively few prisoners, in contrast to the US, where the incarceration rate is high and large numbers of Democrat voters are imprisoned so the current disenfranchisement there benefits the Republicans.[36] However, it may also depend on the type of electoral system in place. In the case of Ireland, the system is proportional representation, single transferable vote, which could potentially mean a prisoner bloc vote could be more significant. They give examples from the 2002 election of Cork South Central, where the victor won by just six votes, and Limerick West, by just one vote and Wicklow, by nineteen votes. In the latter case, one of the candidates was a former prisoner who had been given a presidential pardon, although he lost. The margins were much higher in the 2007 election so it would be difficult for prisoners to determine the result by voting together for a particular candidate. However, Behan and O'Donnell accept that 'in the event that the tight contests of 2002 were repeated in future years, it is possible that prisoners could influence who got elected and perhaps even which parties formed a Government' (Behan and O'Donnell 2008: 330).

The Joint Committee's proposal of using the former address or a declaration of local connection would address this concern, if the law were changed in the UK, as the offender would need to show that there was a genuine connection with the area. As prisoners are often housed far from home, their only connection with the prison area will be that they have been allocated to that particular establishment. The Committee said that it is hard to imagine that prisoners' votes – even if the vote were given to all prisoners – could significantly affect the outcome of an election (at para 188). Adopting the first or second options in the Draft Bill would involve low numbers, so they are very unlikely to affect the outcome of an election. There are few areas in which the vote could be skewed and in such cases voting in an area of local connection or prior residence deals with this problem. The current redrawing of boundaries will reduce the number of constituencies and the government is committed to the principle of equal seats, so that would also limit the impact. The Prison Governors Association has made it clear that there would be no administrative problems in giving prisoners the vote and procedures are already well established to deal with voting by remand prisoners. In any case it would be wrong as a matter of principle to exclude voters on the grounds of the party they might choose to vote for.

From the standpoint of the four key principles of punishment, retribution, deterrence, rehabilitation and public protection, it is therefore difficult to justify disenfranchisement as a punitive measure.[37] In any case, of course, loss of liberty is the punishment and prisoners should not be subjected to further punishment once in custody. Conversely, restoring the vote may offer benefits in protecting the public by promoting rehabilitation. Restoring the vote affirms and strengthens prisoners' status as citizens. As the Court said in *Sauvé*, denial of the right to vote undermines the values of equality, but acknowledging the right strengthens the value of equality essential to democracy. We also have some indications that there would be practical advantages in terms of rehabilitation and reintegration, as being recognised as a citizen would contribute to a change in self-image to an individual with a continuing stake in society. Reflecting on the political process in the period leading up to an election would encourage prisoners to reflect on what is best for the community and on both the burdens and benefits of citizenship.

The fact of voting may be significant in strengthening a sense of participation in the wider society. While there have been no specific studies undertaken on the positive impact of re-enfranchisement of prisoners in those jurisdictions where prisoners have been given an opportunity to vote, the Uggen and Manza study (2004), as we noted in Chapter 3, did show a difference between voters and non-voters in rates of subsequent arrest, incarceration and self-reported criminal behaviour. This was a study of students, rather than prisoners, but it does suggest that voting indicates a sense of being part of society. It highlights an interesting pattern which is worth exploring further and may support the Aristotelian view that participation in the life of the *polis* promotes virtue by strengthening the sense of obligation to a wider community.

As well as challenging the injustice of condemning prisoners to civil and social death, prison reform groups in the UK, such as the Prison Reform Trust and Howard League, and in the US, the American Civil Liberties Union and the NAACP, have all supported restoration of the vote, to serving prisoners in the UK and to former prisoners in the US, in the expectation that it would help their reintegration into society and ultimately their desistance. While the promotion of citizenship may contribute to desistance in giving prisoners an alternative identity, the impact of re-enfranchisement may be limited if the threshold is twelve months, as proposed by the Committee, but it is a step in the right direction.

Historically, groups have fought for the right to vote because the vote matters, both in terms of having a voice in public life, but also because disenfranchisement has been demeaning and insulting to those excluded, principally women, who went on hunger strike to fight for the vote, because it was seen as so valuable. The social instability of the early nineteenth century was also shaped by the fight for electoral reform and the extension of the suffrage to men without property. Exclusion from the democratic process reinforces inequality and while women have now been included, there still remain equality and disparate impact issues, when certain groups are disproportionately incarcerated, notably black Americans in the US and indigenous groups in Australia, as highlighted by the case of *Roach v Electoral Commissioner* [2007] HC 43.

The views of prisoners themselves should also be considered. The numbers involved in voting litigation in the UK suggest that the campaign is supported by many prisoners. The Joint Committee met prisoners to ask their views at HMP High Down and HMP Downview and found that only a few opposed prisoners voting. High Down is a Category B male local prison, holding mostly remand but also some sentenced prisoners, while Downview is a female closed training prison. At Downview, half of the prisoners the Committee met had voted before going to prison and all said they would vote if they were permitted to do so. They deemed the loss of the vote as an extra and illegitimate punishment and felt they were being punished twice. Some prisoners had not voted before but, by engaging in education, they had become politically engaged for the first time inside and did envisage voting in the future if permitted. It was clear that if they did have the right they would exercise it. Those with children said they wanted to vote for their children, to influence the government on their behalf. Others drew attention to the fact that they paid tax in prison and were affected by cuts in public spending, which impacted on prison regimes. Some said prisoners should be given classes on voting. Prisoners thought a ban based on sentence length was too crude, as prisoners convicted of the same crime often received different sentences. Some thought prisoners should earn the basic right to vote by completing a citizenship course, while others saw this idea as patronising, especially as no other citizens have to take such a course to be able to vote. Some prisoners suggested voting could be linked to prisoners' status, so those sent to an open prison might be allowed to vote, while others thought this very unfair, as not all those eligible for open status were actually sent to open prisons. However, it was also noted that politicians were often sent straight to open conditions. At High Down, it was clear that most prisoners saw the vote as a fundamental right. While one respondent thought murderers, and those who have committed serious offences, should not have the vote, others strongly disagreed. Prisoners agreed that voting could play a part in rehabilitation and courses in civic responsibility would help them reintegrate. The prisoners were critical of MPs who voted against the original proposal, saying that it was a reflection of politicians' general hostility to prisoners.

Whether prisoners would actually use the vote if it were restored has also been debated. It has often been noted by observers that voting must be low down on prisoners' priorities and even if the right to vote existed, apathy is likely to prevail, especially given that prisoners may be drawn from groups in the wider community, who may be less likely to vote. Former prisoners and a prison governor were interviewed by the press at the time of the 2011 vote. A prisoner who had been in prison for eighteen years and later worked as a probation officer, said that in both contexts he had never heard a prisoner say:

> 'Oh no, I've lost the right to vote'. Most prisoners don't spend their time in their cells discussing political issues. You're thinking about how much bird you're doing, where your next drugs are coming from, what your next job is going to be. These are people who are totally disenfranchised in every sense. And anyway, what can politicians offer to convicted criminals? It's not like they're going to let them out.[38]

A former governor echoed this view 'I can honestly say that in thirty-two years in the Prison Service I never had a conversation with an inmate about elections' (ibid). But perhaps this is not surprising as they have been excluded from the democratic process. Moreover, if re-enfranchisement were supported by political discussion in prison and the circulation of election materials, this could nurture an interest in the outcome of elections.

It was certainly clear at the prisons visited by the Committee that many prisoners strongly believed that prisoners should be allowed to vote because they were still part of society – despite their physical exclusion – and should have a say in how it is run. The litigation, as we have seen, has engaged over 1,000 prisoners and the lawyer acting for these prisoners did say to the Committee that some were keen to vote, while others were more interested in the financial compensation, which of course was not forthcoming.

But even if the motive for litigation in some cases is pecuniary, this does not negate the principled case for universal suffrage and for felon re-enfranchisement. The case is also not undermined by the claim that prisoners may not use the vote if they are given it. The denial of citizenship through disenfranchisement remains the most important practical and symbolic manifestation of civic death in the UK and in the US. So the argument that if prisoners would not bother to vote even if they had the right is irrelevant and misses the key issue that the right should be available as a matter of principle. There may be a number of reasons, apart from apathy, why electors may refrain from voting, for example, a dismal range of candidates, or as a protest over a particular issue, but the abstention of some voters does not undermine the democratic case for re-enfranchisement. The demographic characteristics of the prison population, the fact that many prisoners are young males, formerly engaged in low-skilled and unskilled work or unemployed, may suggest a low level of involvement in electoral politics, which may persist in prison, but imprisonment may also offer an opportunity to consider the wider issues beyond the institution.

Moreover, the youth vote was deemed to be crucial in influencing the outcome of the 2017 General Election, so interest in politics may change depending on the social and political circumstances. Party preferences may also reflect pre-existing choices and allegiances. The turnout of prisoners may also vary depending on the type of election. Storgaard (2009) found that prisoners' voting in Denmark varied between 20 and 80 per cent for parliamentary elections and was lower for local elections and European referendums.

Behan and O'Donnell found that initially after the vote was restored in the Republic of Ireland, the actual number of prisoners who registered was low, but those who did register had a high turnout (Behan and O'Donnell 2008). The 2007 election was the first election following restoration in which prisoners were able to vote using postal votes. Although the number of prisoners registering was small, there was not a great deal of time in which to register, and, as they point out, many prisoners are serving short sentences and might think it is not worth registering. There were higher levels of registration in prisons for those serving longer sentences and containing some Republican/political prisoners. Registration was lower in remand prisons and open prisons. In fact, only 14 per cent of prisoners allowed to vote actually registered and this meant that only 10 per cent of prisoners eligible to vote actually voted. However, turnout was high in the 2007 election and nearly 71.4 per cent of registered prisoners voted and this was higher than the turnout of 67 per cent outside prison (Behan and O'Donnell 2008: 328–29). They do also note that the level of education is a predictor of political participation and civic engagement and generally there are low levels of education among the prison population.

Behan (2014a) surveyed prisoners in three prisons, looking at voting behaviour, party preferences, political engagement and voting patterns and examined prisoners' experience of postal voting in the 2007 election. This is useful, as we have little information on prisoners' own views, and their views have not been given much attention in the debate on prisoner voting. He found that prisoners were concerned about similar issues as voters outside prison. Those who had voted before going to prison were more likely to vote now. While the prisoners he interviewed were positive about regaining the vote, they still did not feel they belonged in civil society and did not receive any attention from the candidates or parties standing for election and did not receive election material or literature. Some prisoners said they did not vote because of the lack of interest of politicians in penal reform when conditions were still poor.

It is to be hoped that as constituents and potential voters, prisoners would be more likely to engage the attention of their Members of Parliament and this will be particularly valuable if issues are raised regarding the treatment of prisoners and prison conditions. However in the Republic, prisoners did not think this engagement had happened.

A survey conducted by User Voice asked 350 prisoners about their voting behaviour in the 2005 General Election and the latest local election.[39] It found that only 35 per cent of eligible prisoners had voted in the General Election and 44 per cent in the local elections. But 54 per cent said they had voted in the prisoner council elections and 73 per cent reported that they would vote in the next General Election. As we noted in Chapter 3, prisoner council elections are held with a choice of candidates from different parties. It seems, therefore, that this experience of the democratic process had encouraged prisoners' interest in the political process outside.

Because prisoners are already marginalised, excluding them from voting means their social exclusion is further strengthened. In some cases, this means that whole communities may be adversely affected, as some communities are in the US (Clear 2007). Conversely, restoring formal citizenship rights and encouraging prisoners to participate in political life – insofar as they are able within the constraints of imprisonment gives them a voice. On key issues, such as prison reform, the contribution of those who have experienced prison conditions, would be a useful addition, in the same way that involving former prisoners in the academic discipline of convict criminology has furthered our understanding of crime and punishment (Earle 2017).

Prisoner disenfranchisement in the United States

The social impact of felon disenfranchisement as a denial of citizenship rights is highlighted by the experience of the US, where there is a long history of extensive felon disenfranchisement legislation. From 1865 onward, this was overlaid by conflicts over slavery and race discrimination issues and today all the southern states have retained felon disenfranchisement. Modern debates on felon disenfranchisement, as we saw in Chapter 3, have also focused on racial disparity, because of the disproportionate imprisonment of young black males.

Until the 1940s, it was firmly established that the prisoner on conviction loses all rights, except those which the law gives him, as made clear in *Ruffin v Commonwealth of Virginia* (1871) 62 Va (21 Gratt) 790. So as well as losing his property and his civil rights, the prisoner also lost rights over his family and relinquished his status as a citizen. Many states enacted civil death status to make this changed status clear. Because the prisoner had no standing, the courts were reluctant to engage in scrutiny or to critique prison conditions, and they took a 'hands off' approach. Over time these statutes were eroded with property and family rights being restored, but the felon disenfranchisement provisions remained and were re-enacted in specific statutes in the period from 1865 to 1900. These statutes have been seen as a backlash against the Thirteenth, Fourteenth and Fifteenth Amendments which gave voting to rights to former slaves (see Easton 2011). They included a range of residency requirements and a poll tax which had a disparate impact on black Americans, requirements which were not completely removed until the 1965 Voting Rights Act. However, with the continuing disproportionately high numbers of black American men now in custody, the modern apparently neutral felon disenfranchisement laws clearly have had a disparate impact on this group.

The hands-off approach of the courts persisted until 1944 when the landmark case of *Coffin v Reichard* 143 F 2d 443 (6th Cir 1944) ruled that prisoners carry their constitutional rights with them through the door of the prison. While the government has the right to hold prisoners who have committed an offence, it also has a duty to protect them from assault or injury while in custody:

> A prisoner retains all the rights of an ordinary citizen except those expressly, or by necessary implication, taken from him by law. While the law does take his liberty and imposes a duty of servitude and observance of discipline for his regulation and that of other prisoners, it does not deny his right to personal security against unlawful invasion. When a man possesses a substantial right, the courts will be diligent in finding a way to protect it. The fact that a person is legally in prison does not prevent the use of habeas corpus to protect his other inherent rights.
>
> (at 445)

This was reaffirmed by the Supreme Court in the later case of *Wolff v McDonnell* 418 US 539 (1974), where the court said that there was no iron curtain between the Constitution and the prisons, so the court recognises the prisoner is a citizen who retains his constitutional rights when he is sentenced. However, the glaring exception has been the right to vote.

Since that case, the courts have intervened to scrutinise a wide range of issues including due process rights, access to the courts and violence in prison in *Ruiz v Estelle* (1980) 503 F Supp 1295 (1980), and medical care in *Todaro v Ward* 565 F.2d 48 (2nd Cir.1977). Overcrowding was criticised in *Coleman v Schwarznegger/Plata v Schwarznegger* US District Court No. Civ S-90–0520 (4 August 2009) and the right of prisoners to practice their religion in prison was affirmed in *Cutter v Wilkinson* 544 US 709 (2005). However, while the prisoners' rights movement flourished in the US in the 1970s, progress has been uneven since then, with the courts deferring to the prison administration's judgment and authority in a number of cases, on a wide range of matters.

In the US, as noted earlier, there are large numbers of people who are disenfranchised because of their criminal convictions. In many cases, this applies to former felons, as well as prisoners currently serving their sentences, even though post-release disenfranchisement conflicts with Article 25 of the International Covenant on Civil and Political Rights.[40] A large proportion of disenfranchised prisoners in the world live in the US, although the numbers are now declining. The disparity issue has been uppermost in the debates there, as black Americans are particularly affected by the ban and it is thought that as many as 5.8 million black Americans are disenfranchised (Chung 2016). There is also a disparate impact on Latinos and Native Americans, as they are also more likely to be detained than whites (Nellis 2016).[41] There also issues of class impact, as, in some states, it is not possible to regain voting rights even when eligible, unless all outstanding courts' fees and fines have been paid (see Wood and Trivedi (2007). This form of wealth discrimination was unsuccessfully challenged by the ACLU in *Baker v Chapman* No. 03-CV-2008-9007429.00 (2008). So the links between social exclusion and disenfranchisement are clear.

There is considerable variation between states on the scope of the felon voting ban and the conditions for restoration of voting rights. The complexity of the law on restoration may also discourage eligible voters from applying to register. In some cases restoration is automatic, but in others offenders need to apply and to attend hearings. Restoration may also depend on desistance for a specific period. In some states, for example, Virginia, applicants have to prove their civic responsibility through completion of community service. Because the law is so confusing and given the penalties for wrongful registration as electoral fraud, ex-offenders may be deterred from registering or voting. Others, as Barr (2016) notes, may be unaware that they are eligible for restoration of voting rights. Those giving advice also find the rules complex and confusing. A study of election officials in twenty-three states by Wood and Bloom found that election officials unwittingly disseminated misleading advice to the public (Wood and Bloom 2008). Moreover, as McCahon (2016) has argued, many ex-felons may wrongly believe that they do not have certain rights, including the right to vote. The majority of prisoners in local jails are on remand or serving sentences for misdemeanours, and have not committed felonies, so are formally eligible to vote. However, in most jails no help is given to them to negotiate access to voting, so there is in effect *de facto* disenfranchisement. Furthermore, the prospect of change in states may depend on who is elected governor and whether or not he or she is willing to support change.

While the prospect of prisoner voting has been deplored in some quarters as undermining the purity of the ballot box, it could be argued that the opposite is the case. Disenfranchisement arguably undermines the integrity of the electoral process, as it may alter the results of elections if large numbers of potential constituents are excluded. Black Americans are more likely to be Democrat supporters. It is estimated that about 70 per cent of ex-offenders were Democrat voters in 2008.

There has been speculation that in the 2000 election, if ex-felons had been allowed to vote, Gore could have won Florida and that would have turned the election in his favour (Uggen and Manza 2002, Reiman 2005). The issue of disparate impact is especially significant if the victor wins by a narrow majority. In the 2004 election, the results in Florida were very close, and their integrity questioned. Florida was still a swing state in the 2016 election, so the issue remains salient. We do not know for sure if prisoners would 'turn out' to vote and we cannot predict their choice of candidate with absolute certainty, but their absence may potentially affect the outcome of an election if a large section of the constituency is excluded. States with the most repressive felon disenfranchisement laws also tend to have a lower voter turnout (McLeod et al. 2003). In the 2008 election great efforts were made to help ex-offenders register to vote. Moreover, as Phillips and

Deckard (2016) observe, a party was elected in Florida which passed legislation further undermining the black population and its citizenship status.

The levels of felon disenfranchisement in the US remain high with 6.1 million voters in 2016[42] disenfranchised because of a criminal conviction (Uggen et al. 2016: 3). Of this group 4.7 million were working in the community and paying taxes and over 1 million of this group were black Americans who have completed their sentences (ibid). However, there are differences between states and Uggen et al. (2016) estimate that more than 7 per cent of the adult population is disenfranchised in Alabama, Florida, Kentucky, Mississippi, Tennessee, and Virginia: 'The state of Florida alone accounts for more than a quarter (27 per cent) of the disenfranchised population nationally, and its nearly 1.5 million individuals disenfranchised post-sentence account for nearly half (48 per cent) of the national total' (ibid: 3). More people are disenfranchised in Florida than any other state and a challenge is being brought in the District Court, arguing that Florida's felon disenfranchisement laws are unconstitutional. Moreover, the differential incarceration rates for black Americans remain high in the US, so the problem of disparate impact persists (Nellis 2016). Wacquant (2010) has argued that the expansion of the American police, criminal courts and prison 'over the past thirty years have been finely targeted, first by class, second by race, and third by place, leading not to *mass* incarceration but to the *hyper*incarceration of (sub) proletarian African American men from the imploding ghetto' (2010: 74).

The Brennan Center for Justice in New York has been conducting a right to vote project for many years, campaigning to restore the vote to felons on their release from prison. The impetus of the US campaign has been on the denial of the vote post release, because of the wide-reaching impact of the felon disenfranchisement laws. There is some support in the US for change. In Manza, Brooks and Uggen's (2004) survey, 60 per cent of respondents favoured restoring the vote to ex-offenders, while 31 per cent were willing to extend it to current prisoners. In some states both Republicans and Democrats support restoration of prisoner votes.

Felon disenfranchisement increased with the expansion of incarceration and the number of lost voters remains high, despite a recent decline in the imprisonment rate and a relaxation of felon disenfranchisement rules in some states. A Report submitted to the UN Human Rights Committee by a coalition of civil rights groups noted that:

> Despite a decrease in the prison population over the past three years and substantial reform efforts in some states, the overall disenfranchisement rate has increased dramatically in conjunction with the growing U.S. corrections population, rising from 1.17 million in 1976 to 5.85 million by 2010. The growing incarceration rate has been mirrored by the disenfranchisement rate, which has increased by about 500% since 1980. The fact that felony disenfranchisement is so wide-reaching is deeply disturbing, and indicates that these laws undermine the open, participatory nature of our democratic process.
> (ACLU et al. 2013: 1)

The US position is also clearly at odds with the worldwide trend towards re-enfranchisement. Moreover, as Uggen et al. (2016) point out, the disparate impact has also increased. In 1980, only nine states disenfranchised at least 5 per cent of their black American adult population, today twenty-three states do so. While the size of the prison population is now finally shrinking, this will take some time to filter through to reduce the effect on the voting population, because of the provisions limiting the votes of former felons.

Conclusion

While there have been some positive developments in the restoration of the vote in other jurisdictions, in the UK the position has in some respects become worse, with increasing hostility to prisoners' voting rights and to human rights more broadly from the public, the media and successive governments, as well as the major opposition parties. However, during its hearings, some members of the Joint Committee do seem to have changed their views and to have accepted limited re-enfranchisement. The fact that the Committee did recommend change in its Report was encouraging, even if this recommendation has not yet been implemented. But while the majority of the Committee supported some limited change, the Coalition and Conservative Governments have so far rejected a change in the law.

As we have seen, the Strasbourg Court since *Hirst* has consistently rejected blanket bans, but has tolerated exclusions based on sentence length, provided that prisoners serving shorter sentences are able to vote. This approach would exclude many of the applicants in the recent litigation. But it does suggest that even a moderate change on the part of the UK government, such as that proposed in the Draft Bill, would be sufficient to satisfy the court. However, it seems that change is now less likely than at the time of *Hirst*, notwithstanding the many discussions of the issue since then and the conclusions of the Joint Committee. This partly reflects the increasing hostility to human rights jurisprudence and to the powers of the Strasbourg Court.

When the then Prime Minister Cameron was asked for his reaction to the *Delvigne* case in 2015, he stressed that his views were unchanged, that that the Supreme Court had approved the UK ban and that the European Court of Justice had given a further endorsement of the UK's position. However, the decision did not endorse the UK's position, as the UK does not distinguish between offenders convicted of serious and less serious offences. In the *Delvigne* case the restriction only applied to those convicted of serious offences.

Because the Cameron Government was so hostile to change, this has made the right to vote a more significant issue for the press and public than was necessary and encouraged animosity towards prisoners' voting rights and towards prisoners as a group. If a limited change affecting a small group of prisoners had been made, it is likely that the public would have accepted it. Has public opposition been overstated? Lord McNally acknowledged the problem in the Lords debate in June 2010: 'I am not sure that it has support in the editorial columns of the *Daily Express* or the *Daily Mail,* but in the broader general public there is a willingness to consider the experience of other countries, both in rehabilitation of prisoners and the kind of punishment meted to them'.[43] But even if this is over-optimistic and public opinion remains hostile to voting rights, the public have not been presented with clear evidence that the ban is arbitrary and ineffective, or with any arguments in favour of restoration.

From the standpoint of the Council of Europe, the UK has been given more than enough time to introduce change. The prospect of change in the future therefore seems remote. It may depend in part on any future action taken by the Committee of Ministers. However, their enforcement powers are limited. If there were a debate on the options and Parliament did not approve change, then the UK government could go back and say it had been defeated, but its failure to introduce the bill, makes clear its lack of willingness to change. Moreover, if as stipulated in *McHugh,* the courts will not award financial compensation to prisoners or their legal costs, it will be difficult for lawyers to take on these cases in future if they have to act *pro bono.*

The situation has developed into a stalemate, with the UK government refusing to implement change and distancing itself further from the Court and the Convention, while the powers of the Council of Europe and the court to enforce the judgment are limited. If the UK does not comply with *Hirst,* it seems unlikely that it would be expelled from the Council of Europe, as other states including Moldova and Russia remain members, yet they have committed very significant breaches on very serious matters. Examples here would include the torture of detainees in Moldova and atrocities committed against civilians by the Russian federal army in Chechnya, where the Committee of Ministers of the Council has expressed concerns over the effectiveness of compliance measures. Moreover, as noted earlier, new provisions within Russia have given the Russian Constitution supremacy over the Court's judgments.

The UK has moved from delaying compliance to saying that it will not comply. If the Court did demand compensation for applicants who succeed in the Court, then the costs could be substantial, but if the government refuses to pay, the fines are not enforceable. But if it left the Convention, the government could still be liable for obligations prior to that date, although they still may not comply. Non-compliance with international obligations is a significant step, which damages the UK's reputation and sets a poor example to other states, who will be happier about their own failures to comply if the UK, renowned for its commitment to human rights and the rule of law, is also breaching its rights obligations. There is some recognition of this in the latest proposal discussed to cede the vote to those on temporary release.

The media has been particularly adverse to change and reporting on the question of voting rights was principally negative (see McNulty 2014). This issue will be considered further in Chapter 7. From the UK government's standpoint, prisoners' voting rights have been seen as a poisoned chalice. This hostility gathered pace during the lifetime of the Coalition Government and shaped the Conservative campaign in the 2015 election. Unfortunately, in the debates on the Convention, prisoners have been an easy target as they are an unpopular group with the public and the media, so focusing on prisoners' 'exploitation' and 'abuse' of their Convention rights has reinforced public hostility. There has also been relatively little discussion in the media of the fact that the Strasbourg Court has been more willing to defer to states in recent years on criminal justice and other issues, or of the positive advantages of the Convention in protecting the right to life and the right not to be subjected to torture and inhuman and degrading treatment and punishment, well-established and uncontroversial rights in international human rights law which are also valued by the public.

A more measured approach in which the government explained the potential benefits of re-enfranchisement would have helped. For example, the electorate could be made more aware of the implications for rehabilitation and reintegration, the fact that there are no security issues and that the measure is not expensive. They could also have pointed out that other societies have retained or restored voting rights, without endangering society or facing any other problems. In relation to prisoner voting, it is clear that the usual arguments for disenfranchisement are unpersuasive and that there would be no adverse effects, but, on the contrary, benefits may accrue from re-enfranchisement. So public opposition to change could have been addressed more effectively. There are many areas of penal policy where Parliament has exercised a control on the excesses of public opinion, notably in relation to the death penalty, by taking a more restrained and informed approach. But in the voting rights case, the alliance of MPs, the media and public opinion has combined to defeat any significant reform.

This situation contrasts markedly with that of the Republic of Ireland, although both states have become more punitive and seen an expansion of the prison population in recent years. As Behan notes (2014b), there was less public, political or press hostility to prison enfranchisement in Ireland, as well as a much more positive attitude towards Europe and the European Convention. The 2006 Electoral (Amendment) Act, which gave prisoners the right to vote by post in all local, national and European elections and referendums, was passed by a coalition government without much public debate or press reporting, or indeed interest, and with no political opposition in contrast to the UK (Behan and O'Donnell 2008).

As we saw earlier, prisoners may perform acts of citizenship through a range of volunteering activities inside prison, as well as through participation in educational programmes. Political behaviour may also be expressed through participation in prisoner councils whose decision-making powers are limited, but do give prisoners a voice on matters governing prison life and give them experience of democratic structures and processes. While political protests and demonstrations may also offer an opportunity for political engagement, voting remains a key emblem of citizenship status. Whether prisoners would vote may depend, as we have noted, on a number of factors, including their past history of civic engagement. Prisoners with pre-existing political loyalties and commitments may also find time in prison to develop further their political interests, while prisoners with no prior political experience, may discover politics inside prison. These issues will be considered further in Chapters 5 and 6.

Notes

1 The others are Armenia, Bulgaria, Estonia and Russia.
2 *Hirst v UK (No. 2)* App No.74025/01 (6 October 2005) para 50.
3 United Nations Standard Minimum Rules for the Treatment of Prisoners (the Mandela Rules).
4 The purported – and dubious – justification for the age requirement of thirty for women was that women would otherwise form the majority of the electorate, because of the massive loss of male voters during World War I. The age limit for male voters then was twenty-one.
5 *The Times* (24 February 1950).
6 See, for example, *Scoppola v Italy* (No. 3) App No. 126/05 (22 May 2012) in contrast to *Anchugov and Gladkov v Russia* App Nos. 11157104 and 15162/05 (4 July 2013).
7 https://publications.parliament.uk/pa/jt201314/jtselect/jtdraftvoting/103/10302.htm, accessed 26 October 2017.
8 See also *Tovey and others v Ministry of Justice* (2011) EWHC 271 9QB) for further discussion of this issue in the domestic courts.
9 *Smith v Scott, ex p Toner and Walsh and Chester v Secretary of State for Justice and another* (2009) EWHC 2923 (Admin) and (2010) EWCA Civ 1439.
10 See, for example, the recent review of sentencing by the Law Commission (2016) and the work of the Sentencing Council www.sentencingcouncil.org.uk/, accessed 14 June 2017.
11 HC Deb, 3 November 2010, Vol. 517, col. 921.
12 HC Deb, 20 December 2010, Vol. 520, col. 151.
13 HC Deb, 24 October 2012, Vol. 551, col. 923.
14 Press release: Labour's policy is that prisoners should not be given the vote, 22 November 2012.
15 Radio 4, World at One, 11 February 2011.
16 BBC Interview, 20 February 2011.
17 *Daily Mirror* column, 26 January 2014.
18 In a speech to an Amnesty conference in 2012, but which was reported in the popular press in August 2017 (*The Daily Mail,* 6 August 2017, *The Express,* 7 August 2017 and *The Sun,* 8 August 2017).
19 The French Criminal Code was amended in 1994 to limit the ban to ten years, but Delvigne had been convicted under the previous code.
20 Case C-6501/13 *Thierry Delvigne v Commune de Lesparre-Médoc and Préfet de la Gironde* [2015] Opinion of AG Cruz Villalon, para 124.
21 *R (on the application of Chester) v Secretary of State for Justice; McGeoch v The Lord President of the Council and another* [2013] UKSC 63.
22 HC Deb, 10 February 2011 Vol. 523, col. 586.
23 HC Deb, 22 June 1981 Vol. 7 cc 28-109.
24 HC Deb, 22 November 2012, Vol. 553, col. 745.
25 The House of Lords Select Committee on the Constitution *Oral Evidence Session with the Rt Hon. Michael Gove MP, Lord Chancellor and Secretary of State for Justice,* Evidence Session No. 1, 20 December 2015, pp. 17–18.
26 HC Select Committee on the European Union Justice Sub-Committee, *The Potential Impact on EU Law of Repealing Human Rights Act,* Evidence Session No. 8 (2 February, 2016), pp. 11–12 cited in Simson Caird (2016).
27 HC Deb, 2 November 2017, Vol. 630.

28 See, for example, *R v Horncastle and another, R v Marquis and another, R v Carter* [2009] EWCA Crim 964, See also Lord Hoffmann, *The Universality of Human Rights*, Judicial Studies Board Annual Lecture 19 March 2009, where he criticised the way the court had sought to extend its jurisdiction by seeking to impose uniform rules on member states.

29 *Al-Khawaja and Tahery v UK* App Nos. 26766/05 and 22228/06 (15 December 2011).

30 Decision of the Committee of Ministers (24 September 2015).

31 http://doc.ksrf.ru/decision/KSRFDecision230222.pdf

32 See, for example, *Washington v State* 75 Ala 582 (1884), *Shepherd v Trevino,* 575 F.2d 1110 (5th Cir 1978) and *Bailey v Baronian* 120 R.I. 394, A. 2d 1338 (1978).

33 *August and another v Electoral Commission and others* CCT 8/99 [1999] ZACC 3.

34 *Minister of Home Affairs and others v NICRO and others* CCT 03/04 [2004] ZACC 10.

35 Section 113 Social Security Contributions and Benefits Act 1992.

36 On 29 September 2017 there were 3,593 prisoners in the Republic of Ireland including remand prisoners and the imprisonment rate was 75 per 100,000 of the population (ICPS 2017). http://prisonstudies.org/country/ireland-republic, accessed 26 October 2017.

37 For further discussion see Easton (2006).

38 Jon Kelly 'Would prisoners use their right to vote?', *BBC News Magazine* 10 February 2011.

39 www.uservoice.org/wp-content/uploads/2013/06/Summary-of-The-Power-Inside. pdf; Baz van Cranenburgh, *A Market Research Summary*, So What? April 2010).

40 www.hrw.org/legacy/reports98/vote/usvot98o-06.htm, accessed 23 October 2017.

41 See *Farrakhan v Gregoire* 590 3d 989 (9th Cir. 2010) for further discussion of disparate impact issues.

42 This compares with 3.1 million disenfranchised because of a criminal conviction in 1996.

43 Reported in *The Guardian* 20 September, 2010 where it was also noted that Nick Clegg was willing to support change.

5

DISCOVERING POLITICS IN PRISON

Introduction

This chapter will consider the role of the prison in raising and increasing political awareness. Reference will be made to the prison as a potential and actual source of political radicalisation, with reference to Islamist extremism. Prisons have been seen as major sources of recruitment for al-Qaeda and other terrorist groups around the world. In recent years, prisons have become more strongly associated with radicalisation and there has been more interest in developing measures to combat this. The formulation of policies to address the problem in other states, including the US, Spain, France and the Netherlands will also be considered.

The role of the prison in deradicalisation will additionally be discussed. In this context, sectarian political subcultures in Northern Ireland offer a good example of the role prison and prisoners can make in contributing to the resolution of conflicts. The population of offenders convicted under the Terrorism Act may include those serving shorter sentences, as well as those who are released on licence, so what happens on release is of concern. But because of the relatively small size of the group of TACT offenders, it is difficult to formulate reliable information on what is effective with these offenders in reducing the risk of future offending. Prisoners held for terrorism-related offences still constitute a small proportion of the prison population. However, the research on desistance, which is well-established in relation to non-terrorist offenders, may still be relevant to this group. Moreover, we now have a range of interventions used to assess risk and to promote disengagement. The response to these prisoners needs to be carefully calibrated to avoid increasing a sense of victimisation and resentment.

In the UK, terrorism is defined in the Terrorism Act[1] as follows:

(1) In this Act "terrorism" means the use or threat of action where –
  (a) the action falls within subsection (2),
  (b) the use or threat is designed to influence the government [F1or an international governmental organisation] or to intimidate the public or a section of the public, and
  (c) the use or threat is made for the purpose of advancing a political, religious [F2, racial] or ideological cause.
(2) Action falls within this subsection if it –
  (a) involves serious violence against a person,
  (b) involves serious damage to property,
  (c) endangers a person's life, other than that of the person committing the action,
  (d) creates a serious risk to the health or safety of the public or a section of the public, or
  (e) is designed seriously to interfere with or seriously to disrupt an electronic system.
(3) The use or threat of action falling within subsection (2) which involves the use of firearms or explosives is terrorism whether or not subsection (1)(b) is satisfied.
(4) In this section –
  (a) "action" includes action outside the United Kingdom,
  (b) a reference to any person or to property is a reference to any person, or to property, wherever situated,
  (c) a reference to the public includes a reference to the public of a country other than the United Kingdom, and
  (d) "the government" means the government of the United Kingdom, of a Part of the United Kingdom or of a country other than the United Kingdom.
(5) In this Act a reference to action taken for the purposes of terrorism includes a reference to action taken for the benefit of a proscribed organisation.

Terrorism refers to an act or acts of violence for political, religious or ideological purposes. The Federal Bureau of Investigation defines a terrorist incident as 'a violent act or an act dangerous to human life in violation of the criminal law of the United States, or of any state to intimidate or coerce a government, the civilian population or any segment therefore, in furtherance of political or social objectives'.[2]

Offenders convicted of terrorism-related offences in the UK, who are categorised as Category A, are held in the high security estate, to prevent them escaping and to limit their influence on others. Many Islamist extremist prisoners, including Abu Hamza, have been held in Belmarsh. The policy of dispersal within the high security estate was introduced following the escape of IRA prisoners from HMP Whitemoor in 1994 and the findings of the subsequent Woodcock Report

(Woodcook 1994). This policy designed for IRA prisoners, has also been applied to Islamist extremists since 9/11 and 7/7. However, UK anti-terrorism law has now been broadened to encompass acts preparatory to terrorism, the encouragement of terrorism and its glorification, and advocating it without direct involvement, as well undertaking training for terrorist purposes.[3] This has meant that there are more offenders convicted of preparatory offences, usually serving shorter sentences and moving towards their release and these offenders will usually be held outside the high security estate. So the potential for radicalisation is broader and may mean that other prisoners, both Muslim and non-Muslims, are more vulnerable to radicalisation by extremists.

Prison radicalisation

In considering the issue of radicalisation, we need to be aware of the diversity of the population of 'terrorist offenders', as those being held will include those who have committed violent acts, as well as those engaging in activities preparatory to the commission of those acts, including fund-raising, and the encouragement and glorification of terrorism. Among committed extremist offenders, the prison and probation population will include both leaders and followers. The wider prison population at risk of radicalisation may include those drawn to terrorist groups because of their own prior criminality, as well as those vulnerable because of their personal circumstances. Prisoners already imprisoned for terrorist offences can also become more radicalised in prison.

Radicalisation does not always entail religious conversion, as is the case with Islamic converts, but may be purely political, as, for example, in the case of the Weathermen or Weather Underground group, which was active in the US in the 1960s, and far right extremist groups in Europe (Dearey 2014: 38). The US Department of Justice defines prisoner radicalisation as 'the process by which prisoners during the course of their incarceration adopt extremist views, especially beliefs that violent measures must be employed to achieve the political components of militantly religious and political objectives'.[4] However, religious conversion does not always mean radicalisation. Prisoners may convert to Islam for opportunistic reasons, such as protection, or for better living conditions, and they may disengage with the religion on leaving prison. Others may convert because religion genuinely helps them psychologically to deal with their imprisonment.

By 2013, there were 120 TACT prisoners, 90 per cent of whom were al-Qaeda influenced, and thirty of these prisoners were from other groups, including animal rights groups, and other domestic extremists (Pickering 2013: 11). On 31 March 2017, there were 186 prisoners being held on terrorism-related offences and domestic extremism/separatism in Great Britain, a rise of 15 per cent over the previous year, of whom 155 had been convicted, 29 were on remand, one was an extradition case and the other a deportation case (Home Office 2017). Fifty-nine prisoners held for terrorism-related and domestic extremism/separatism offences were released from prison in the year ending December 2016 (ibid). The majority of TACT prisoners are being held for Islamist extremism, involving both domestic and international terrorism, but TACT prisoners also include extreme right-wing and other groups, and the number of extreme right-wing prisoners has increased (Liebling and Straum: 2013: 17). However, most of the available research and literature is on the presence and dangers of Islamist extremism in prison.

The UK has already had experience, in the 1970s and 1980s, of dealing with those convicted of terrorist offences, when dealing with sectarian prisoners during the Northern Ireland conflict. However, there was little interest in the role of prison radicalisation before 9/11, but we now have much more material on Islamist extremists in prison. An Extremist Prisoners Working Group was set up in 2006, after the July 2005 London bombings. It has focused on support for Muslim chaplains, and helping staff to identify extremism, on the formulation of counter-radicalisation measures and resettlement programmes. A Prison Service Extremism Unit was also established in February 2007 to address the issue of radicalisation and extremism in prison and more recently, a Counter-Extremism Taskforce was set up, in April 2017, to deal with radicalisation and extremism in prison.

Many examples of prisoner radicalisation have been identified in Europe, the UK and the US. In the UK, the 'shoe bomber' Richard Reid, convicted for trying to blow up an aircraft with explosives hidden in his shoes, Muktar Said Ibrahim, convicted of attempts to bomb the London transport system, and Jermaine Grant, accused of plotting terrorist attacks in Kenya, were all held at Feltham, where they are thought to have been radicalised. However, the move towards violent extremism may be a gradual process, continued outside prison, so while Reid converted to Islam inside prison, he attended Finsbury Park mosque on his release, where he heard the sermons of the radical preacher Abu Hamza and others, as did Ibrahim. Terrorist attacks may be committed by small groups organised around friendship and kinship networks.

In France, there is evidence that the perpetrators of the major terrorist attacks there in recent years had met each other in prison. Amedy Coulibaly, who killed the hostage at the *Hypercacher* store siege in Paris in 2015, had met Cherif Kouachi, in Fleury-Mérogis prison, when Coulibaly was serving a sentence for armed robbery. The Kouachi brothers, Cherif and Said, were responsible for the Charlie Hebdo murders in 2015. Mohamed Meris, responsible for the Toulouse attack in 2012 was also thought to be radicalised in prison as was Mehdi Nemmouche who attacked the Jewish museum in Brussels. Abdelhamid Abaaoud and Salah Abdeslam, involved in the November 2013 Paris attacks, met in prison in Belgium. In the early 1990s Khalid Kelkal was radicalised in a French prison, and sought to radicalise others there. He later joined a radical Algerian group, the GIA, Groupe Islamique Armée, and, in 1995, was involved in the assassination of an imam in Paris and attempted to bomb the high-speed train link between Paris and Lyon.

In the US, Kevin James was radicalised in New Folsom Prison in California, when he was twenty-one. He became the leader of a radical prison group, Jam'iyyat Ul-Islam (JLS), the Assembly of Authentic Islam, which aimed to establish an Islamic caliphate in the US. It targets 'infidels' and enemies of Islam and supporters of Israel. James was later involved in armed robberies to obtain funds for terrorism. In prison he recruited others, for example, Levar Haley Washington, subsequently convicted of acts preparatory to terrorism, including the procurement of weapons through robberies. José Padilla, a gang member from Chicago, was also radicalised in prison and was later arrested on suspicion of planning to explode a dirty bomb. Several of the prisoners released from Guantánamo have also subsequently been involved in terrorist attacks around the world. Those already with extreme views may also have an opportunity to consolidate and develop them inside. For example, Hitler wrote *Mein Kampf* in prison in 1923–24 and al-Azzawi, emerged as a leader of al-Qaeda, while in prison in Iraq.

The dangers of prisoner radicalisation have also been highlighted by the media. A report in *The Times* discussed the threat of radical imams influencing prisoners, while Anthony Glees has described Britain's prisons as 'a state-funded breeding ground for extremism' (see Gibbons 2014). Examples were given of an imam then working in British prisons, who was a member of Al Hima Media, whose members have expressed the view that women who have sex before marriage should be killed and who have supported violence against women, and another imam whose party included a supporter of the killing of homosexuals. Glees stresses the need to vet imams, to examine their qualifications carefully and to require them to preach in English and to avoid political issues, although NOMS has said it does check chaplains very carefully. Steve Gillan, the former leader of the Prison Officers Association has also warned of the danger of young people being radicalised in prison (ibid). In one incident reported in 2014, a Muslim prisoner, at the category B Isle of Wight prison, who had not been convicted for terrorist-related offences, was found with drawings resembling the ISIS flag, a map of the prison and details of an escape plan which involved taking an officer hostage. He was moved into the Close Supervision Centre after this incident.[5]

Neumann (2010) distinguishes between internal and external drivers of radicalisation. Internal refers to the efforts of individual prisoners or prison gangs, based on religious affiliation, to convert others or to take on leadership roles, including leading Friday prayers or representing Muslim prisoners in the prison in discussions with staff, while external drivers would include extremist material sent into prisons, as well as links to websites outside, and the influence of visitors who promote extremism. In some cases, radical imams have also obtained access to prisons. He describes prisons as 'places of vulnerability' because they constitute an unsettling environment, where prisoners lose their own social networks. This means that prisoners with no prior involvement in politically inspired violence run the risk of being recruited and radicalised by politically motivated offenders, who recreate their command structures inside prison and mobilise support outside. Younger people from lower-income groups have been seen as particularly vulnerable and this group is over-represented in the prison population. However, the 'radicalised' come from a wide range of backgrounds, including doctors and other professionals, and from older age groups as well. The perpetrator of the Westminster Bridge attack in 2017 was middle-aged rather than a young man in his twenties. Neumann (2010) found substantial evidence of prison radicalisation and plots originating in prisons in Europe, as well as in the US, and states such as Afghanistan.

The assumption that prison is the venue for radicalisation underpins the UK government's counter-terrorism strategy, CONTEST, which includes Protect, Prepare, Pursue and Prevent. The Prevent strategy aims to identify and to counter radicalisation, which it defines as the process by which a person comes to support terrorism and forms of extremism leading to terrorism.[6] Extremism is defined in the Prevent strategy as vocal or active opposition to fundamental British values, such as democracy, the rule of law, individual liberty and mutual respect and tolerance of different faiths and beliefs. It also includes calls for the death of members of the British armed forces in the UK or overseas. Violent extremism is the endorsement of violence to achieve extreme ends. Prisons are included in the Prevent strategy because some of those convicted of terrorist-related offences have tried to recruit others. Furthermore, some prisoners convicted for non-terrorist offences, but who have a prior association with terrorist networks, have also engaged in radicalisation and recruitment of others in prison.

The issue of radicalisation was considered by the House of Common Home Affairs Committee in its 2012 Report, *Roots of Violent Radicalisation*. It included prisons in its study of drivers for recruitment to terrorist movements, with links to Islamic fundamentalism, Irish dissident Republicanism and domestic extremism. It also looked at the role of universities and the Internet. It took oral and written evidence from a range of groups and individuals and it also visited Belmarsh and spoke to prisoners and staff. At that time, the research base on the causes of radicalisation was limited, so much of the evidence was anecdotal. But the Committee found a sense of grievance and a perception on the part of respondents that their concerns were ignored by mainstream political parties. The Report also suggested that violent extremism within the Muslim community was declining (at para 21), although this seems over-optimistic in the light of subsequent attacks in London, Paris, Brussels and Barcelona. Although it recognised the Internet and the impact of radical preachers as crucial drivers for radicalisation, it observed that there may also be a process of self-radicalisation. It also noted that universities have been complacent regarding the presence of radicals especially as in universities, like prisons, individuals are more vulnerable because they may be away from home for the first time.

Evidence was given to the Committee of a man remanded to Belmarsh who was held in a cell near to Abdullah al-Faisal. Within three days, he was persuaded to undertake a martyrdom mission and when he left prison he went straight to Yemen to look for a training camp. There he was sent to a madrassa, but they sent him home. The Report notes that it is well established that in prison a person can be drawn into networks and friendships which increase the likelihood of criminal activities. It acknowledges that there are examples of people recruited into gangs linked to terrorist purposes in the US, but it is 'difficult to find firm evidence or to quantify the impact' (at para 35). Its visit to Belmarsh also suggested that 'being recruited to a self-identified Muslim grouping within prison was more about association and personal safety than about than radicalisation' (ibid). The issue was later reconsidered by the Acheson Review, led by Ian Acheson, whose assessment of the threat of Islamist extremism in prisons, probation and youth justice and of the capability of NOMS to deal with this threat, was published in 2016 (Ministry of Justice 2016b).

The Acheson Review

While the full contents of the Acheson Review are classified, a summary of its findings was published. The Report uses the term 'Islamist extremism' to cover violent and non-violent elements of extremism. It uses the definition of extremism from the 2011 Prevent Strategy document of vocal or active opposition to fundamental British values and demands for the death of members of the armed forces (2016b: 2). It sees Islamism as the imposition of an expansionist and politicised version of Islam under which society is to be ordered according to an interpretation of Sharia law, which is anti-Western, hostile to other religions and other strains of Islam and is totalitarian. Radicalisation is the process by which adherents of this belief come to adopt it.

The Review found evidence that Islamist extremism was a growing problem within prisons and emphasised that a central, wide-ranging and coordinated strategy is necessary to combat it. Expressions of extremism, it argued, should be reported systematically, with sanctions to deter such behaviour. NOMS policy should be changed to reflect this and there should be greater coordination with the police. Its main finding was that the then prevailing system in which TACT and Islamist extremist prisoners were dispersed across the prison estate should be reviewed, and the containment of known extremists within dedicated specialist units should be considered. The Review also envisaged a future expansion of the number of prisoners convicted of offences of terrorism and extremism, as more people return from fighting in Syria, Iraq, Yemen, Afghanistan and Somalia.

It identified a number of elements of the problem in prison, including Muslim gang culture, levels of violence, drug trafficking and criminality associated with these groups and with TACT offenders, overt support for Daesh, and prisoners threatening staff and other prisoners. It argued that some Islamist Extremist prisoners act as 'emirs', exerting a controlling and radicalising influence on the wider Muslim prison population, with aggressive encouragement of conversions to Islam. Also of concern was unsupervised collective worship, where there was pressure on supervising staff to leave the prayer room, prisoners attempting to engineer segregation by landing, wing or even prison and attempting to prevent staff searches by claiming that their dress was religious. The Review further noted that books and material promoting extremism were found in chaplaincy libraries and were held by individual prisoners, and there was intimidation of prison imams by prisoners. In addition, prisoners exploited officers' fears of being called racist, and also abused Prison Rule 39 to smuggle illicit material in and out of prison. PR 39 prohibits prison staff from opening correspondence between prisoners and legal advisers, unless there is a reason to believe the rule is being abused. The Review recommended that an

Independent Counsel be appointed to consider how to prevent this. It also pointed out that the policy of dispersal, originally used for IRA prisoners, has not been updated to deal with the Islamist Extremism threat. There are differences between the two groups, including the fact that the number of IRA prisoners was relatively few and outside of Northern Ireland, they were unlikely to have the support of other prisoners.

The Review visited fourteen different establishments in the UK, including public and private prisons, from outside the high security estate, as well as prisons in the Netherlands, France and Spain, where Islamist extremist prisoners are separated from the wider population. It found many UK prisons struggled to manage faith-related disruption. The Review recommended more support for Category B and Open Estate prisons, and better training for staff. It found that 'cultural sensitivity' among NOMS staff towards Muslim prisoners inhibited effective confrontation of extremist views. It recommended that staff, whose roles relate to counter terrorism at the national strategic level, should also have operational prison experience, and relations between the police and security services and NOMS should be strengthened. Probation was also considered. Although the National Probation Service deals with high-risk offenders and Community Rehabilitation Companies lower risk offenders, the CRCs do need to be aware of problems and risks offenders, so proper training and sharing of information is essential. The Review pointed out that the work of risk management of extremism is in its infancy. More attention needs to be given by those working in youth justice to the emerging threats of the radicalisation of those aged under eighteen. More inter-agency cooperation is needed and the Review argues that intelligence from prison may be useful when dealing with serious terrorist incidents. Within prison, the smuggling of mobile phones is a persistent problem, but possession of mobiles by TACT and IE prisoners should be given special attention. The Review also found that there was little data on religious conversions, or the reasons for them, and a lack of management control over access to extremist materials.

The Review interviewed fifty Muslim prison chaplains. At that time, there were sixty-nine full-time, sixty-five part-time and 110 sessional Muslim prison chaplains, two-thirds of whom were from the traditional and conservative Deobandi denomination, which could mean that chaplains from other denominations feel marginalised. The review found that there was a weak understanding of Islamist extremism among the chaplaincy, but it also acknowledged the useful work imams undertook. It was clear that faith was very important to prisoners and could be transformative in improving their lives.

The key recommendations of the Review included the need for an independent advisor on counter-terrorism issues in prisons, responsible to the Secretary of State, a new security category for TACT and IE prisoners managed centrally, and the removal from the general prison population, of the subset within this group, who pose a particular and enduring risk to national security, through their subversive behaviour, beliefs and activities. They should be held instead in specialist units where deradicalisation interventions can be implemented. It also advocated more staff training, systematic recording of extremist beliefs and threats of violence, stronger vetting of prison chaplains and greater support for frontline staff in dealing with disruption or abuse of faith activity. There should also be an increased focus on the identification and removal of sources of extremist literature, on the safe management of Friday prayers, with sanctions for the abuse or misuse of acts of worship, a review of Rule 39 procedures, improving the capacity to respond quickly to serious violent incidents and improved coordination with the police, who should be given primacy to deal with serious prison incidents. The use of in-cell technology instead of corporate worship, it argued, should be considered, as well as making governors more accountable for peaceful worship in their prisons, for example, by checking the content of sermons.

In its response to the Acheson Review, the government said it was implementing eleven of its recommendations and partially implementing and continuing to review the other three recommendations (Ministry of Justice 2016c). It notes that the problems identified reflect wider safety issues of violence and discipline, also raised in the White Paper *Prison Safety and Reform* (Ministry of Justice 2016a). However, it did acknowledge that Islamist extremism is an acute risk to staff and prisoners. The government has said that the highest risk terrorists, the potential and actual radicalisers, will be separated from the mainstream population to prevent the risk of radicalisation. All extremists will be encouraged to disengage through interventions and individual case management and those who elect not to do so will be monitored and risk managed. Staff training and faith teaching is also being strengthened to prevent radicalisation.

Recent developments

Since the Acheson Review was published, there have been further major terrorist incidents linked to Islamist extremism in Manchester and London, in the space of a few months in 2017, as well as one linked to far right extremism. However, there have also been further measures to defeat prisoner radicalisation. Specialist units have been established within the high security estate to allow greater separation and management of extremists who pose greatest risk to other prisoners. Ways of improving the identification and management of extremist prisoners are being considered.

A Directorate of Security, Order and Counter Terrorism was established in 2016, to address extremism in the context of prison and probation. This was part of the government's wider counter-terrorism and counter-extremism agendas and prison safety and reform plans. It also deals with problems of disorder within prisons as well as the threat of phones, drugs and drones entering prison. The Counter-Extremism Taskforce is a joint unit formed between the Prison and Probation Service and the Home Office, but will also work with the police and other agencies. It was set up in 2017 and builds on the work of the directorate and uses intelligence from prison and probation staff and information from counter-terrorism experts to assess the threat of prisoner radicalisation and advises prisons on how to combat specific threats and how to manage the most dangerous extremists. It will train prison and probation staff on how to discourage offenders' involvement in extremism, how to identify extremist literature and to challenge extremist behaviour.

Its establishment was expedited in response to the 2016 White Paper *Prison Safety and Reform,* which had highlighted the dangers of extremism in prison to staff, other prisoners and society and need to manage a wide range of offenders 'from highly motivated terrorists convicted of extremely serious offences, to prisoners who may be vulnerable or susceptible to extremist ideology' (Ministry of Justice 2016a: para 115). The atmosphere in prison, it noted, is one in which individuals are vulnerable to extremist ideologies, both Islamist and extreme right-wing ideas. It said that it intended the unit dealing with the threat of extremism in prisons to encourage closer working with its law enforcement and policy partners (ibid: para 230). It also stressed that governors and frontline staff will be given training and skills needed to challenge extremist views and 'the most subversive individuals will be removed from the mainstream prison population and held in specialist units to protect others from their poisonous ideologies' (at para 231). Prison safety was also considered by the House of Commons Justice Committee in 2016, and in its response, the government has emphasised that it is working with the Home Office to strengthen the response to the risk of radicalisation and extremism in prisons (House of Commons Justice Committee, 2016).

The Prison and Probation Service has revised its counter-extremism and extremism prevention strategy in response to the Acheson Review and combating extremism remains a priority. A new extremism awareness training package for all prison officers has been introduced on identifying, reporting and confronting extremism (NOMS 2017: 16). Prison officers are also given briefings on Recognising Extremist Activity in Prisons by Prevent staff. The process for recruiting prison chaplains is also being strengthened. There are already pre-appointment checks for all prison chaplaincy posts, including a counter-terrorism check and security clearance. Efforts are being made to remove extremist literature from prisons. Prison governors are responsible for peaceful worship, including Friday prayers, and can use existing powers to remove individuals from corporate worship, if they behave subversively, or promote beliefs which run counter to British values. But the government does not favour in-cell alternatives to corporate worship. It also does not intend to change current processes dealing with potential abuse of R 39.

Governors have been instructed to ban extremist literature from prison and extremist texts have been removed. They have also been instructed to remove anyone from communal worship who promotes extremist views. The most dangerous extremists will now be held in specialist units in the high security units, apart from the general prison population. The vetting of chaplains has also been tightened, with pre-employment vetting checks for chaplains introduced in February 2017. This move towards specialist units is an important shift, although this can also be problematic. The Ministry of Justice announced in April 2017 that it was establishing three separation centres, the first at HMP Frankland, which is now open and whose inmates include Anjem Choudary, followed by two others at HMP

Woodhill and Full Sutton, with a capacity for twenty-eight prisoners.[7] They will be used for prisoners who pose a risk to national security by encouraging others in the commission, preparation or instigation of an act of terrorism where the risk can only be managed by separation, and this will be assessed every three months. The procedures governing the new separation centres are set out in the *Separation Centre Referral Manual* (PSI 05/2017).

The problem of managing radicalisation, however, is exacerbated by staff cuts. In a BBC interview on 7 April 2015, Chris Phillips, the former head of the National Counter-Terrorism Security Office, said that staff shortages were making it harder to deal with Islamic radicalisation, as extremists are not properly monitored, so safety is being compromised. The then Home Secretary, Theresa May, rejected this claim, although she did say she wanted new extremism officer roles in prison. It is certainly clear from the recent incidents of disorder in prison that staff find it difficult to maintain order and do not have sufficient time and resources to address properly additional issues such as potential radicalisation.

The treatment of Muslim prisoners

The development of policies on prisoner radicalisation and deradicalisation has highlighted the broader issue of the treatment of Muslim prisoners in prisons in England and Wales. Muslim prisoners are the fastest growing religious group in prison and they constituted 15 per cent of the prison population in 2017. In 1994 Muslim prisoners were 5 per cent of the prison population of England and Wales, 8 per cent in 2004 and 12 per cent in 2008 (HMIP 2010: 9). Muslims are also over-represented in the prison population in the UK, France and the Netherlands. Muslim prisoners in the UK are a heterogeneous group and include birth Muslims and converts, Muslims from Asian, black, white and mixed heritage groups, British Muslims and foreign nationals, from states including Pakistan and Somalia. The increase in Muslim prisoners in the UK has been attributed to a range of factors, including demographic drivers, the fact that the Muslim population is generally younger and concentrated in inner-city areas, with high levels of social deprivation. The Young Report noted that Muslim prisoners see themselves as subjected to differential treatment, because of their faith; for example, they are more likely be stopped and searched outside, and felt that they had been stereotyped as terrorists because they were Muslims (Young 2014). This has raised the question of whether Muslims are in effect a suspect community.[8] Some Muslim communities feel unfairly targeted by the Prevent strategy, although it does now focus more on other forms of extremism. The fact of the increased number of Muslim prisoners in the UK could also, as Acheson notes, 'chime with the radicalisers' message of the victimisation of Muslims' (Ministry of Justice 2016b: para 14).

However, until relatively recently, there has been little information on Muslim prisoners in the UK. Since 2010, the subject has received more interest with a Thematic Review from the Prison Inspectorate in 2010, as well as the Young and Lammy reviews of young black and Muslim men in the criminal justice system as well as smaller scale studies.[9] In addition, the question of equality and diversity in the prison system has received more attention, with increased awareness of the needs of Muslim prisoners. In compliance with the equality duty imposed on prisons, regular reports on equality matters have been published. The Mubarek Report published in 2006, following the death of Zahid Mubarek, murdered by his cell mate, had also raised awareness of the need to address equality issues (Keith 2006). However, this may also, in some cases, mean that staff may be reluctant to engage with prisoners because of concerns over being seen as racist.

A common theme emerging from these studies is that Muslim prisoners complain of discrimination and of being seen as fundamentalists. A Thematic Review of Muslim prisoners' experiences was conducted by the Prison Inspectorate and its findings were published in 2010 (HMIP 2010). It is based on information from prisoner surveys and inspection reports over a three-year period and in-depth interviews with a sample of 164 male Muslim prisoners from eight prisons, including local prisons, training prisons and Young Offender Institutions and interviews with the Muslim chaplains in those prisons. Thirty per cent of the interviewees were converts who had a stronger sense of religious and ethnic identity. There was a higher number of black converts. Two-thirds of the prisoners interviewed described themselves as Sunni Muslims, others saw themselves as Shia Muslims or did not know what they were.

The HMIP Report notes that at the time of its research less than 1 per cent of the Muslim prison population were in prison for terrorist-related offences (2010: 4). The Lammy Report (2017) also refers to 175 Muslims convicted of terrorist offences between 2001 and 2012, a small proportion of Muslim prisoners.[10] However, Muslims constitute the majority of TACT offenders. Figures for 2017 suggest that 90 per cent (105) of the 183 offenders in custody for terrorism-related offences on 31 March declared themselves as Muslim.[11]

The investigations of the Prison Inspectorate indicate that Muslim prisoners report more negatively on their experience in prison and particularly on the issues of safety and relations with other prisoners. White Muslims were more positive, with black and mixed heritage Muslims least positive. Asian Muslims reported more negatively on safety and respect. However, converts were less critical than birth Muslims of the treatment of Muslims in prison or the media. The Thematic Review recorded that Muslim prisoners feel less safe in prison than non-Muslims. 23 per cent of Muslim prisoners said they had been victimised in prison compared to 25 per cent of non-Muslims (HMIP 2010: 17). Muslims were more likely to report victimisation by staff, especially in dispersal prisons. Differential perceptions were widest in high security dispersal prisons, where there is the greatest focus on security and extremism. But Muslims were more positive than non-Muslims in reporting that their faith needs were met in prison. However, they resented the presence of so many staff at Friday prayers and especially the presence of female officers, or staff talking during the service, or walking on the carpet of the mosque with their shoes on. Muslim prisoners were also more likely to report unfairness on the Incentives and Earned Privileges Scheme.

The way Muslims are perceived – particularly the association of Muslims with terrorism – was the major problem cited by prisoners in interviews. Specifically, they thought there were differences in treatment because they were Muslim; for example, they felt that they were observed more than other prisoners. Public and official discourses around terrorism, extremism and radicalisation had a negative impact on their experience of safety and respect. Muslim prisoners were also unhappy over the media coverage of Muslims and its effect on staff and other prisoners. For example, they said the media depicted Islam as violent, failed to distinguish between 'good' and 'bad' Muslims or to note that Muslims are also fearful of terrorism. Muslim prisoners thought staff had little idea how to relate to them other than as extremists. Staff focused on them as potential threats to national security, although the majority were not convicted of terrorist offences. For example, in one prison they were not able to pray together. Some tried to hide their religion from others. The suspicion of Muslims among non-Muslim prisoners was also noted by Earle and Phillips (2013).

The Thematic Review discussed different motives for conversion, including dietary benefits and to obtain protection, to get more time out of one's cell, as well as the desire to change one's life. Some prisoners said there was an increase in conversion at Ramadan to obtain better food. Of those prisoners interviewed, 30 per cent were converts, some wanted the discipline and structure of Islam, while others wanted protection through their membership of a group with a powerful identity, and some sought material advantages, but even if they joined for that reason, in time they became genuine practising Muslims. The Review noted that Islam can be a positive force to help prisoners deal with prison and help them move towards reform. The converts emphasised more than birth Muslims the positive role of Islam in enabling them to cope with the trials of prison (2010: para 511).

Some prison staff were concerned about the conversion and intimidation of non Muslims by Muslim gangs in dispersal prisons and Young Offender Institutions, as well as the pressure on Muslim prisoners to adhere to a stricter form of Islam, but the Review found little evidence of this. However, prison staff were reluctant to challenge inappropriate behaviour and had insufficient training on this. Although staff were aware of the dangers of radicalisation, they lacked the knowledge and confidence to manage Muslim prisoners. Inspectorate reports on staff in the high security estate have also highlighted the problem of balancing the need for vigilance on potential radicalisation with the need to build effective relationships with prisoners.

The Thematic Review also considered the role of Muslim chaplains.[12] Chaplains were valued by prisoners, although the chaplains themselves thought staff lacked an understanding of Islam, and there was not enough time for them to fulfil their pastoral duties or to support prisoners, especially in view of the large numbers of recent converts. There was a perception that they were not trusted by the prison authorities and were also sometimes treated with suspicion by prisoners. They were also critical of media reports which they thought demonised Muslims and were not happy with the way prayer was seen as a sanction which could be withdrawn for unrelated misdemeanors. They thought more training was needed on Islamic beliefs and culture, rather than more diversity training. The chaplains also thought that prison staff had negative misconceptions of Islam. Some chaplains had been interviewed about their potential to radicalise others. While Muslim chaplains are seen by the government as part of the strategy to deal with extremism in prisons, this also means some prisoners do not trust them.

Staff training in the Prison Service to identify and deal with signs of possible radicalisation began in 2007. But the Report warns of the danger of a blanket security-led approach to all Muslim prisoners in strengthening the stereotype of Muslims as potential extremists. Staff need training to focus on Muslims as individuals with specific risks and needs, rather than as part of a distinct suspect group. This suspicion of Muslim prisoners as actual or potential extremists can be counterproductive, if it fuels resentment and disaffection, so prisoners are more likely to re-offend or move towards extremism. Similarly, the negative representations of Muslims in newspapers can strengthen Muslim identity and alienation further, although the extent of this negative representation has been debated.[13] However, the Report does note some improvements in Muslim prisoners' perceptions, for example at Belmarsh (2010: para 4.18). The Thematic Review recommended a NOMS national strategy for Muslim prisoners, supported by national and local policies outlining how the needs of Muslim prisoners will be met, for example, allowing more time for chaplains, and cautioned that prisoners should not be banned from Muslim services for unrelated misdemeanors. This final recommendation has now been implemented.

Liebling and Straub (2013) conducted research at HMP Whitemoor from January 2009 to March 2011. They discovered that staff were apprehensive about dealing with TACT offenders. On the one hand, staff wanted to be watchful of signs of radicalisation, but they also felt that they had to be careful not to alienate prisoners, especially if conversion to Islam was itself seen as a risk. Some prisoners did describe the prison as a 'recruiting drive for the Taliban' and some officers agreed, but researchers found it difficult to ascertain the actual risk, as much of the evidence was anecdotal and indirect. Liebling and Straub note that '(A)n environment that was perceived as a continuation and extension of a life dominated by feelings of alienation, misrecognition and unfairness offered fertile ground for cultivating hatred of the state or society' (ibid at 21).

A study of the outcomes for young black and/or Muslim men once they have entered the criminal justice system, in prison and on release, was undertaken by the Young Review in 2013 and its report was published in 2014 (Young 2014). The Review studied young black and Muslim men aged eighteen to twenty-four and considered their experience of negative stereotyping: young Muslim men were stereotyped as extremists, as likely to be engaged in terrorist activity, while young black men were stereotyped as gang members and as drug dealers. Both groups are over-represented in the prison population. Despite a long history of equality policies in the Prison Service and the equality duty imposed by the Equality Act 2010 to eliminate discrimination and to promote equality, the Review notes that it is clear these groups continue to experience differential treatment in prison because of their race, ethnicity or faith (2014: para 74). There was also a lack of support for effective rehabilitation.

The Young Review stressed that ethnicity, faith and culture play a key role in promoting sustained desistance from crime. In Spalek and El-Hassan's (2007) earlier study of a small sample of prisoners who converted to Islam, the respondents suggested that it helped them rebuild their lives. But the Young Review reported that if three or four prisoners were seen praying together, then security reports were made. Black, Asian and minority ethnic prisoners thought that they were more likely to receive warnings and adjudications and that they had been downgraded on the Incentives and Earned Privileges scheme for trivial issues.

The Review found prison officers focused on issues of verbal abuse, rather than attitudes or stereotyping. But Muslim prisoners were more likely than non-Muslims to see perceptions of other prisoners as problematic and said converts were treated with suspicion. It notes that the work of imams is especially important in promoting a better understanding of Islam and helping to resolve Islamophobic incidents in a constructive way. The Report stresses the need to build social capital within communities, for example bringing in former offenders as mentors, but they may face problems in getting access to the custodial estate. More disaggregated information and monitoring, it argues, is needed on ethnicity and faith.

Since the Young Report was published, the Lammy Review has also been conducted to review the treatment of and outcomes for black, Asian and minority ethnic individuals in the criminal justice system. It was set up in 2016 and covers prosecutorial and court systems, prison and secure youth institutions and rehabilitation services. It has called for evidence, visited establishments and organised round tables and published interim findings. It found disproportionate contact with the criminal justice system for BAME adults and young offenders in relation to being tried in the Crown Court instead of the magistrates' courts, custodial remands in the Crown Court, custodial sentencing and adjudications for prison discipline (Uhrig 2016). Black and Asian men were more likely to be held in the high security estate for public order offences than white men. Black and mixed ethnic men and mixed ethnic women had adjudications brought against them at higher rates than white groups (ibid: 25). The final Report highlighted the high number of young BAME offenders in custody and the fact that BAME offenders are more likely to go to prison for drugs offences (Lammy 2017). It acknowledges that the factors occurring prior to entry into the criminal justice system contribute to the over-representation of BAME offenders in custody. The Lammy Report makes thirty-five recommendations, including better monitoring and recording of individuals in the criminal justice system, including their religious affiliation, reconsideration of prosecution and deferred prosecutions of BAME young offenders and more recruitment of BAME staff, to improve both representation and trust.

So we have had several reviews of Muslim and BAME prisoners and an array of equality initiatives and policies, but the sense of differential treatment remains, and where there are differences, this can feed into the narrative of victimisation. There has also been an increased focus on equality and diversity and greater support for Muslim prisoners, through recruitment of more chaplains. There were over 200 Muslim prison chaplains by 2013, compared to fewer than 100 in 2008 (Pickering 2013: 12). There has been a Muslim advisor post at NOMS since the late 1990s.

Segregation versus integration

Whether terrorist prisoners should be held separately from other prisoners, and whether they should be concentrated in a particular prison, has often been debated. Politically motivated prisoners may be viewed by states as different from ordinary offenders and are often held separately. They may also be detained and punished under different laws, for example, emergency legislation or counter-terrorism laws, which will be discussed in more detail in Chapter 6. These prisoners usually attract more external interest than ordinary prisoners and, in some cases, may benefit from early release under amnesties, at the cessation of conflict. Concentrating prisoners in a particular prison can also attract outside attention on the prison, as occurred in the case of Guantánamo and in relation to the hunger strikers at the Maze prison.

If prisoners are able to mix freely with other prisoners they may be able to circulate materials, to form networks and to mobilise support. There is also the danger that those on the periphery of a group could become more involved through contact with the more extreme offenders, and they, in turn, may contribute to the radicalisation of those previously not engaged in extremist politics. Separation is useful not just because it inhibits radicalisation, but also because it limits contact with organised crime and professional criminals, which is important as crime may be used by terrorist groups for fundraising. Holding prisoners in a specific unit means specialist staff can be utilised, specific interventions targeted and observation of the group can prove a useful source of information and knowledge. So it may be cost-effective in terms of the use of resources. However, separation can also promote cohesion and solidarity within the group, which may make deradicalisation harder, and increase their sense of injustice if these prisoners are treated differently from other prisoners. During the conflict in Northern Ireland, the concentration of sectarian prisoners in specific blocs allowed them to maintain hierarchies and command structures, exert control over their members, discourage informants, organise escapes and strikes, and to intimidate staff and their families outside the prison.

Notwithstanding the negative aspects of segregation, the concentration of prisoners in Northern Ireland also expedited the peace process, as we shall see in Chapter 6, as the leadership was able to promote the cessation of armed conflict in favour of political means among Republicans inside the prison and ultimately outside, in the wider community. But if a group has loose cells rather than a clear structure, as is the case of groups like al-Qaeda, as Neumann (2010) has noted, then bringing adherents together in prison may also allow more formal structures to develop. Separation of prisoners may be harder in the UK at the present time because, as noted earlier, there are now more TACT prisoners convicted for their involvement in preparatory acts, who may be serving shorter sentences, and dispersed across the whole prison estate, rather than held in the high security prisons. The TACT prison population also includes women and a range of age groups which makes separation on the basis of TACT offences harder to implement.

Complete isolation, or solitary confinement, is difficult to implement because of conflicts with international human rights law, and such treatment would augment prisoners' sense of victimisation, and may also increase external support. It may also not preclude further self-radicalisation. Anders Breivik, who has been held in isolation in a Norwegian prison, argued at his appeal, that his views had become more extreme in custody, in part because of his isolation.

The issue of separation has also been discussed in the domestic courts. In *R (Bary and others) v Secretary of State for Justice* [2010] EWHC 587 (Admin), the claimants were held in a special Detainee Unit, apart from the rest of the prisoners, who had very little contact with them. They were not accused or convicted of offences within the UK, but were accused or convicted of terrorist offences overseas, and were being held in the Unit pending extradition or deportation. The governor, Ferdie Parker, issued a notice in 2008 imposing tighter restrictions limiting them to the Unit, except for doctors' appointments. In a letter, he had said that he was worried about radicalisation, especially when a new prisoner, Omar Othman, was transferred to the Unit. The Divisional Court found 'that Mr Parker's concerns about possible radicalisation of young Muslim prisoners in the main part of Long Lartin were not only genuine, but also reasonable. We think that the recognition of this possibility in the HMIP report of January 2008 is particularly important. Therefore, we have no doubt that Mr Parker's concerns about the possible effect if Mr Othman had been given free access to the main prison were fully justified, even if he had no hard evidence or intelligence to base them on at the time he took his decision' (at para 78). The claim that the decision was disproportionate and unreasonable and breached Articles 3 and 8 was rejected.

The management of extremist prisoners in Europe and the United States

The problem of prisoner radicalisation is not unique to Britain, of course, but is also faced by states around the world, in Europe, as well as the Middle East and the US. How the problem is addressed reflects cultural, historical, political and financial pressures. It may also depend on local political structures, which may include tribal ones, and whether the state is a Muslim-majority state. However, there are also some common themes and challenges and the experience of other states can offer insights into possible developments in the UK. For this reason, the Acheson Review visited prisons in the Netherlands, Spain and France to see how they deal with extremists. The favoured approach in these states has been to separate Islamist extremist prisoners in high security conditions. As well as being seen as the safest option for achieving good order in the prison, this strategy has also meant that it is possible to target counter-radicalisation measures more effectively using specialist staff and to promote rehabilitation, where possible, and to enable surveillance of the high-risk group. Instead of offering the corporate worship of Friday prayers favoured in the UK, visiting imams counsel prisoners individually and run group study classes.

In the Netherlands, there has been a segregation policy since 2006 for prisoners convicted of terrorist offences who are held in separate units to prevent the radicalisation of other prisoners. These units are located at Vught prison in North Brabant, where Mohammed Bouyeri the murderer of filmmaker Theo van Gogh is held, and De Schie prison in Rotterdam, which holds remand and convicted terrorist prisoners in a separate unit with its own facilities, to prevent them radicalising others. The numbers of terrorists held by the Netherlands is much lower than in Spanish and French prisons. Although the number of cells is limited, and they are used for leaders rather than followers, with thirty prisoners held in the units in the Netherlands between 2006 and 2009, it is expected that the number of these segregated prisoners will expand in future. Staff are transferred after four years in these units to work in other areas of the prison system.

The regime in these units is stricter than for other prisoners. But prisoners are regularly subject to risk assessments, based on the Violent Extremist Risk Assessment (VERA-2) tool, adapted to the Netherlands, to see whether they can be moved to an ordinary wing. VERA-2 examines beliefs and attitudes and looks for a range of possible indicators, including a commitment to an ideology justifying violence, a perceived sense of victimisation and grievance, of personal or group injustice, a rejection of democratic society and its pluralist values, the dehumanisation of targets, hostility to national collective identity, lack of empathy, a network of family or friends involved in violent action, and the glorification of violence. It also considers whether the individual possesses violent extremist materials, or has personal contact with extremists and the identification of a specific target for attack. Also taken into account are offenders' willingness to die for their cause, their history of violence, their involvement in weapons training or their family or friends' involvement, as well as their own commitment and motivation. But VERA-2 also looks at protective factors which reduce the risk, such as a personal or a family rejection of violence.

In Spain, the issue of the management of terrorist prisoners has focused principally on the treatment of prisoners from the Basque separatist group, ETA, Basque Homeland and Freedom. ETA was responsible for the murder of the prime minister in 1973 and has been involved in numerous deaths and kidnappings. The group announced a permanent ceasefire in 2011, and it claimed in April 2017 that it had disarmed. By April 2016, 386 ETA prisoners were held in France and Spain. Normally in the Spanish prison system, prisoners would be housed near home where possible, but as ETA prisoners come from the same region, it is thought that housing them together would strengthen the control of the ETA hierarchy over prisoners and make it harder for supporters to leave the group (Torres Soriano 2014). ETA is less interested than Islamist extremist groups in radicalising other prisoners. But a policy of dispersal is favoured, as it is thought that this can help to promote dissent within the organisation and the prospect of transfer nearer home can be used as an incentive to break with the group. Pursuing a policy of reintegration through incentives has been challenging because of prisoners' fear of being punished by ETA. The Spanish government's dispersal policy has been challenged by kidnappings and demonstrations, demanding that these prisoners be held nearer to their homes and that they be given conditional early release. This issue was considered by the Strasbourg Court in 2013, in *del Río Prada v Spain* App No. 42750/09 (21 October 2013), which found that there had been breaches of Article 7 and Article 5, in relation to an ETA prisoner whose sentence had been retroactively extended and who was denied early release. The prohibition on early release in this case was unlawful. In response to this judgment, the Spanish High Court did order the release of some ETA prisoners. But so far there has not been an amnesty. But while a dispersal approach is used in Spain for ETA prisoners, Islamist extremists are held in a small number of high security prisons.

In France, in the last few years, specialist units for terrorist offenders have opened at Fresnes, Fleury-Mérogis, Osny and Lille prisons, with an enhanced regime. The units employ specialist staff with a knowledge of Salafism and there is now a greater focus on rehabilitation than in the past, as only those deemed capable of change will be held there. In France the religious faith of prisoners is not normally recorded, but it is estimated that 60 per cent of the prison population is Muslim, compared with 8 per cent of the population of France as a whole.

Practice varies in other European states. In Belgium, for example, there is a combination of specialist terrorist wings or units, where deradicalisation programmes are offered to prisoners, and dispersal across the high security estate. In Italy, terrorists are held in three prisons with high security wings and kept apart from other prisoners. In Norway, most terrorists offenders are usually dealt with by dispersal. But segregation may be used in the most serious cases, for example Anders Breivik who is subject to individual segregation for twenty-two to twenty-three hours a day in Skien prison. But the prison system does not yet have separate terrorist units. Breivik successfully challenged his conditions in the Oslo District Court in 2016,[14] but the Bogarting Appeals Court, in 2017, rejected the claim that his rights under Article 3 were violated. His isolation did not constitute torture or inhuman or degrading treatment under the Convention. His separation was justified to protect him from other prisoners and because of the risk to other prisoners of violence from him. He then appealed to the Norwegian Supreme Court, which in June 2017, upheld the finding of the Court of Appeal that the conditions in which he was held did not amount to inhuman treatment and did not breach Article 3.[15] His lawyer has indicated that he will take his case to the Strasbourg Court.

In Germany, the approach varies between the federal states, although generally efforts are made to isolate and separate extremist prisoners, to prevent further radicalisation and to develop deradicalisation programmes. In the past, Germany has used special terrorist wings, for example, in the 1970s, to deal with the Red Army Faction. The treatment of these RAF prisoners, their extended pre-trial detention and the conditions in which they were held, specifically their isolation, raised concern at that time but was unsuccessfully challenged in Strasbourg in *Ensslin, Baader and Raspe v Germany* (1978) DR 64, when the European Commission on Human Rights rejected their complaints as inadmissible. Ensslin, Baader and Raspe committed suicide in 1977, while being held in Stuttgart's Stammheim prison. Ulrike Meinhof was also held there and she also killed herself in 1976. The group was held apart from other prisoners, rather than being individually isolated. The RAF wanted to politicise prisons and ran a campaign publicising their conditions, as well as participating in hunger strikes, to improve those conditions. Concerns over their incarceration and the conditions in which they were held ultimately attracted more supporters to the group. Even harsher conditions of isolation were imposed on the RAF members Krőcher and Mőller, imprisoned in Switzerland, but the Court did not consider that they reached the level required to breach Article 3.[16]

The Strasbourg jurisprudence suggests that the threshold for a breach of Article 3 in relation to segregation is set quite high, although, as we saw in Chapter 2, segregation can have adverse effects on the mental health of the prisoner. The court will look at the particular conditions, the duration, the objective pursued and the effects on the individual. In the case of Ramirez Sanchez, or Carlos the Jackal,[17] held in France, eight years of isolation in the view of the Court did not reach the threshold for a breach of Article 3 and was ameliorated by the high number of visits he was permitted. The view of the Strasbourg Court is that segregation is permitted only within limits, but not total isolation or complete sensory deprivation.[18] Issues to be considered include the duration of isolation, its impact on the prisoner's physical and mental health and the objective pursued.[19] It will examine whether the long-term effects of isolation can be ameliorated by giving the prisoner access to the same facilities as other high security prisoners.[20] There should also be regular reviews of the need for the individual's segregation.

In the US, a combination of dispersal and concentration is used for prisoners convicted of terrorism-related offences, as they are mostly held in units in specific prisons. Although much attention has been focused on Guantánamo, which former President Obama[21] described as the 'number one recruitment tool' for jihadists as it became a symbol of oppression of Muslims, there are also many prisoners held in prisons on the mainland for terrorism-related offences, including those involved in the bombing of the World Trade Centre. By the end of 2011, there were 362 federal prisoners on terrorism-related charges, 269 involved in international terrorism and 93 for domestic terrorism (Hamm 2013a). Following criticism of the Bureau of Prisons for its failure to monitor communications, there has been a move towards segregation. So most of these prisoners are now held in two new Communication Management Units (CMUs) in federal prisons in Marion, Illinois and Terre Haute, Indiana. These prisoners are confined under very strict conditions, with limited visits and only allowed to speak English. They are held separately to avoid them radicalising other prisoners or hatching plots inside.

Hamm notes that Islam is the fastest growing religion among prisoners in the West, including the US, where, he says, the research on prison radicalisation suggests that 240,000 prisoners have converted to Islam since 9/11 (Hamm 2009: 670). His review of the literature found two contrasting views, the first, which sees prisons as incubators for Islamic terrorism and is very concerned over prison Islam, while the alternative approach focuses on the potential of Islam to rehabilitate prisoners.

The view from federal law enforcers, including the FBI, is that prisoners have been targeted as terrorist recruits by Saudi-backed Wahhabi clerics. The fact that the Saudi government is spending a substantial amount to promote Wahhabi Islam – the austere form of Islam on which al-Qaeda ideology is based, has been highlighted and copies of the Wahhabi Koran are given to charities and mosques and distributed to prisoners. This view, which Hamm describes as 'alarmist', reflects the discovery by the FBI in 2005 of a plot to attack military sites and synagogues which originated from JLS (Jam'iyyat Ul-Islam), a gang of Sunni Muslims at New Folsom Prison. This was the first prison gang in the US with a terrorist agenda which sought to radicalise other prisoners. The alarmist view was also expressed in the Report *Out of the Shadows: Getting Ahead of Prisoner Radicalization* published in 2006 (George Washington University Homeland Security Policy Institute et al. 2006). The Report draws from the testimony of law enforcement experts who consider prison Islam as a clear and present danger to US security. Congress passed the Violent Radicalization and Homegrown Terrorism Prevention Act in 2007, calling for the establishment of a national commission to study and make recommendations on the mitigation of violent radicalisation and ideologically based violence in prison. The Department of Homeland Security set up a unit in 2007 to address the danger of home grown terrorists and included the threat from Islamist extremist prisoners and from prison Islam or 'Prislam'. Ballas (2010), in a report on prisoner radical- isation in the US for the FBI, refers to the role of prison Islam in blending prison inmate culture with religious practice and which rests on a radical strand of Islam and which foments plots within prison. He stresses that prisons contain a captive audience of alienated young males, who may be easily influenced by extremist leaders and many are from minorities who already feel subject to discrimination in America, or are concerned at the treatment of Muslims overseas: 'This perceived oppression, combined with a limited knowledge of Islam, makes this population vulnerable for extremists looking to radicalize and recruit' (2010: 1). He also refers to a shortage of qualified religious providers, which allows prisoners with a limited knowledge of Islam to assert themselves as leaders. Once a terrorist plot has been conceived inside prison, then the parolee can take it outside and use street gangs to obtain firearms to be used in crimes for funding an attack, as well as operatives from the international jihadist movement.

Sinai (2014) argues that prison gangs who use the Koran to justify their activ- ities in US prisons give inmates the benefit of protection and a sense of being part of a wider community outside. 'This form of "Jailhouse Islam" is unique to prison because it incorporates into the religion the values of gang loyalty and violence' (Sinai 2014: 41). Goldmann (2014) stresses that while criminals usually cannot continue their activities in prison, terrorists can as they have a captive audi- ence. So when extremists interact with prisoners, opportunities arise to combine religious fervour with traditional criminal tendencies, as the latter group already know how to use weapons. As some prisoners may already have anti-social and anti-government views and racist tendencies, they are good targets for recruitment and may have been abandoned by friends and families so are alienated and socially isolated. They are more likely to identify with the group and exaggerate the differences between their group and others. The process of radicalisation in prison is similar to that outside, as individuals who see their future as uncertain are more likely to seek a group to reduce that uncertainty and to give them direction. Terrorist groups are also becoming more interested in criminal enterprises to raise money for their activities and prison gangs are an effective means to promote radicalisation. Gang membership gives affiliation, loyalty and protection. But a prisoner who joins just for personal protection is more likely to cut ties on release than one who feels the need to belong.

Hamm (2009) is critical of the alarmist view, which sees prisons as incubators for radicalisation, because it is not based on solid research, such as interviews with prisoners and officers. He favours the rival view, that Islam 'has a moderating effect on prisoners, that plays an important role in prison security and rehabilitation', which is based on verifiable data (2009: 699). He argues that Islam encourages inmates to reflect on and restructure their lives and helps prisoners adapt to prison. It can meet prisoners' spiritual needs and enhance self-discipline. Some convert on the advice of cellmates, fellow gang members and parents, rather than foreign terrorist groups. Many prisoners adopt a religious faith in prison for the first time.

Hamm discusses the results of a two-year study of prisoner radicalisation in US prisons, which looked at the role of gangs, charismatic leaders and the processes by which inmates progress from radicalisation to operational terrorism. Based on these case studies in Californian prisons, he argues that self-help programmes may be useful in combating terrorist recruitment. In New Folsom Prison a terrorist plot was hatched by a gang of Sunni prisoners, with a leader inspired by al-Qaeda. At that facility few rehabilitation programmes were available, there was also a shortage of chaplains and a gang problem and the prison was overcrowded. But at Old Folsom Prison there was an inmate-led Islamic Studies Program with a deradicalisation agenda which provided a counterweight to Islamic extremism. Hamm argues that these inmate self-help programmes can be more effective than state measures to prevent radicalisation.

However, while it is difficult to generalise from so few examples, it is clear that the existence of a positive deradicalisation or rehabilitation programme does not negate the potential of prisons to radicalise. Even if the numbers radicalised in prison are relatively few, they can of course cause massive harm, as exemplified by the title of Hamm's book on the topic, *The Spectacular Few* (Hamm 2013b).

A Report from the International Centre for the Study of Radicalisation and Political Violence (ICSR) discussed findings from fifteen countries, including the UK, Netherlands, Spain and the US, Algeria, Egypt and Afghanistan, to see what could be learnt from other states in dealing with terrorism (Neumann 2010). This Report recognised that prisons provide fertile ground for radical religiously framed ideologies to flourish, but also makes the point that conditions which favour radicalisation are exacerbated by overcrowding and understaffing, which make it harder to detect radicalisation and also 'create the physical and ideological space in which extremist recruiters can operate at free will and monopolise the discourse about religion and politics' (ibid: 2). The Report reaches no firm conclusions on whether such prisoners should be held separately from others. Most of the states in the study combined dispersal with partial concentration, dispersing terrorist prisoners across a few high security prisons. The programmes used in the various states included counselling, discussion of theological issues and improved prison regimes for those participating in programmes. It may also mean states offering incentives for change, although this may be politically unpopular. Early release for political prisoners was offered in Northern Ireland as part of the peace process and included in the Good Friday Agreement. These provisions divided the public and politicians, especially in the face of sporadic continuing instances of violence, and were opposed by the families of victims.

Obviously, more research is needed on prisoner radicalisation to ascertain the extent of problem. However, most observers would agree that religious conversion is not the same as radicalisation. Also if groups such as Jam'iyyat Ul-Islam operate as gangs, they can be dealt with by normal gang control measures. Imams also have an important role to play in encouraging a more moderate form of Islam. Furthermore, greater scrutiny post-release is needed to track inmates with suspected terrorist links, with multi-agency cooperation and multi-disciplinary responses.

Deradicalisation in prison

Deradicalisation is the process by which a person rejects an extremist ideology and thereby reduces the risk of future engagement in terrorist activity. The prospects of success of deradicalisation strategies vary, depending on the target group, whether leaders or followers, and their motivation for the initial radicalisation, whether opportunistic, instrumental, political, or spiritual. In some cases, it may be possible to prevent the commitment progressing to action even if the commitment to the ideology remains. The management of prisoners held for offences under the Terrorism Act in the UK is part of the wider counter-terrorism strategy. Deradicalisation may take place at a group level, as in the case of the IRA, as well as at the individual level. But there are still active dissident groups in Northern Ireland committed to the use of violence to achieve their goals.

The prison context may also offer opportunities to deradicalise not available outside in the wider society for, as we shall see in Chapter 6, the action of the IRA leadership inside prison was a key element in the Northern Ireland peace process. Leaders of the IRA were able to promote disengagement and the pursuit of nonviolent means to achieve their aims, because there was a strong leadership with a hierarchical command structure, and this leadership increased awareness of the value of achieving the group's goals through democratic political structures, rather than by armed campaigns. The potential for this may be more limited in relation to

Islamist extremist groups because of their looser structure. However, the time spent in prison also offers space to consider political issues and following educational courses can also be valuable in promoting critical reflection. In some cases, prison may also offer a welcome opportunity to escape a violent conflict. Prison officers are in a unique position in dealing directly with those who have acted on their extremist beliefs. Even if officers are unable to directly influence inmates' political views, the humane and egalitarian treatment of prisoners makes it harder to sustain a narrative of victimisation.

The ICSR report proposed a mix of different kinds of programmes combining religious re-education and vocational programmes, a focus on reintegrating prisoners into mainstream society, to give them the means to start a new life, to form new social networks, and to find a means of 'locking prisoners into multiple commitments and obligations towards family, community, and the state' (Neumann 2010: 3).

However, if the issue of deradicalisation is treated primarily as a matter of desistance and as part of the process of rehabilitation, then existing sources of knowledge of what works to reduce re-offending can be used. What works with other offenders may be effective with radicalised offenders in contexts where they have similar profiles, attitudes and behaviour to other offenders. While there are already distinct specialist programmes for specific classes of offenders, such as sex offenders, for example, they may still use similar tools to those employed in relation to 'ordinary' offenders, including CBT and support on leaving prison.

At present, the research base on TACT offenders is too small to conduct rigorous large-scale studies and it is too early to conduct longitudinal studies, unlike other groups of offenders. In the treatment of the group, security issues and risk assessments predominate, reflecting that it may be impossible to change some members of this group, but it is important to consider rehabilitation as well, where this is feasible. Because younger offenders may grow out of crime, interventions need to be carefully framed to prevent a spiral of deviancy amplification. This raises the issue of whether terrorists are fundamentally different to other offenders, and if there are similarities in terms of the role of subcultures and their search for alternative sources of status, the criminological literature may be useful in exploring ways of combating extremism. Political prisoners usually do not see themselves as criminals, but may share some common characteristics and acts of violence are clearly criminal acts, regardless of motivation. Recidivism may be the result of a wide range of factors and involves complex issues, but the literature on desistance, rehabilitation and deterrence suggests that some prison programmes may work for some individuals, even if not all, and in that respect can sometimes succeed. There are, of course, the same methodological problems of measuring recidivism, encountered in other studies of desistance, of proving the effectiveness of deradicalisation programmes, especially as some of these programmes are relatively new. Issues to consider are whether the time span used to measure deradicalisation is disengagement for two years after release, or for a longer period and how it should be tested.

The limited effect of imprisonment in deterring professional criminals is well-established, so it is perhaps not surprising that some of the leading figures in Islamist extremist groups have been imprisoned on several occasions, and the fact of their repeated imprisonment may be seen by them and others as further proof of the persecution of Muslims. The deterrent effect of a long sentence of imprisonment is also weak for those willing to kill themselves to pursue their goals. However, for younger offenders, who may grow out of crime, it is important to intervene to prevent their radicalisation while in custody.

Lloyd (2013), a member of the Extremism Team at NOMS, notes that most commentators distinguish between leaders and followers, but there are also those whose criminal history is motivated by criminality rather than politics. Although some terrorist attacks have been committed by those without a prior criminal history, making them harder to detect, in some of the recent attacks the offenders did have previous criminal convictions. The TACT prison population is heterogeneous and it includes amateurs and more sophisticated terrorists. Terrorists are a diverse group, comprising a range of different groups and different types, in terms of group structure, their history of violence and the motivations of their members. Their participation in attacks may vary from peripheral to central roles. Some terrorists may be more educated and skilled than 'ordinary' criminals. However, terrorist offenders, says Lloyd, are motivated by ideologies, rather than personal gain, so may be eager to publicise their beliefs, whereas ordinary criminals may be more reclusive to avoid detection.

An Interventions Unit was set up at NOMS in 2008, which included psychologists, probation officers and Muslim chaplains, to deal with the whole range of offending, to draw on practice elsewhere and from the literature on desistance (Dean 2014). It has formulated a range of interventions including the Healthy Identity Interventions (HII Foundation and HII Plus), and religious deradicalisation programmes, such as Al Furqan, to promote desistance, as well as Extremism Risk Guidance.

HII has been used in UK since 2012 and is delivered on an individual basis with two facilitators per prisoner. HII looks at what motivates individuals to engage and offend, and their attitudes and beliefs which enable offending (NOMS 2013). Its aims are preventing future offences, encouraging participants to challenge ideologies, examining the factors which motivate offenders and enabling them to move on with their lives. It sees identity as a key issue. The programme addresses how to meet personal needs, other than through involvement in terrorist groups. HII uses an evidence-based framework for those convicted of Terrorist Act offences, or other offences, where the motivation is deemed to be extremist. This intervention may also be used if the recipient is not convicted of these offences, but there are concerns regarding the offender's engagement with extremist ideologies, which may be identified by using the Extremism Risk Screening Guidance.

Modules include Cognitive Behavioural Therapy (CBT) and mindfulness and group and individual sessions. These aim to help offenders to manage their thoughts, emotions and feelings associated with conflict and to address their distorted beliefs.

The HII programme also prepares participants for more intense interventions. It draws on established approaches used in offending behaviour courses and the 'What Works' literature, including the Risk–Need–Responsivity model and Good Lives Model. The Risk–Need–Responsivity model matches the intensity and duration of intervention to the risk and need level of the individual and targets those most at risk. The Good Lives Model assumes individuals seek to satisfy the same needs as others, but the ways they try to achieve this leads to harmful behaviour, so the intervention supports meeting these needs without harming others. The desistance literature concentrates on understanding why individuals reach a point in their lives when they decide they no longer wish to offend. It focuses on changing identity and developing alternative identities is seen as the key to desistance. So it is therefore important that the intervention addresses the circumstances which make people engage with extremist causes, or ideologies, and make them willing to offend on their behalf, and facilitates circumstances which promote disengagement and desistance. By 2014, about one-third of convicted extremist offenders had completed the Healthy Identity Intervention. However, some prisoners refuse to take part in HII and if individuals are coerced into participation, it is questionable whether it would be effective. Participants are more likely to collaborate if they see that doing so is in their own interest.

The NOMS Intervention Unit contributed to the development of the Extremism Risk Guidance (ERG22+) which identifies specific features – individual and social circumstances which link to the individual's offending – to assess their engagement, and the circumstances which favour engagement with an extremist group cause or ideology, the willingness to offend on the group's behalf, their capability and the circumstances which enable them to commit a particular offence. The major sources of information for risk assessment are individual interviews with an offender, although some prisoners have refused to participate in ERG22+.

While ERG22+ is used in England and Wales, the Violent Extremist Risk Assessment (VERA-2), is utilised in many other states, including Australia and the Netherlands. So compared to 2001, we now have improved risk assessment measures such as VERA-2, discussed earlier, and ERG22+, as well as deradicalisation programmes, including HII, but we do not as yet have sufficient information on their effectiveness, although this may be available in the future. Which is the best programme may depend on the political and social context. In some cases, as Dean (2013) notes, prisoners may not disengage from the ideology or political cause, but may desist from terrorist behaviour. There may be different degrees of engagement and disengagement between offenders, but clearly establishing a new identity is crucial. The wider context of prison life is also important. Treating prisoners as citizens, as we have argued, can promote good order within the prison and undermine the narrative of victimhood. Furthermore, equality and diversity policies may play a role in reducing perceptions of victimisation.

Use may also be made of court reports and reviews from prison and probation staff and information from other third parties. Risk assessments are still subject to development as the research base on terrorist offenders, as we have noted, is smaller than for other type of offences. Risk assessments may themselves be risky if they underestimate or over-estimate the risk, which could have catastrophic effects on public safety or infringe the human rights of suspects. The ERG Guidelines focus on personal and group identity, group conflict and managing threats. HII and ERG have been influenced by the research on terrorist offenders, which highlights the need for status, in some cases a geographical displacement, and an over-identification with the relevant group. Factors which may undermine involvement include the positive influence of families, disillusionment with the leadership of the group, and a perception of poor treatment by the group. Risk assessments will focus on identifying those at risk, even where offenders are convicted for non-terrorism offences if, for example, they have a prior association with an extremist group and it is thought that they may be involved in recruitment in prison.

Desistance will require a process of de-identification with a group or ideology and a dis-identification to define themselves in opposition to it. We know from studies of desistance of ordinary offenders that the process is not smooth and disengagement may mean lapses and reversals. The aim of intervention is to enable individuals to meet their personal needs legitimately, challenging attitudes and beliefs which are harmful, for example, and their demonisation and dehumanisation of others. Reducing identification with the group makes it harder for them to see others in a stereotypical way. It is also important to increase their tolerance and acceptance of events and emotions and their sense of personal responsibility, so their focus is on their own personal identity, rather than the group's. Promoting alternative ways to realise their goals, or to express their commitments and values without needing to harm others, is essential. Using ex-offenders can also be valuable in giving authority to discussions as part of a deradicalisation programme, but it may be difficult for reformed terrorists to obtain access to prisons and there may be fears of the risk of their re-engagement.

The UK approach has favoured supporting imams' work to combat radicalisation, by giving prisoners access to a more moderate form of Islam. So a religious deradicalisation programme, Al Furqan, was devised in 2011 to offer an alternative interpretation of the Koran and to challenge misinterpretations of Islam. It scrutinises key texts, examines periods of peaceful coexistence with other faiths in Islamic history, focuses on tolerance and includes the duties and obligations of Muslims in a non-Muslim state. However, it was stopped at the end of 2015 because of concerns over its content. Efforts have also been made to develop a programme to further prisoners' understanding of Islam, through the Tarbiyah programme, but this was revised following criticism in the press that some of the materials used could promote violence. Some offenders may have a very limited knowledge or understanding of the Koran, but simply identify with Muslims as a group.

Prison radicalisation has received more attention in the last few years, but what happens after prison is, of course, also crucial in promoting desistance, especially now that there are more TACT prisoners serving short sentences and those prisoners serving longer sentences will also be released on licence back into the community. Many currently in prison will be released over the next decade. Major breaches of licence conditions will mean a return to custody, although minor breaches may result in a warning. In the UK more attention is now being given to developing work after prison, as the process of disengagement and deradicalisation clearly needs to continue outside, for example, by establishing links with community groups, and including discussion of theological issues.

The Prevent duty guidance, revised following the Counter-Terrorism and Security Act 2015, does cover both prisons and probation, although the emphasis is on risk assessment and risk management rather than rehabilitation (HM Government 2015). TACT offenders on release are subjected to Multi-Agency Public Protection Arrangements (MAPPAs) which in the past have focused primarily on violent and sex offenders (Wood and Kemshall 2007). But where offenders are radicalised in prison, it may be difficult for probation staff, or the police, to assess whether an offender has been caught up in a radical group for reasons other than belief, for example, protection in prison, or for instrumental reasons, to get better food, more time off work to attend prayers, and is a 'convenience' Muslim, so they may be more likely to relinquish the association with extremism on release than if they are ideologically committed to the group's agenda.

The issues discussed earlier, of disproportionate outcomes for young Muslim and BAME men highlighted by the Young Review and Lammy Report, still need to be addressed. Young notes the problems with payment by results in the *Transforming Rehabilitation* Agenda, as there are no incentives within TR to address disproportionate outcomes for young black and/or Muslim men. Families also need to be engaged as part of the desistance process, but if drugs and alcohol are involved in the offender's history, Muslim families may be reluctant to accept an offender back into the family. So where aftercare is a key issue, work with families can assist in reintegrating the offender into the community. Sharing of intelligence between prisons, the police and the probation service is crucial, but those convicted of minor offences will not necessarily be subject to such intense surveillance and close supervision as those convicted of more serious offences. While all prisoners now receive twelve months' supervision and support on leaving prison, the findings of a recent study by the Inspectorates of Probation and Prisons suggest that support is uneven and limited and not enough is being done to help prisoners, or to manage risks (Criminal Justice Joint Inspection 2016). If prisoners leave prison with little financial, social and emotional support, then this gap may be filled by radical groups who target them. The shoe bomber, Richard Reid, and Mutkar Ibrahim, leader of the July 2007 London bomb plot, were both radicalised in prisons, but were then further radicalised on their release at the Finsbury Park mosque which, at the time, was strongly associated with extremist preachers.

Conclusion

As we have seen, prisons clearly have the potential to radicalise and have done so in a number of cases, but they also have the potential to deradicalise offenders. Just as the isolation of offenders from the external world increases their vulnerability to radicalising pressures, imprisonment also affords time for reflection and for prisoners already radicalised, the opportunity to develop individual critical awareness. This is more likely to occur when conditions outside are favourable to a new approach, as in Northern Ireland, where prisoners contributed to the peace process developing outside the prison walls.

The key points that emerge from the research on the issue are the need for well-ordered prisons with high levels of safety, and adequate staffing and resources to stem the process of radicalisation. Monitoring radicalisation is much harder in overcrowded and disorganised prisons and in these prisons it is easier for groups and individuals to influence others. Moreover, a lack of safety may make prisoners more vulnerable to radicalisation, if they seek protection from others, and in the absence of meaningful activities, they may be more likely to embrace extremist ideologies. Staffing is also important to control the flow of material and contraband coming into prison, and easy access to translators is also needed. While prisons have been given more funding for counter-terrorism, prison overcrowding and staff cuts, the increases in prison violence, and the availability of drugs, as we saw in Chapter 2, have contributed to recent instances of disorder. It proved difficult during the riots in 2016 for smaller numbers of staff to maintain good order in prison and this may also impact on the processes of monitoring of radicalisation and deradicalisation strategies. So the issues of radicalisation and deradicalisation have to be seen as part of the wider debate on prison reform and prison conditions. Furthermore any issues of discrimination – or perceptions of discrimination – in the prison environment may also feed into the extremist narrative of victimisation, so race and religious equality training in prisons are essential elements of a deradicalisation agenda. Tracking prisoners on release and providing post-release support to reintegrate are also important. We also need to consider the prison's deradicalising potential in the broader context of the rehabilitative potential of prisons in supporting the individual to find another identity. While TACT offenders are still a minority of the prison population, as we have seen, their effective management is critical.

The relationship between terrorists, political prisoners and ordinary criminals is complex. Not all political prisoners are terrorists and political prisoners may be imprisoned in some cases because of their beliefs rather than actions. Terrorists may see themselves as political prisoners, or as freedom fighters, rather than ordinary offenders, and of course there have been instances where prisoners formerly engaged in armed resistance, have on their release, become elected leaders and law makers, notably Martin McGuinness and Nelson Mandela. The relationship between political prisoners and ordinary criminals will be explored further in Chapter 6.

Notes

1 Terrorism Act 2000, as amended by the Terrorism Act 2006 and Counter-Terrorism Act 2008.
2 www.fbi.gov/stats-services/publications/terrorism-2002–2005, accessed 30 December 2017.

3 Terrorism Act 2006.

4 US Department of Justice (2004) cited in Sinai (2014: 36).

5 Reported in *The Guardian*, 26 October 2014.

6 HM Government (2015) *Prevent Duty Guidance: Guidance for specified authorities in England and Wales on the duty in the Counter-Terrorism and Security Act 2015 to have due regard to prevent people from being drawn into terrorism*, www.legislation.gov.uk/ukdsi/2015/9780111133309/pdfs/ukdsiod_9780111133309_en.pdf, accessed 23 July 2017.

7 www.gov.uk/government/news/dangerous-extremists-to-be-separated-from-mainstream-prison-population, accessed 21 July 2017.

8 See, for example, the debate between Pantazis and Pemberton (2009, 2011) and Greer (2010).

9 For example, Spalek and El-Hassan (2007), Earle and Phillips (2013), Young (2014) and Lammy (2017).

10 Lammy (2017: 11). See also Home Office (2013) Terrorism arrests – analysis of charging and sentencing outcomes by religion: www.gov.uk/government/publications/terrorism-arrests-analysis-of-charging-and-sentencing-outcomes-by-religion/terrorism-arrests-analysis-of-charging-and-sentencing-outcomes-by-religion, accessed 8 November 2017.

11 Home Office, *Operation of Police Powers under the Terrorism Act 2000 and subsequent legislation* (31 March 2017).

12 For further discussion of the role of the Muslim chaplaincy, see Gillat-Ray and Ali (2013).

13 See, for example, Bleich et al. (2015).

14 *Anders Behring Breivik v Ministry of Justice* (20 April 2016 i Oslo tingrett).

15 *Anders Behring Breivik v Ministry of Justice* Supreme Court HR-2017-1127-U (case no. 2017/778) (8 June 2017).

16 *Kröcher and Möller v Switzerland* (1982) 34 DR 25.

17 *Ramirez Sanchez v France* App No. 59450/00 (4 July 2006).

18 The UN Rapporteur on Torture has stressed that isolation should be used only in exceptional circumstances and for not more than 15 days.

19 *Rohde v Denmark* App No. 69332/01 (21 July 2005).

20 See *Ocalan v Turkey* App No. 46221/99 (12 May 2005), *Ocalan v Turkey (No. 2)* App Nos. 24069/03, 197/04, 6201/06 and 10464/07 (18 March 2014).

21 Press Conference, The White House (22 December 2010).

6

THE TREATMENT OF POLITICAL PRISONERS

Introduction

The relationship between political prisoners, imprisoned for their political beliefs or political actions, and the 'ordinary' prison population will be considered in this chapter, as well as the question of whether the former group should be treated differently. However, while there are clear examples of political figures imprisoned for their political activities, many prisoners become political because of their experiences in prison or because of contact with politicised prisoners, as we saw in Chapter 5. The presence of key figures from a political movement in prison may mobilise other prisoners. Imprisonment has also been used as a means of silencing political opposition, most notably in the twentieth century. The use of prison for this purpose is still evident, despite greater international monitoring and surveillance of detention and the formal ratification of human rights instruments. The relationship between political and non-political prisoners will be considered, with reference to the contrasting contexts of the Gulag in Stalinist Russia and the more recent conflict in Northern Ireland, which generated a substantial body of research and analysis. Obviously there are many other examples of political prisoners, for example, the PKK in Turkey and ETA in Spain, while in the UK, we could include, *inter alia*, those imprisoned during the miners' strike in 1984–85 and for participation in animal rights campaigns.

Defining a political prisoner

The term 'political prisoner', usually refers to an offender, whose offence is motivated by political ideologies, and whose imprisonment is linked to their political beliefs or activities. The term covers a wide range of groups, those imprisoned as conscientious objectors, and those punished for civil disobedience which is non-violent, as well as those who use violence, who would today be defined as terrorists. Some political prisoners may advocate violence, but not practice it. Definitions of political prisoners may vary and prisoners of war imprisoned in the course of armed conflict might also be included in a broad definition. The Parliamentary Assembly (of the Council of Europe) offers a definition in Resolution 1900 of 2012, which states that a person deprived of his or her personal liberty is to be regarded as a 'political prisoner':

a. if the detention has been imposed in violation of one of the fundamental guarantees set out in the European Convention on Human Rights and its Protocols (ECHR), in particular freedom of thought, conscience and religion, freedom of expression and information, freedom of assembly and association;
b. if the detention has been imposed for purely political reasons without connection to any offence;
c. if, for political motives, the length of the detention or its conditions are clearly out of proportion to the offence the person has been found guilty of or is suspected of;
d. if, for political motives, he or she is detained in a discriminatory manner as compared to other persons; or,
e. if the detention is the result of proceedings which were clearly unfair and this appears to be connected with political motives of the authorities.[1]

While members of terrorist groups convicted for terrorist offences may consider themselves to be political prisoners, this definition explicitly excludes them:

4. Those deprived of their personal liberty for terrorist crimes shall not be considered political prisoners if they have been prosecuted and sentenced for such crimes according to national legislation and the European Convention on Human Rights.

The Resolution then invites states to reassess the cases of any alleged political prisoners and to release or retry them. The right to freedom of political thought and conscience is protected by Article 9 of the European Convention and the right to freedom of expression by Article 10 of the Convention, but these rights may be limited where it is necessary in a democratic society, in the interests of public safety, to protect public order, health or morals, or to protect the rights and freedoms of others. So the state would need to show an adverse effect on national security. The right to freedom of opinion and expression is also protected by Article 19 of the UN Universal Declaration of Human Rights.

The term 'political prisoner' is also used to refer to offenders whose motivation is political, and the context here is significant, as the offences may be committed in the course of a political uprising, and the aim of the action is to change the policies of the state or to challenge the authority of the government. So the relationship between the offence and a political objective is highly important. But political prisoners may include those who have committed no offence, but are imprisoned for their political beliefs, as in the above definition. In the case of the Gulag considered below, many of the detainees had not committed offences to achieve a political objective, but were deemed to be guilty of this, as we shall see, under Article 58.

Amnesty refers to those who commit crimes, including violence, for political reasons as political prisoners, while those detained for their beliefs, and who do not commit violence, are described as prisoners of conscience. Amnesty International began in 1961, by demanding the release of two students who had been imprisoned in Portugal, during the Salazar regime, for raising a toast to freedom. Initially Amnesty focused on the release of political prisoners, but the organisation now deals with a wider range of human rights issues, including the death penalty and discrimination, but imprisonment still remains a key concern, as it campaigns on prison conditions and the ill-treatment of prisoners, including torture, as well as on unfair trials and arbitrary detention. Amnesty defines prisoners of conscience as persons imprisoned for their beliefs or views: 'someone who has not used or advocated violence but is imprisoned because of who they are (sexual orientation, ethnic, national or social origin, language, birth, colour, sex or economic status) or what they believe (religious, political or other conscientiously held beliefs).'[2] But these features might be seen as applicable to many political prisoners. There are also disagreements over whether the category 'political prisoner' should include those who commit or incite violence, rather than merely expressing political ideas, but for Amnesty, prisoners of conscience are essentially non-violent. The organisation will assist political prisoners, including those who have committed violence, but only in relation to fair trial issues and to protection against torture.

So the minimal definition of a political prisoner would be a person detained for involvement in political activity, for holding or expressing political views. A person incarcerated for their political beliefs who has not committed a crime would clearly be a prisoner of conscience, but most studies of political prisoners have concentrated on those who have committed offences in the furtherance of their political goals. The adjective 'political' indicates a relationship to government, so political prisoners are usually engaged in activities challenging a regime or policy.

Political prisoners may also see themselves as prisoners of war, as combatants captured in the course of armed conflict and therefore entitled to the special protection for prisoners of war, which is well established under international humanitarian law and international human rights law. The rights of prisoners of war have been formally protected by successive Conventions which give wide-reaching rights, although they may be difficult to enforce in practice. So the treatment of prisoners of war in World War II, for example, varied greatly, according to where they were captured, with those in Europe generally treated better than those in the Far East. These Conventions can be seen as rudimentary Prisoners' Rights Charters, covering basic rights to food, sanitation, freedom from ill-treatment, the right to receive post and other goods. This has meant that prisoners of war have been able to maintain some semblance of normality to make confinement more bearable.

For example, one way prisoners have negotiated their constraint is to organise classes. Education has long played a part in prison life, even in the most extreme conditions, and continues to be a way in which prisoners can redefine themselves as ordinary citizens, as we saw in Chapter 3.

This can be illustrated by the example of prisoners of war who organised and attended classes when imprisoned in Germany and in the Far East. One camp in Germany, Stalag Luft VI in Heydekrug, had an extensive library and demand for courses was so high it was known as the 'Barbed-Wire University' (Gillies 2011: 260). It was easier to provide education in Europe than the Far East, where conditions were much poorer and resources very limited. In European POW camps, students took exams which were set and marked by the Exam Boards at the University of London. Oxford University also established a Diploma for POWs, although the questions would be checked and censored by the prison adminis- tration. The British Red Cross provided books for prisoners, to which they had a right under Article 39 of the 1929 Convention Relative to the Treatment of Prisoners of War, the precursor to the 1949 Geneva Convention. While there was a strong demand for languages, students also studied accountancy, law, science and the humanities and proper exam rules and standards were applied. For prisoners studying provided not only an escape from boredom, but also an opportunity to acquire new skills and some went on to develop their studies further after the war, with many achieving degrees.

The use of political imprisonment

Political imprisonment has a long history, as religious and political dissenters have been hounded and imprisoned in Europe. Early examples given by Neier (1995), in his review of political imprisonment, are the persecution of Thomas More in the sixteenth century and John Lilburne in the seventeenth century in England. In France in the seventeenth and eighteenth centuries, prisoners did not remain in custody for long as they were either killed or freed. However, in the eighteenth century political dissenters were held in the Bastille, alongside ordinary prisoners, and the lines between them were often blurred.

In the late eighteenth century, in the 'September massacre' in Paris, in the first week of September 1792, over a thousand prisoners were murdered by the *sans- culottes* over four days, while the prisoners were on their way to the prison or already incarcerated. While the intended targets were those suspected of being for- eign spies and counter-revolutionaries, clergymen and members of the nobility and of the Swiss Guard, in fact most of the victims were 'ordinary' criminals who were unhappily incarcerated at the same time. These massacres – which included disem- bowelling and rapes – sparked international outrage. They occurred in the context of the Austro-Prussian invasion of France and the Prussian victory at Verdun and reflected fears that if the Prussians reached Paris they would liberate the prisoners. The Reign of Terror, in which thousands seen as enemies of the regime were killed, executed or died in prison awaiting trial, lasted until 1794. Those deemed to be a political threat were held, in very poor conditions, at the Conciergerie in Paris, awaiting execution. The Conciergerie was nicknamed the antechamber to the guillotine. The revolutionary court was also housed there and the prison could accommodate up to 1,200 prisoners. Its most famous inmates included Marie-Antoinette, Charlotte Corday and the revolutionary leaders Danton and Robespierre.

The number of political prisoners remained high in the nineteenth century in both Europe and in the US where many political activists were imprisoned. American prisons were crowded with abolitionists, those challenging Jim Crow laws in the southern states in the 1880s and 1890s, as well as suffragettes. Anarchists were held in the state penitentiary at Joliet in the 1880s after the Haymarket incident in 1886, where in a demonstration over a police attack on striking workers, a bomb exploded, killing four police officers, seven civilians and injuring many. Eight anarchists were charged and convicted; four of them were hanged, one killed himself and three were given long prison sentences, but were later pardoned. Their supporters strongly denied their involvement with the bombing, but claimed they were arrested for their political views and that their trial was unfair, but this has been subject to much debate.[3]

In Russia, the imprisonment of political prisoners was used long before the mass incarceration of the Stalinist period. In the nineteenth century anyone suspected of political activity in Russia was detained with many political activists imprisoned, hanged, and exiled to Siberia. In Tsarist Russia, large numbers were imprisoned for their political beliefs and activity, but there were fewer political prisoners than in Stalinist Russia and conditions generally were better. In response to this intense repression, the Tsar, Alexander II, was eventually assassinated. It was, of course, a time of developing socialist and utopian and anarchist ideas in Europe and the political prisoners included Alexander Herzen, who was a member of a Fourierist utopian group, and Dostoevsky.

Dostoevsky was also imprisoned first in 1849 in the Peter and Paul Fortress, in St Petersburg where a death sentence was commuted just before the time of his scheduled execution. He was then held at Omsk prison in Siberia for four years, for taking part in a literary group, the Petrashevsky Circle, who were studying the works of the French socialists. This was followed by a period of compulsory military service in Siberia. In Omsk he wrote his *Memoirs of the House of the Dead*, based on his experiences in prison, where he was shocked by the violence of both the guards and the other prisoners (Dostoevsky 2008).

The anarchists, Bakunin and Kropotkin, were both imprisoned for political activities in the Peter and Paul Fortress. Bakunin was held there from 1851 to 1854, before being transferred to another prison, and then exiled to Siberia in 1857, from where he later escaped.[4] He had previously been held in Kőnigstein Fortress near Dresden and in Prague. Kropotkin was incarcerated in the Fortress in 1874, where he was initially denied pen, ink or paper, but, following external pressure, he was allowed writing materials and completed a scientific report he was doing on explorations in Finland. He was also able to read a large library of historical materials left at the fortress by earlier generations of political prisoners.

Kropotkin was held in isolation and the guards were prohibited from speaking to him, although prisoners communicated by tapping the walls. He was allowed to exercise outside for half an hour each day. His brother was also arrested, imprisoned and sent to Siberia for twelve years for writing a letter critical of the political repression in Russia. Kropotkin was moved to another prison in 1876 and then to a military hospital with a prison attached, as he had become so ill while incarcerated. There he managed to escape and fled to Europe, where he also sampled French prison life, when detained as a result of his continuing activism (Kropotkin 1899).

In 1882 Kropotkin was held for a few months in prison in Lyon and then was transferred to Clairvaux. He records in his autobiography that in France at that time it was thought that for political prisoners the loss of liberty was so hard that no additional punishments were needed (Kropotkin 1899). They were held in separate quarters from other prisoners, wore their own clothes, were not compelled to work and were able to smoke and to buy good quality food and wine. Kropotkin was able to write and recorded his experiences of imprisonment and a critique of prison conditions in his autobiography and in an essay on prisons. While serving his time there, he taught other political prisoners science and languages. Although the political prisoners did not have regular contact with ordinary prisoners, they did speak to those working in the pharmacy. Kropotkin argued that French prisons were more humane and enlightened in their treatment of ordinary prisoners than those in England. The physical conditions and work available were better and prisoners were not flogged for insubordination. Consequently French prisons were less degrading, but they still did not prevent recidivism. He also noted the plight of elderly prisoners, whose only contacts on release were their former friends so inevitably they moved back to a life of crime (Kropotkin 1899: 463).

On his release from Clairvaux in 1886, he published his book, *In Russian and French Prisons,* in English, where he describes the impact of imprisonment, inducing physical and mental depression through sensory deprivation, and isolation and meaningless work (Kropotkin 1887). He argues that the impact of prison discipline also undermines the will of prisoners, which makes it harder for them to resist the pressures of returning to a criminal life on release. He is critical of prisons as institutions for breeding anti-social attitudes and behaviour and says that even reformed prisons do not reform prisoners. Instead the thief learns more skills and becomes more embittered against society and this will happen as long as prison as an institution exists. He describes prisons as 'universities of crime, maintained by the state' (1899: 468). Society is wrong and unjust in its prevailing system of punishment, but also foolish, he claims, as 'it maintains at its own expense these universities of corruption, under the illusion that they are necessary as a bridle to the criminal instincts of man' (ibid: 70).

Notwithstanding the widespread use of imprisonment in the nineteenth century to neutralise critics of political regimes, the twentieth century is usually seen as the era of mass political imprisonment, as political imprisonment was widely used by states around the world including the US, China, Russia, Latin America, the Middle East, South Africa and in Europe, to deal with their critics. For example, in the

US, Eugene Debs, leader of the socialist party was sentenced to ten years for making an anti-war speech and this was upheld by the US Supreme Court.[5] In *Schenck v United States* 249 US 47 (1919), the validity of the criminal conviction of Schenck and Baer for distributing anti-war leaflets to potential conscripts was upheld. The case stressed the importance of the context, or circumstances, so the freedom of speech tolerated in time of peace may not be appropriate when the country is at war. The opinion of Justice Oliver Wendell Holmes in that case, and the formulation of the clear and present danger test to justify limits on free speech, has often subsequently been cited in support of political imprisonment. At the time, there had been a spate of letter bombs in the US, with radicals being arrested and in some cases deported, with the Bolsheviks, the Industrial Workers of the World (IWW) and other political groups being blamed for these acts. In the UK the philosopher Bertrand Russell was also imprisoned for his anti-war activities, but as Arthur Balfour had intervened, he received better treatment than many others.

In World War II, Japanese Americans were interned in the US. Later during the Vietnam war, anti-war protesters were also detained. The relationship between political protestors and conscientious objectors has frequently been reviewed in debates on civil disobedience and while the right to disobey has often been defended, whether they should be punished or exonerated is more problematic (see Dworkin 1977). The persecution of political opponents, of course, may be counter-productive in boosting support for the ideas of detainees. This happened in Northern Ireland where the internment policy consolidated support for Republican groups, and more recently in 2017 in Spain, with the imprisonment of members of the Catalan government by the Spanish government. In November 2017, around 750,000 protestors demonstrated in Barcelona against the imprisonment of the Catalan leaders for their role in the fight for Catalonia's independence from Spain. Some of the demonstrators bore placards saying the detainees were political prisoners. In South Africa, the incarceration of leading figures mobilised resistance outside the prison, while the political prisoners used the time spent in incarceration to develop their political ideas (Buntman and Huang 2000, Buntman 2003).

Political imprisonment reached its peak in Europe during the Nazi and Stalinist periods. When the Nazi Party was elected in Germany in 1933, it embarked on a programme of detention of a wide range of groups, including communists, social democrats, critics of the regime as well as 'asocials' or ordinary criminals, and Jews, which culminated in its mass extermination programmes. In Russia, Stalin initiated a decades-long programme of executing and imprisoning his political opponents and those accused of crimes against the state. Political imprisonment was also used in East Europe after the Hungarian uprising in 1956, the Prague spring in 1968 and in Poland, after the introduction of martial law to suppress Solidarity in 1981, where political prisoners remained active in prison and helped to bring down the regime.

However, the development of international human rights and international criminal law and the associated institutions set up to protect human rights since the late 1940s have made it harder for states to use political imprisonment as a strategy to deal with opponents, although there remain problems of enforcement. These institutions emerged in response to the revelation of the atrocities of the Nazi camps and the evidence given at the Nuremberg trials, where defendants were tried for war crimes and crimes against humanity. International human rights instruments, including the UN Universal Declaration of Human Rights, the European Convention of Human Rights and the later International Covenant on Civil and Political Rights, protect freedom of thought, conscience and religion, freedom of opinion and expression, as well as freedom of assembly and association.

It is also harder now than in the past for states to conceal this persecution from non-governmental organisations and from the world's media and social media. But there is still a problem of enforcement of human rights standards. The reports of the Committee on Human Rights and the Committee for the Prevention of Torture record the continuing persecution of individuals and groups critical of prevailing regimes in states who have ratified these Conventions and illustrate the limits of international human rights law in practice, in securing protection of political freedoms.

While the use of political imprisonment has declined, other even more violent methods, including killing by death squads have been used in Latin America along with the abduction and murder of political activists who were detained and never seen again, in, for example, Argentina, Guatemala and El Salvador. There have also been many examples of journalists critical of the regime in Russia who have met with a sudden death and been murdered by persons unknown. Less violent but effective means to ways to control dissent may include restricting access to work, education and travel. For example, a *Berufsverbot* was used in Nazi Germany from 1933 to bar political opponents from certain occupations, and again by West Germany in 1972, so people deemed to hold radical political views or members of radical groups were not allowed to work for the Civil Service. This was imposed in response to the activities of the Red Army Faction, formerly the Baader-Meinhof group, which had been active since the late 1960s and had been involved in bombings and kidnappings in Germany in the 1970s. The leaders of the group were imprisoned, as we saw in Chapter 5, and Baader, Meinhof, Raspe and Esslin were held in a separate wing apart from other prisoners and committed suicide, although their treatment was not seen by the European Commission of Human Rights as reaching the threshold for a violation of Article 3.[6] The dismissal of a civil servant because of her political beliefs was successfully challenged in Strasbourg in *Vogt v Germany* App No. 17851/91 (26 September 1995), where the Court found breaches of Article 10, the right to freedom of expression and Article 11, the right to freedom of association.

The modes of punishment and control used by states on political opponents and dissidents will be shaped by the political and economic context of those societies as well as their legal framework. While the imprisonment of political opponents has declined as a strategy and has been displaced by other measures, it can be resuscitated, of course, if required, as seen in Turkey recently where large numbers of the regime's critics and eighty-one journalists were imprisoned in 2016 after the failed coup. If the political opponents are foreign nationals, for example, states may seek to deport rather than incarcerate them.

Political imprisonment has resulted in a substantial body of literature which has enhanced our understanding of imprisonment. As well as factual records of imprisonment and life histories, we also have literary works, for example, Oscar Wilde's *Ballad of Reading Gaol* and *de Profundis*, the poetry of Verlaine and Jean Genet's play *Haute Surveillance*. Victor Serge's autobiographical novel, *Men in Prison*, was based on his experience in prison in Paris before World War I and later in Russia in the late twenties.

The literature of confinement is broader, covering asylums – a popular theme in Gothic fiction – as well as prisons. For example, Nerval wrote his novella, *Aurélia*, which describes his descent into insanity, while incarcerated in an asylum. In feminist literature, confinement has been used to describe the constraints of domesticity, for example, by the narrator in Charlotte Perkins Gilman's *The Yellow Wallpaper*, first published in 1892.[7]

However, with few exceptions, notably Angela Davis, the bulk of prison literature, as Dearey (2010) notes, is written by men. In addition to prisoners' own life histories, we have a corpus of novels on the experience of imprisonment, such as Dickens' *Little Dorrit,* which have added to our knowledge of prison life and of the relations between prisoners and between prisoners and the outside world. Others, such as Gramsci (1995), who was given a twenty-year sentence in 1928 following a show trial, have used their time inside prison to develop their political ideas. Lenin was also in prison for a year in St Petersburg, where he completed most of the work on his book, *The Development of Capitalism in Russia*. He was held in relatively good conditions and later in exile received an allowance from the state. Trotsky also worked on his political writings while detained in St Petersburg.

The relationship between political prisoners and ordinary prisoners

The relationship between political prisoners and ordinary criminals is highly complex. As we shall see, some political prisoners have sought to distance themselves from ordinary offenders, while others have found common ground. The attitude of political activists reflects their ideological frameworks, as well as their understanding of crime and perceptions of the class struggle. Attitudes towards ordinary prisoners from the Left have ranged from denunciation to romanticisation of the offender.

Within Marxism, hostility towards the lumpenproletariat is found in Marx's work in *The German Ideology* (1846), *The Eighteenth Brumaire of Louis Bonaparte* (1852) and *Capital* (1867). While Marx (1853) does recognise the impact of social and economic deprivation of individuals who commit crimes, he still sees crime as an expression of the immiseration and brutalisation of the working class, and a reflection of the excesses of individualism and perceives the lumpenproletariat as parasitic upon the proletariat, who suffer most from the impact of crime. The earlier Bolsheviks had thought that most ordinary criminals were proletarian rather than bourgeois, so once reformed they would be natural allies for the revolution. But political prisoners were deemed incapable of reform. For Lenin, crime was an expression of the problems of the transition to socialism, but needed to be confronted. Solzhenitsyn refers to Lenin's demand in 1918 that the number of prison places be expanded and sentences increased (2003: 179). For Stalin, deviant behaviour was in conflict with communism's goals and values. Initially Stalin thought crime did not exist in socialist society but later he saw all crime as anti-Soviet and sympathetic to capitalist ideology, with devastating consequences for those on the receiving end of his criminal justice policies, and of course, critics of Soviet society were also criminalised.

Within criminology, radical criminologists have focused on the problems of social inequality, poverty and deprivation which they see as criminogenic.[8] Hudson (1998), and others, have further argued that social deprivation should be taken account of in the sentencing process, with reduced penalties for the socially deprived.[9] Offering materialist analyses of crime and punishment, Marxist theorists have focused on the historical development of punishment to reflect the needs of the dominant class and to facilitate the accumulation of capital. Punishment is construed as a means of reasserting control over the working class, of inculcating work discipline through the experience of prison labour and providing a source of cheap labour for private companies. The prison has been seen as a means of absorbing surplus labour, where necessary, and in regulating and controlling the working class, especially as the provision and commitment to social welfare has declined (Rusche and Kirchheimer 1939, Wacquant 2009). Realist criminologists have highlighted the negative effect of crime on working-class life.[10]

The link between the labour movement and prisoners has also been problematic as trade unionists in the UK and US have often been hostile to prisoners as workers, despite the fact that the fight for trade union rights led to the sanctions of imprisonment and transportation of those involved. This hostility reflects concerns over the role of prison labour in undercutting workers' pay and access to jobs, as prison labour offers a cheap source of labour and also awareness of the impact of crime on working-class communities. The AFL/CIO[11] has opposed the use of prison labour in public and private sectors as unfair competition with free labour. It has also strongly opposed privatised prisons and using prisons for profit. It includes prison and police officers among its members, but it has also supported prison reform.[12]

Penal servitude has a long history in the US and when slavery was abolished, an exception was made for it in the Thirteenth Amendment to the Bill of Rights: 'Neither slavery nor involuntary servitude, except as a punishment for crime whereof the party shall have been duly convicted, shall exist within the United States, or any place subject to their jurisdiction.' McLennan (2008) charts the development of convict labour in the nineteenth century in which prisoners directly worked for private contractors or were leased to them, sometimes working in factories alongside free workers. The system was successfully challenged by 'free workers' and others, as the system was seen as degrading and the working conditions were brutal. In 1883 in New York the state took control of the operation of prison industries. In Europe the protection of prison labour is enshrined in the European Prison Rules, which prescribe that 'In all instances there shall be equitable remuneration of the work of prisoners' (EPR 26.10) and that the interests of prisoners shall not be subordinated to the pursuit of financial profits from industries involved in prison work (26.8).

Prisoners' groups in the US, such as the Missouri Prison Labor Union (MPLU), have continued to campaign for minimum wages, improving working conditions as well as the abolition of the death penalty. The IWW has also treated prisoners as incarcerated workers, with common interests with workers outside, and their members have in the past been imprisoned for their activities.

But Marx's negative view of the lumpenproletariat was rejected by many anarchist groups and theorists. For example, Bakunin (1872) saw the relationships among the poor and the dispossessed as an embryonic form of collective life and includes 'the riffraff and the rabble' within his hopes for the future. What Marx saw as the lumpenproletariat, as a dangerous class of potential strike breakers, Bakunin saw as the 'flower of the proletariat', reflecting his divergent views on law and the state. He explained what he meant by this term:

> By the *flower of the proletariat,* I mean above all that great mass, those millions of the uncultivated, the disinherited, the miserable, the illiterates, whom Messrs. Engels and Marx would subject to their paternal rule by a *strong* government – naturally for the people's own salvation! All governments are supposedly established only to look after the welfare of the masses! By flower of the proletariat, I mean precisely that eternal "meat" (on which governments thrive), that great *rabble of the people* (underdogs, "dregs of society") ordinarily designated by Marx and Engels in the picturesque and contemptuous phrase *Lumpenproletariat.* I have in mind the "riffraff," that "rabble" almost unpolluted by bourgeois civilization, which carries in its inner being and in its aspirations, in all the necessities and miseries of its collective life, all the seeds of the socialism of the future, and which alone is powerful enough today to inaugurate and bring to triumph the Social Revolution.
>
> (Bakunin 1872: 294)

Bakunin's interest in the criminal class was shared by many anarchists of the time and subsequently by modern anarchist groups. At a practical level, close contact between anarchist groups and professional criminals in the past was often necessary to execute criminal acts, including assassinations and robberies. But also from an anarchist perspective, the disregard of the law, epitomised by the criminal, may well be welcomed rather than scorned. As Horowitz notes: 'Criminality often pervaded the anarchist movement – not merely because the anarchist relied on theft, assassination, insurrection, but because of his exaltation of lawlessness' (Horowitz 1964: 601). In contrast to Marxism, anarchism has not perceived the criminal as the enemy of the proletariat. However, in engaging in insurrectionary acts, anarchists may not define themselves as criminals motivated by self-interest, but rather as motivated by altruistic reasons, the desire to change society and as Angela Davis (1971) has observed, this is the key difference between ordinary and political prisoners.

In the late nineteenth century, as noted earlier, many of the leading figures in anarchism, such as Kropotkin and Bakunin, had been imprisoned in France and Russia and during the 1890s, anarchism flourished in France. This period was marked by bombings and violence. The explosion at the Café Terminus near Gare St Lazare in 1894, injured twenty, one of whom later died. It was the work of Emile Henry and was intended to avenge the execution of Auguste Vaillant who, in 1893, had thrown a bomb into the *Chambre des députés*. Vaillant had committed that crime to avenge the execution of the anarchist Ravachol in 1892. Paris was paralysed by fear because of the violence, but each execution of the perpetrators also attracted more support for the movement. But over time the futility of violence was recognised by the majority of the anarchist movement. The *Confédération générale du travail* (CGT), the confederation of French trade unions, was founded in 1895, in the year following the last anarchist attacks and increasingly, many anarchists moved into the trade union movement and syndicalism, and sought to merge anarchist theory with non-violent practice.

While political prisoners have often distanced themselves from ordinary offenders, there have been occasions where they have found common ground and the experience of imprisonment has stimulated activists to consider the problems faced by ordinary prisoners negotiating the stresses of custody. In a study of women prisoners in Northern Ireland, Moore and Scraton (2014) found that Republican women acknowledged the vulnerability of ordinary women prisoners. They note that 'it is possible to recognize the particular context regarding the imprisonment of those with political motivation without stigmatizing or excluding those who have been imprisoned through different routes' (ibid: 95). They acknowledge the difference between political and ordinary prisoners, but the latter 'experience a criminal justice process which reflects and sustains institutionalized structural inequalities' (ibid: 96). So imprisonment can be construed as political, if there are disproportionate numbers of particular ethnic groups or poorer groups held in custody, and if imprisonment reflects social inequalities, which raises questions regarding the issues of class bias, racism or legacies of colonialism. It also means prison itself can become a site of political struggle.

The gulf between ordinary and political prisoners should be not be overstated as ordinary prisoners can still be seen as victims of an unequal society and ordinary prisoners may themselves be politicised in prison, as political prisoners may mobilise ordinary prisoners. This can be illustrated by the case of the civil rights movement which during the 1960s and 1970s, contributed to the development of the prisoners' rights movement in the US. Many members of the movement were themselves incarcerated and prison became a site for the struggle for civil rights (Davis 1971). While the movement is principally associated with rights for Black Americans, it also influenced the women's movement and gay rights movement. For civil rights activists, the experience of imprisonment deepened their own political commitment, but their presence in prison affected fellow prisoners, as, for example, in the Attica riot in 1971 considered earlier. Black civil rights activists, including George Jackson, Angela Davis and Malcolm X, also recorded their experiences contributing to the literature on imprisonment. Jackson's, *Soledad Brother*, was published in 1971 as was Angela Davis's critique of American prisons which she later developed into demands for the abolition of prison, co-founding an abolitionist group Critical Resistance, while Malcolm X published his record in 1987.[13] But while the writings of political prisoners have been critical of prison as an institution and of prison conditions, not all political prisoners are hostile to individual officers. As Crewe (2009) observes, while political prisoners may be opposed to state institutions and their representatives, they may recognise the humanity and decency of individual officers. He gives the example of Nelson Mandela's relationship with a particular officer on Robben Island.

The 1970s was a key era of litigation on prisoners' rights in the US, as prisoners challenged their conditions in court and used class actions to improve their conditions. For example, in *Holt v Sarver* (1970) 308 F. Supp. 3633 E.D. Ark, the court accepted that conditions in Arkansas prisons constituted cruel and unusual punishment and demanded that the prison authorities improve them. Ordinary prisoners may be politicised by their experience of prison life, especially if the regime is oppressive. The 1970s was a period when the courts were more willing to become involved in the supervision of prison conditions, and the Supreme Court was much more activist and intervened to protect and consolidate suspects' and prisoners' due process rights. At the end of the decade, a class action was also heard in *Ruiz v Estelle* (1980) 503 F. Supp 1295, challenging the conditions in Texan prisons.

The prisoners' rights movement was also supported by radical lawyers, originally from the civil rights movement, who saw the criminal justice system as oppressive towards black Americans and the prisons dominated by black and poor offenders. George Jackson was in prison for years for a minor theft. After his death in 1971, a terrorist group was formed, the George Jackson Brigade, who committed bombings and armed robberies, and sought political change, and whose members were also later imprisoned (Burton-Rose 2010).

The politicisation of ordinary prisoners in the late sixties and early seventies was exemplified by the Attica riot in 1971 and the other riots in that period and campaigns for prisoners' rights. In the early 1970s the Prisoners Union was established in San Francisco to protect prisoners' rights. It had 3,000 members by 1993 and published a magazine, *The Outlaw*. Some prisoners' unions in the US remain active today in challenging their conditions even if not formally recognised by the prison authorities. However, prisoners' unions, as we saw in Chapter 2, may be a stronger expression of political activity and resistance than Prisoner Councils which perform a much more limited role in challenging conditions.

Some former political prisoners have gone on to campaign for prisoners' rights on their release. Linda Sue Evans was a member of the Weathermen group, later called the Weather Underground Organisation. She was imprisoned in 1970 on conspiracy charges and then in 1987 given a forty-year sentence for charges of false identification in obtaining firearms and harbouring a fugitive. This concerned her involvement in an armed robbery, in which two police officers and a guard were killed. In 1990 she was sentenced for five years on conspiracy charges in relation to earlier bombings in Washington. Her sentence was commuted by Bill Clinton in 2001 and since her release she has become actively involved in fighting for prisoners' rights and voting rights. While incarcerated, she had campaigned for the rights of lesbian and women prisoners, demanding education for women prisoners and more support for prisoners living with HIV/AIDS. Nadya Tolokonnikova, a member of the group Pussy Riot, was imprisoned in Russia for 'hooliganism', following a performance at a Moscow cathedral which included criticism of Putin, and she has since founded a group, Zona Prava (Zone of Justice), fighting for prisoners' rights and better prison conditions. These campaigns to assist prisoners raise the broader and unresolved question of whether activists should be engaging in prison reform or focusing on alternatives to imprisonment.

As we saw in Chapter 2, some sections of the Left have been ambivalent or disinterested in ordinary prisoners. For example, in France during the May 1968 student uprising, there was little evidence of work with or campaigns for prisoners. The focus among student leaders was instead on finding common ground with workers and the workers' support for students culminated in a general strike, which resulted in the police repression of strikers, as well as of the student demonstrators. Some students were imprisoned, but were released quickly as part of the ongoing negotiations. When the Minister of the Interior, Christian Fouchet, demanded that *'Paris vomir la pègre qui la déshonore'* (Paris vomit out the criminal underworld which dishonours it), the students responded with *'Nous sommes la pègre'*[14] (We are the underworld), but they did not engage with prisoners. Later in the early 1970s, members of a Maoist group, la Gauche Prolétarienne, including Alain Geismar, were imprisoned for involvement in the group's magazine, *La Cause du Peuple*, and as a result became more interested in the plight of ordinary prisoners. An Information Group on Prisons (GIP), whose members included Foucault, was set up by la Gauche Prolétarienne to examine the nature of prisons. This group later dissolved itself to allow prisoners to speak for themselves and was replaced by a Comité d'Action des Prisonniers in 1972 (Christofferson 1999).

However, some anarchist groups have identified more closely with non-political prisoners, in part reflecting their own experience of imprisonment. Many anarchists were imprisoned in the UK in the 1890s and the early twentieth century, for example, the Walsall anarchists in 1892, whose trial began at the time of Ravachol's confession.[15] However, because the anarchists in that period focused primarily on pamphlets rather than books, their ideas have received less attention than the socialist movement, where there is a substantial literature. The Anarchist Black Cross group originated first in Tsarist Russia to support political prisoners and prisoners of war. There are arguments over the exact date the group started, but it seems to be in the period from 1905 to 1907. They later supported those imprisoned by the Bolsheviks. It was originally called the Anarchist Red Cross, but changed its name to avoid confusion with the International Red Cross. The group collapsed in the 1930s, but was revived in the UK in the 1960s.

Now there are ABC groups worldwide, including the US, Toronto, Berlin, Moscow and in Belarus, where the group assists prisoners detained for political activity. They are also active in the UK, with groups in Brighton, London, Bristol, Cardiff and Leeds. The London ABC aids prisoners whether or not they are anarchists. It says it aims to 'support prisoners, political prisoners, people in detention centres and just people fucked over by the capitalist system'.[16]

In the UK, the Bristol ABC group helps prisoners and publishes pamphlets on how their experience as prisoners affects them on release, for example, 'On the Out' written by an ex-prisoner. They have also published work on Close Supervision Centres and have supported a day of solidarity with transgender prisoners. The Bristol ABC group raises money, writes to prisoners, supports international political prisoners and sees prison as a weapon of the state. It focuses mostly on those wrongly convicted, or imprisoned for political activity, or in conflict with the prison system.

The Leeds ABC group offers assistance to those resisting the prison regime, who they see as part of the class struggle, as well as helping imprisoned anarchists and ordinary prisoners who become political activists while in prison, such as John Bowden.[17] Some prisoners may see themselves as political prisoners following their experience of incarceration for non-political crimes.

In the UK, there is a range of other groups working with prisoners as part of its political agenda, including the Campaign against Prison Slavery, which is abolitionist, and which has campaigned against forced labour in prison and the Incentives and Earned Privileges scheme. There is also an Animal Liberation Front support group to help imprisoned ALF members, the Empty Cages collective and the abolitionist group, Community Action on Prison Expansion. So we now can find a number of links between some political groups and prisoners in the UK, reflecting a range of issues.

In the US, many anarchist groups also write to prisoners, particularly to those imprisoned as a result of their political beliefs or actions. ABC groups expanded there in the 1980s and small groups merged to form the ABC Federation in 1995. Their perspective on political prisoners is clearly enunciated:

> Political prisoners and prisoners of war are not in prison for committing social crimes, nor are they criminals… All are in prison as a result of conscious political action. Building resistance, building and leading movements and revolution… for making change.[18]

The Federation says that prisoners who go to prison because of political action demand priority, over other prisoners, including those who become politicised in prison. But they acknowledge that all prisoners struggling against repressive prison systems should be supported. There is also a Black and Pink group in the US supporting LGBTQ prisoners and a Green and Black Cross group, who support defendants who are environmental activists and mostly give advice on how to deal with police encounters.

Although the plight of prisoners has attracted attention from these groups, the most extreme example of incarceration of large numbers of prisoners for 'political crimes' in Stalinist Russia, attracted relatively little attention from the rest of the world at the time.

The Gulag: *zeks, urkas* and 58ers

The contrast between political prisoners and 'ordinary criminals' is well illustrated by the experience of the Gulag in Stalinist Russia. Gulag is an acronym of *Glavno Upravlenie Lagerei* which means Main Administration of Corrective Labour Camps.[19] It was run by the NKVD, the People's Commissariat for Internal Affairs, who were the secret police. The Gulag Prison Agency was set up in 1934 to deal with the need for rapid industrialisation and to provide labour for the emerging industrial production process. New legislation had been passed to allow for the arrest and exile of the intelligentsia and party members. By 1940, the economy depended on prison work and the Gulag retained a crucial economic role throughout the Stalinist period.

The use of forced labour as a punishment, or penal servitude, has a long history in Europe and had been used already in Tsarist Russia. Although the Bolsheviks in the 1920s did experiment with penal reforms, focusing on education for young offenders, Stalin favoured deportation with hard labour. In 1918 Lenin had also advocated forced labour for all aged from sixteen to fifty to meet the needs of the new state and 1918 is usually taken as the starting point of the Gulag.

Marx had envisaged that prisons and the police would be superfluous after the Revolution, with the withering away of the state and in the context of a society in which needs are met. At worst, crime and policing matters would be dealt with by other means, if they could not be discounted. But despite discussions about the withering away of the prison as a state institution during the revolutionary period in Russia, it survived the revolution and flourished after 1917, with the construction of new prisons as well as the retention of the old prisons and conditions deteriorated with many dying in the poor conditions. Stalin was in power for nearly thirty years and prison numbers were high throughout his regime. By the 1940s there were 478 camps of varying sizes. While the official aim of the Gulag was for the prisoner to work for the common good, to redeem oneself through hard labour, in practice conditions were so harsh prisoners often died.

It is not clear how many prisoners were held in the camps or how many died there, because of the secrecy of the regime and the lack of official records and archives, even though the inmates were given numbers. Official records, where they do exist, are likely to be underestimates, as camp officials may not have wished to record the many deaths resulting from the extremely harsh conditions. Furthermore, many perished in transit. Conditions also worsened during the war with the increasing food shortages.

Some have suggested 7 to 8 million were incarcerated there, others say the figure is much higher and there were also special colonies for prisoners of war, kulaks and other groups.[20] Bacon (1996) says 12 million were incarcerated between 1934 and 1947. Conquest (1990) estimates that by the end of 1938, there were nearly 7 million political prisoners in the Soviet Union, one in every 15 or 16 adults. Many of those in prison were executed, many died from the harsh conditions, the cold, hunger and disease and 3 million are thought to have died in Kolyma alone. There were amnesties in 1941, but this was to release prisoners for the war effort, and again in 1953, after Stalin's death.

As Applebaum (2003), says the division between political and ordinary criminals then and later was arbitrary. Ordinary theft could be redefined as a political act and what many would see as an ordinary crime, such as theft, could be treated as political if deemed to be theft of state property. Non-political offenders could also be reclassified by the police as political prisoners, in the late 1930s, if the demand for quotas of labour had not been met.[21] The treatment of political prisoners, who were seen as counter-revolutionaries, was often harsher than for ordinary criminals and clouded in greater secrecy.

Political prisoners in the Stalinist period sentenced under Article 58 of the RSFSR Criminal Code (1934) were referred to as '58ers'. Article 58 covered subversive activities and 'counter-revolutionary crime' and included anti-Soviet attitudes and activities, promulgating anti-Soviet propaganda, destruction of socialist property and sabotage. It was also used to incarcerate farmers denigrated as kulaks who were sent to the camps as part of the process of dekulakisation, the abolition of the peasantry as a class.

Article 58-1 stated that:

> "Counterrevolutionary" describes any action directed towards the overthrow, subversion, or weakening of the power of worker-peasant councils or of their chosen (according to the Constitution of the USSR and constitutions of union republics) worker-peasant government of the USSR, union and autonomous republics, or toward the subversion or weakening of the external security of the USSR and the fundamental economic, political and national gains of the proletarian revolution. In consideration of the international solidarity of interests of all workers, acts are likewise considered "counterrevolutionary" when they are directed at any other workers' government, even if not part of the USSR.
>
> If the perpetrator escapes across the border then adult members of the family may be punished by deprivation of liberty for 5 to 10 years and confiscation of property.

Article 58 also covered offences of espionage, undermining of state production, transport, trade or monetary relations, the perpetration of terrorist acts against representatives of Soviet authority, or workers' and peasants' organisations, as well as counter-revolutionary sabotage. If a person was sought, but not found, their relatives could be arrested instead. Second terms were also given out in 1938, without a further trial. Prison terms were extended for the 58ers when the need for more labour for particular projects arose and again after the War to meet the camps' own requirements for labour.

These prisoners had often received severe sentences for often trivial reasons, and what constituted anti-Soviet behaviour was construed broadly. Examples given by Solzhenitsyn of prosecutions and convictions under Article 58 included a lecturer who did not mention Stalin in his lectures and was denounced by a student, a sixteen-year-old who made a mistake in Russian in a wall newspaper, for which he received a five-year sentence, children who knocked a poster off a wall while fighting, and a man who hung his jacket on a bust of Lenin, who was given ten years (2003: 240). The minimum age of criminal responsibility under Article 12 of the Criminal Code in 1926 was twelve, and sentences for very young offenders were also very harsh. Solzhenitsyn gives the example of a child who was given five years for stealing twelve cucumbers. But for Article 58, there was no minimum age and he cites the case of a boy aged six years given a custodial sentence under it (ibid at 275). Religious education was also deemed a crime under Article 58-10, which covered counter-revolutionary propaganda. Earlier in the 1920s and 1930s women who were bringing their children up in their religious faith were arrested and convicted. As Solzhenitsyn says, Article 58-10 was interpreted broadly and had no maximum limit on the associated penalty. But non-political offenders and habitual criminals were also arrested for trivial offences and given harsh sentences. He includes the example of farmers who had mowed a field for the state and went back a second time to get clippings for their own cows, but were caught and executed (ibid: 133).

Political prisoners included many cultured and highly educated prisoners, professionals and intellectuals as well as peasants, or kulaks, and workers sentenced for failing to meet their work targets, or because of goods missing from the workplace, and members of political groups such as the Basmachi, a central Asian resistance movement against the Soviets, which had been active in the 1920s.

The Gulag held a wide range of prisoners but the ordinary prisoners were referred to as '*zeks*', which is an abbreviation of the Russian word for prisoner, *zakyluchennyy* (*заключенный*). Among the *zeks* the toughest prisoners were referred to as *urkas*. There was a strict division between the *zeks* and 58ers, both formally and in the perceptions of both officials and the prisoners themselves. Different penological theories were applied to the two groups. Gulag commentators, including Fyodor Mochulsky, the director of Pechorlag forced labour camp from 1940 to 1946, refer to the strict division between political prisoners and ordinary criminals (Mochulsky 2011). The non-political prisoners were held in different barracks and the two classes of prisoners experienced different conditions.

The labour camps also included women, who often formed surrogate families to make life more bearable while in exile. Hutton (2001) refers to the case of Natalia Sats, imprisoned in Siberia in 1937, after her husband denounced her as a traitor. During her incarceration Sats formed close relationships with non-political prisoners and said that unlike the other political prisoners, she was not repulsed by the women convicts. She attributed her psychological survival to her surrogate family and artistic work as she authored plays and organised concerts and other activities.

Because the prevailing view was that *zeks*, or non-political prisoners, could be reformed through re-education and were more trustworthy, they were often used to control other prisoners and assist the officers, while political prisoners were deemed more dangerous to society and untrustworthy, even though many were incarcerated for very minor crimes and were usually physically weaker than the *zeks* who, as Mochulsky (2011) notes, were encouraged to bully the 58ers. The majority of the *zeks*, he says, were hardened criminals and more dangerous and violent than the 58ers and often unwilling to work and exploited other prisoners, forcing them to work for them (Mochulsky 2011: 52). Unsurprisingly the atmosphere within the camps was volatile with frequent revolts over food which was always in short supply. Some *zeks* deemed reliable were allowed to move freely around the camp. Those who worked for the camp administration received reduced sentences and privileges and some stayed on as prison employees at the end of their sentences.

Gulag prisoners, including ordinary prisoners and some political prisoners, were also drafted into penal battalions during the war. These *shtrafniki* were seen as expendable and assigned to the most hazardous engagements such as clearing minefields and very few survived. Soviet soldiers who had been captured by the Germans and liberated by the Allies were returned by the Allies to Russia in 1946 and 1947 and were shot or incarcerated in the Gulag. Alexander Perchersky, who led the escape from Sobibor in 1943, was convicted of treason after the war for allowing himself to be captured by the Nazis and sent to the Gulag until 1953.

Despite the severe punishments for challenges to conditions in the camp, there were many examples of resistance as cited by Solzenitsyn, including mutinies, hunger strikes and escapes, even though the prospects of survival outside in Siberia were slim and if recaptured, escapees were beaten and given another ten years. In most cases, though, prisoners submitted to their punishment. He sees the fact that there was no overt public opposition outside as significant in reducing the prospect of resistance (2003: 352). The fear that anyone could be arrested regardless of guilt or innocence, was widespread, as the scientist Vladimir Tchernavin (1935) records in his account of his imprisonment. However, he did manage to escape with his wife and son and the details are recounted in Tatiana Tchernavin's memoir (1934). The repression effectively silenced internal criticism in Soviet society, while outside the country, there was a reluctance to challenge the excesses of the Soviet Union, the reasons for which have been much debated.[22] This reluctance of other states to condemn the regime reflects, to some extent, as Neier (1995) notes, the prevailing view at that time, that the internal affairs of states were not a matter of international concern.

Prison work was seen as reformative, but in practice, conditions were so harsh that offenders would die prematurely. Even for those who did survive, it was difficult for political prisoners to re-integrate on their release, because 58-ers were seen as politically suspect and there was a fear of being tainted by association. Many stayed in the area where they had been incarcerated, lacking the resources to return home, while others were sent into internal exile on release.

When Stalin died in 1953, the number of forced labour camps was reduced and conditions in the remaining camps were relaxed. One and a half million prisoners – both *zeks* and 58-ears were released in the 1953 Amnesty. This marked the beginning of the end of the Gulag, which was consolidated in 1956, as part of Kruschev's de-Stalinisation of Russian society. The camps had also become an economic drain on society by this time, because of the high numbers incarcerated and the problems of finding profitable work for prisoners made it harder to care for them. The high recidivism rate of ordinary offenders and the highly developed gang subculture of the *vorý v zakone* (thieves in law) at the top of the inmate hierarchy, with its own rituals, and frequent use of violence, suggested that the camps were failing to meet any rehabilitative goals.

Some of the camps survived and in the 1960s and 1970s, dissidents were held at Perm-36. Most of the remaining political prisoners in the Soviet Union were finally released in 1987 and 1988, by Gorbachev who freed them as part of his efforts to show the world he was taking a radical new approach, with economic and social reforms, as well as greater openness. It also meant that for the first time prisons were more open to researchers and King (1994) was allowed access to fourteen institutions, including remand prisons and corrective labour colonies. But he found levels of overcrowding and prison industries becoming less profitable, with the collapse of the command economy and prisons struggling to cover the costs of feeding their prisoners.

While the Gulag might seem a unique Soviet phenomenon, with its close alignment between the state and prison life, the similarities between the Gulag and modern Western prisons have been observed by Christie (2000), Pratt (2002) and others. For example, in the US, the incarcerated population and the numbers on probation and parole have reached unprecedented levels, and this rise has paralleled the increasing involvement of private companies in prison industries and in the construction and running of prisons for profit. The work of Mauer (2001) and Wacquant (2009) has highlighted the use of mass imprisonment in the US to absorb surplus labour. But the involvement of private companies in punishment has also expanded in the UK.[23]

Since the dismantling of the Gulag, the prison population in the Russian Federation has been reduced and more alternatives to custody developed. Within Russia, a range of penal measures are now used, but the Russian incarceration rate remains one of the highest in the world, at 428 prisoners per 100,000 of population,[24] peaking in 2000, and the penal system is still used to silence and exile those seen as a threat to the regime.

Relatively little research has been undertaken on contemporary Russian and East European prisons by Western scholars, because of the problems of accessibility, with most contemporary penal research focusing on Western Europe and the US. However, the work of Piacentini (2004) and others has increased our understanding of the contemporary Russian penal system. The 1990s was a period of penal reform, but also unrest with riots at Krasynoyarsk in 1991. A new Soviet Penal Code was introduced in 1992, which led to improved visits, better food and the right to make phone calls. When Russia joined the Council of Europe in 1996, new laws safeguarding prisoners' rights and prison reforms were a requirement of membership and were introduced. Further penal reforms were initiated in 2010. However, as in the West, formal rights do not necessarily entail substantive rights. Reforms were needed for Russia to join the Council of Europe. A Department for Human Rights and a new office of a Prison Ombudsman were established. There has also been a moratorium on the death penalty since 1997 and improvements in due process rights with legal representation for defendants. This modern framework is oriented much more towards justice and European penal standards, but incarceration rates have remained very high and conditions are still inadequate in many prisons.

The history of the Gulag has cast a long shadow over the post-Soviet prison system. As Slade (2016) says, 'The legacies of the Gulag can still be found in low trust in the institutions of criminal justice, in the guiding philosophies of punishment, the architecture of prisons and in the framing of interpersonal relations between prisoners' (Slade 2016: 941). There are also concerns over the continuing use of imprisonment to silence diverse critics of the regime, such as the former oligarch Mikhail Khodorkovsky, eventually released in 2013 and now in exile, as well as the Pussy Riot protestors and several journalists.

Since the economic restructuring and reforms of the 1990s, prisons have been under-funded and rely on the barter of goods, services and knowledge to survive. Because of the problems of underfunding, following the collapse of the centralised economy, prisons find it difficult to cover the living costs of prisoners, which means prisoners have to work in order to live, just as they did in the past in the Gulag. Although Piacentini argues that there are insufficient international human rights provisions to protect against forced labour in the context of imprisonment, some of the prisoners she interviewed valued working for the local community and thought it assisted their rehabilitation. Prisoners work in local farms and industry on a day-release basis and also rely on support from their families. Some prison industries are contracted out to the private sector in Russia and, as in the West, it is difficult to find enough good quality work for prisoners. Prisoners are still physically excluded, with penal colonies in the north and east, while most of the population is concentrated in western areas. Those prisons geographically furthest from Moscow are less well-funded and under less surveillance. Piacentini visited prisons in Omsk and Smolensk and found that Western penological knowledge was more prevalent in Smolensk than in Omsk, where older Soviet penal attitudes prevailed amongst the staff.

While human rights discourse and the pressure to meet rights standards to comply with the Convention and the European Prison Rules has had some impact on prison reform, conditions in many prisons remain very unsatisfactory, with poor medical care and overcrowding, and rights violations still persist. Many cases have been brought against Russia in the European Court of Human Rights which has found breaches of Article 3 in numerous cases.[25] There is also increasing reluctance on the part of the Russian government to implement the prescriptions of the Strasbourg Court and new constitutional reforms have been introduced to assert the primacy of Russian law. The failure to provide adequate health care and the high risk of TB, HIV and hepatitis in Russian prisons have been highlighted. Amnesty (2017), in a recent report, has also drawn attention to the poor conditions in which prisoners are transported in 'Stolypin' coaches, to distant penal colonies, which amount to cruel, inhuman and degrading treatment as they are housed in overcrowded carriages with limited access to toilets. The journeys can take as long as one month in some cases. Prisoners may be held far from home, especially female prisoners, as there are fewer women's prisons. Piacentini and Pallot (2014) in their discussion of the use of 'in exile' imprisonment in Russia found that 33.4 per cent of women prisoners were sent out of their region while the figure for men was much lower (2014: 27). In their survey they found that the average distance for a woman prisoner from her home was 486 kilometres. In exile imprisonment is still being used to crush political dissent.

Amnesty International is very critical of the Russian Federal Penitentiary Service and notes that conditions in Russian prisons are among the worst in Europe: 'It is time for the Russian authorities to remove the last vestiges of the GULAG and bring their prison system in line with international human rights standards' (2017: 6) In 2016 alone, as it observes, there were sixty-four judgments against Russia relating to places of detention. In *Polyakova and others v Russia* App Nos. 3509009, 35845/11, 45694/13 and 59747/14 (7 March 2017) the Strasbourg Court found breaches of Article 8 in the allocation of these (male and female) prisoners far from home making it difficult for them to maintain family contact. The same conclusion was reached in the earlier case of *Khodorkovsky v Russia and Lebedev v Russia* App Nos. 11082/06 and 3772/05 (25 July 2013). It points out that there have also been several cases on failures to provide adequate medical care in detention.[26]

The Gulag and subsequent developments have been discussed to consider the relationship between political and non-political prisoners and to highlight the state's treatment of opponents. The scale and brutality of the camps are striking and extreme, but the issue of the appropriate treatment of political prisoners has also arisen in the UK.

The struggle for recognition as political prisoners in Northern Ireland

Although here the focus on political prisoners has been principally on Republican and loyalist prisoners held during the Northern Ireland conflict, UK prisons have also held miners during the miners' strike and activists involved in protests on a range of issues, including animal rights, as well as in the past, those imprisoned because of the politics of sexuality.

The situation in Northern Ireland at first sight might appear quite different to that of the Gulag, insofar as many of those incarcerated in Russia were innocent, and some did not know with what offences they had been charged and others had been subjected to show trials, if tried at all. While the criminal justice process in Northern Ireland has been criticised for its failings, clearly those detained did have more due process rights, although there was a period of internment without trial and there were miscarriages of justice. In Northern Ireland political prisoner status – a key demand in the conflict – also meant improved treatment in contrast to the Gulag. But the treatment of prisoners in Northern Ireland during the conflict is of interest in highlighting the differences between political prisoners and ordinary prisoners. The conflict also highlighted the issue of whether the activities of paramilitary groups, whose actions are motivated by political objectives, should be dealt with by ordinary criminal law, rather than emergency measures or counter-terrorism law. Both these issues will now be considered in more detail.

The demand to be treated as political prisoners was a key aim for those members of the provisional IRA imprisoned for sectarian political activities, and pursuit of this goal led to further conflict, and to hunger strikes. It is estimated that 20,000 to 30,000 people were incarcerated for politically motivated offences during the Troubles, from 1968 to 1998 (McEvoy 2001). In the post-1968 conflict, over 3,700 men women and children were killed, mostly by paramilitary organisations – both Republican and loyalist, and 10 per cent of killings were by state forces.

During the conflict over 50 per cent of convicted prisoners were imprisoned for politically motivated offences (McEvoy 1998). The refusal to accept paramilitary prisoners as political prisoners led to problems within the prison system and extended the struggle outside and attracted worldwide attention. Communities in the north mobilised to support political prisoners and to protect their rights.

Most of the debate on the politics of imprisonment in Northern Ireland has been on politically motivated prisoners and this has meant that the treatment of ordinary prisoners has been given less attention. However, some of the paramilitary prisoners were at the forefront of challenges to the prison system so they did have an impact on prison conditions, which assisted all prisoners, and as a part of the peace process, these prisoners shaped the political landscape outside the prison. The case, for example, of *Campbell and Fell v UK* (1984) 7 EHRR 165, affected the conditions of the wider (non-political) prison population. Even when applicants did not succeed, the issues were at least aired in the courts and, in some cases, demands were later met, so they paved the way for subsequent litigation. For example, in *McFeeley*[27] most of the issues raised then were deemed inadmissible by the Commission, but interference with correspondence was later found to breach Article 8 in *Silver and others v UK* App No. 5947/7 (25 March 1983). Although the modes of resistance used by the political prisoners in Northern Ireland, as we shall see, were dramatic and effective, ordinary prisoners in the period were also resisting imprisonment through direct action – as we saw in Chapter 2, as well as through legal challenges, consolidating procedural due process rights and gaining improvements in prison conditions.

McEvoy (2001) refers to three stages in the use of imprisonment in Northern Ireland during the conflict: reactive containment from 1969 to 1975, marked by mass arrest and detention under special powers and the use of interrogation techniques such as hooding. The conditions in Castlereagh holding centre in East Belfast were challenged in *Ireland v UK* (1978) 2 EHRR 25, where the Commission and Court disagreed over whether these techniques constituted torture or inhuman and degrading treatment. Conditions at Castlereagh were also criticised by Amnesty and the UN Human Rights Committee and continued to attract concern until the Centre closed in 1999. The second stage, from 1976 to 1981, was criminalisation, in response to the Gardiner Report (1975), when the loss of political status led to blanket and no-wash protests and hunger strikes. The Diplock Report had also recommended using the criminal justice system to deal with political violence, instead of internment, which had been subject to widespread international criticism (1972: 13). The third stage, from the 1980s, was managerialism, where the focus was on efficiency and value for money.

The Maze prison, formerly known as Long Kesh, was opened in 1971 to house those interned without trial in the early 1970s, in Nissan huts, described by inmates as 'the cages'. It was located at the site previously used for the Long Kesh Detention Centre and for an RAF airfield. During the period of internment from 1971 to 1975, internees wore their own clothes, associated freely with each other and with sentenced paramilitary prisoners who were also held there, and were accommodated in huts according to their political groupings. An attempt to prevent a visit to one of the huts resulted in inmates setting fire to the prison. Internment was one of a raft of measures to deal with terrorism in Northern Ireland and it finally ended in December 1975. By the mid-1970s, there were 1,500 prisoners in the Maze, housed in the new H-blocks. Internees and prisoners had organised themselves in compounds with officers in command. The Maze closed in 2000, and was demolished in 2006, although one of the H-blocks was kept as a memorial.

In 1972, the Conservative Government gave paramilitary prisoners convicted of offences related to the conflict, 'Special Category Status', which was intended to prevent a threatened hunger strike by prisoners and as part of the negotiations. SCS prisoners were in effect treated as political prisoners, although not formally recognised as such, and held in the Maze alongside internees. These prisoners did not have to do prison work or to wear prison uniforms, and were kept in compounds away from other prisoners and given extra privileges, including food parcels and extra visits.

Although this policy did not go as far as formally recognising paramilitary prisoners as political prisoners, it did clearly demarcate them from other prisoners. However, the policy was criticised by the Gardiner Committee and others, who described the policy as a serious mistake and who thought it unfair that prisoners who are politically motivated should be given privileges not available to other prisoners. It was also wrong to suggest that a political motivation means an offence is less serious or more justifiable than one committed by a non-political prisoner. Obviously, from the victim's standpoint, the harm of offences of violence, or other offences, is not diminished by the political motivations of the perpetrator. The Gardiner Report (1975) recommended the removal of Special Category Status. This was implemented in 1976. It was also thought that holding SCS prisoners together encouraged radicalisation. When the policy changed in 1976, these prisoners were treated as 'common criminals' and their claim to be treated as political prisoners was denied. The view of the government was clearly expressed by Margaret Thatcher in her response to the subsequent hunger strikes: 'Crime is crime is crime, it is not political'. But the focus had already shifted towards the criminalisation of these prisoners by the mid-1970s.

The removal of special category status led to resistance and conflict including hunger strikes, which resulted in the death of ten prisoners, as well as the deaths of some off-duty prison officers in reprisal. McEvoy et al.'s (2007) study of the Maze described a range of modes of resistance, including escape attempts, lengthy legal challenges, hunger strikes, self-harm, violence, riots and the creation of alternative communities. Most prisoners were Catholic and the majority were members of the IRA. Prisoners saw themselves as prisoners of war and the prison became a place to continue the struggle.

The protests included a 'blanket' protest, where prisoners wore only blankets. This was followed by a protest in which they smeared their cells with their excrement. The protestors used the term no-wash protests to describe this resistance, but they were frequently described by observers as 'dirty' protests. So their bodies, as McEvoy says, can be seen 'as practical and symbolic subjects of their resistance' (McEvoy 2001: 83). Today, of course, prisoners' bodies are used to smuggle mobile phones and drugs into prison and are seen as suspect and subjected to searches. About 300 prisoners were taking part in the protest by 1978, demanding the right not to wear prison uniforms and freedom of association with other Republican paramilitary prisoners, the right not to work and to organise their own educational and recreational facilities, and to weekly visits, letters and parcels and the restoration of lost remission. Prison uniform embodied the criminalisation of the political prisoner. Although the protest was undertaken mostly by male prisoners, thirty women in Armagh prison also joined the protest. So the protests expressed the refusal to be criminalised. Prisoners also organised Gaelic classes to mark their differences from other prisoners and as an expression of cultural resistance. The history of the use of Gaelic as part of the struggle both inside and outside prison is charted by Mac Ionnrachtaigh (2013). In the Maze, attempts to conduct visits in Gaelic were thwarted by prison service instructions that demanded English be used for security reasons.[28] Loyalist prisoners, who also wanted to be treated as political prisoners, did refuse to wear uniforms and mounted a clean protest, keeping their cells pristine. However, this was called off after five months as it was thought these strikes looked too similar to the Republicans' position, and the loyalists also had a more ambivalent attitude towards the state.

The applicants in the *McFeeley v UK* case, discussed earlier in Chapter 2, were also involved in the no-wash protest. While the European Commission on Human Rights said in *McFeeley*, that the applicants were not entitled to achieve the status of political prisoner under national law or the Convention, it criticised the UK government's inflexibility, pointing out that they could have provided some other form of clothing, so prisoners could at least go outside. Following the case, the government did do this, as well as making other changes. After the *McFeeley* decision, some prisoners stopped their protest, others continued and paramilitary commanders in prison decided to embark on a hunger strike and to call off the no-wash protest. Seven prisoners, including McFeeley, had begun the strike in October 1980 and it was called off in December when a settlement was proposed, and it seemed the government had conceded to their demands. But the strike was later resumed in March 1981, when prisoners thought they had been duped and the government had reneged on their offer. The hunger strikers included Bobby Sands who died after sixty-six days on the strike.[29] Ten men died of starvation before the strike ended in October 1981, and three days after the strike was called off, the government announced changes to policy, including paramilitaries being allowed to have their own clothes, free association with other wings in each H-block and increased visits. But while the prisoners never achieved their goal of official recognition as political prisoners, most of their demands were met following the end of second hunger strike, so they effectively achieved political status even if this was not acknowledged as such by the government. The death of Sands had resulted in more support for the Republican movement and encouraged more prisoners to engage in hunger strikes. These hunger strikes engendered worldwide criticism of the British government and mobilised support outside in the community. Obtaining the support of groups and public outside was essential to demonstrate the legitimacy of their claims, and to resist the state's depiction of these prisoners as criminals. Resistance inside the prison clearly affected politics outside, as well as public opinion in the UK and internationally, which the state could not ignore.

The strikes also propelled Sinn Féin into electoral politics, as Bobby Sands was elected as an MP for Fermanagh-South Tyrone during the strike. He received 30,000 votes as the Anti H–Block candidate in April 1981, although he died shortly afterwards. Following Sands' election, new legislation was introduced, enacted in section 1 of the Representation of the People Act 1981, to stop prisoners standing for election:

> A person found guilty of one or more offences (whether before or after the passing of this Act and whether in the United Kingdom or elsewhere), and sentenced or ordered to be imprisoned or detained indefinitely or for more than one year, shall be disqualified for membership of the House of Commons while detained anywhere in the British Islands or the Republic of Ireland in pursuance of the sentence or order or while unlawfully at large at a time when he would otherwise be so detained.

In the by-election held after Sands' death, his election agent Owen Carron was elected in Sands' constituency and Gerry Adams was later elected as MP for West Belfast. However, Sinn Féin policy has consistently supported abstention, so elected members have refrained from taking up seats in Westminster.

The support in the community engendered by the hunger strike strengthened the political base for Sinn Féin and helped them to become a political force.

However, the immediate impact was an increase in violence and the bombing of the Grand Hotel in Brighton, during the 1984 Conservative Party conference, was seen as retribution for the death of Bobby Sands and the other hunger strikers. But the strikes also increased pressures on the UK government to negotiate to end the conflict, resulting in the Anglo-Irish Agreement in 1985 and later the Good Friday Agreement in 1998.

In the past prisoners on hunger strike had been force fed in English prisons, for example, the suffragettes from 1909 to 1914. The Price sisters were force fed in 1973–1974, which led to demonstrations and protests, but the policy was then abandoned following their case. The World Medical Association had prohibited force feeding in 1975 and its Malta Declaration adopted in 1991 and revised in 2006 affirms that force feeding of hunger strikers is ethically unacceptable.[30] The Strasbourg Court has not ruled out force feeding if intended to save lives, but the manner in which it is administrated may violate Article 3. The issue was addressed by the Strasbourg Court which held in *Nevmerzhitsky v Ukraine* App No. 54825/00 (5 April 2005), where it ruled that in this case, the way a prisoner was force fed in the Ukraine, including the use of restraints, did amount to torture and violated Article 3. The prisoners in Ugelvik's (2014) Oslo study saw hunger striking as pointless because they would be force-fed.

It is clear that the Maze prisoners achieved concessions through their struggles. Separation from other prisoners was one of their demands and this separation made it easier for them to organise and even to conduct a successful escape of thirty-eight prisoners from H-Block 7 in September 1983, with soil from the tunnelling hidden in the cells. An officer was stabbed and later died from his injuries and others were injured in the course of the break-out. This was the largest escape from a British prison and it showed the challenges facing staff in maintaining control of the prison.

McEvoy (2003) sees the strike and the consequent changes as a turning point in relations between prisoners and prison officers. It meant prisoners controlled the compounds for most of the working day, and were able to create sites of resistance. The morale of staff was low and further undermined by threats from the IRA to kill off-duty prison officers and their families, as prison officers were seen as a legitimate political target. Twenty-one prison officers had been killed from 1976 to 1981.

However, paramilitary prisoners were also crucial to the peace process in Northern Ireland in the late 1990s. There had been secret negotiations between the British and Irish governments and the IRA, in the early 1990s, to start the peace process and there had been both IRA and loyalist ceasefires in 1994, although the IRA ceasefire was broken by the bombing of Canary Wharf in 1996 and the loyalists also found it difficult to control the actions of some of their groups. Nonetheless, leaders were also going into prison every week to discuss future ceasefires and the peace process and to prepare prisoners for change. The Republicans had been moving towards political engagement, and some ex-Maze prisoners were now at the heart of the Sinn Féin leadership. Mo Mowlam, the then Northern Ireland Secretary, also visited prisoners in the Maze to discuss the Belfast agreement in early 1998 and prisoners were involved in the negotiations. But despite the ongoing peace process in the 1990s, there were still attacks on loyalist prisoners in prison.

The role of 'political' prisoners in the peace process in Northern Ireland has been well documented. Morrison (2014) argues that prisoners played a key role 'in the gradual acceptance of peaceful politics by the majority of those within the Irish Republican Movement' (2014: 75). But the key role for prisoners had begun earlier, when the movement became politicised as it shifted towards engagement in democratic political participation, alongside armed struggle, combining 'armalite and the ballot box'. Prison, Morrison argues, was a key element in the politicisation of this movement. In the 1970s many Provisional Republicans from the both the leadership as well as the rank and file members, including Gerry Adams, were in prison or interned and were very well organised inside prison, conducting debates on how the movement was faring and discussing different strategies. This enabled the leadership to encourage other prisoners to consider alternative political routes, and to reflect on the experience of other revolutionary movements. He refers to Adams stressing the need to develop political consciousness in prison and to see armed struggle as a means to an end rather than an end it itself. A contributor to *Republican News* in the period 1975–1977, who called himself Brownie, but is widely believed to be Gerry Adams, developed this notion of a political struggle and was critical of the leadership. In the Maze, the prisoners *de facto* political status meant they controlled their own blocks and education and that they had the space to discuss and develop their political ideas. Morrison (2014) argues that these discussions led to the acceptance of political rather than armed struggle within the Republican prison population. Also in the 1970s and 1980s, he stresses, the prison population was highly regarded by the Republican community outside: 'From the origins of Irish Republicanism right up to today the role and authority of the Republican prisoners has been both influential and respected by the membership' (Morrison 2014: 84). Moreover, once released, prisoners spread the notion of a political rather than armed response across the wider community. There was already a dissatisfaction with the leadership who failed to achieve their demands in the ceasefires in 1974 and 1975, and a feeling that new strategies were needed. The emerging new leadership gradually took over, with those from the North ousting those from the South. Ferguson (2014), who interviewed former prisoners from both sides, argues that many prisoners were more active in peace-building than the politicians and played a crucial role in shifting the direction of the struggle and influencing attitudes towards it. It had previously been Republican policy to abstain from taking part in elections to Westminster, Stormont, or Dáil Éireann in the Republic, and the new approach rejected this. Ferguson also argues that having this time and to think about the future of the movement while in prison, its political ideology and strategy, encouraged 'a reformulation of the conflict inside the prison walls', to consider ways of achieving their political goals without violence (Ferguson 2014: 281).

The Good Friday Agreement, or Belfast Agreement, in 1998 was accepted by the majority in an all-Ireland referendum, which led to constitutional changes and the creation of the Northern Ireland Assembly. Paramilitary prisoners were given a privileged status as the Agreement included a commitment to release prisoners who were members of paramilitary groups within two years, on licence, as well as requiring the decommissioning of weapons:

1. Both Governments will put in place mechanisms to provide for an accelerated programme for the release of prisoners, including transferred prisoners, convicted of scheduled offences in Northern Ireland or, in the case of those sentenced outside Northern Ireland, similar offences (referred to hereafter as qualifying prisoners). Any such arrangements will protect the rights of individual prisoners under national and international law.
2. Prisoners affiliated to organisations which have not established or are not maintaining a complete and unequivocal ceasefire will not benefit from the arrangements. The situation in this regard will be kept under review.
3. Both Governments will complete a review process within a fixed time frame and set prospective release dates for all qualifying prisoners. The review process would provide for the advance of the release dates of qualifying prisoners while allowing account to be taken of the seriousness of the offences for which the person was convicted and the need to protect the community. In addition, the intention would be that should the circumstances allow it, any qualifying prisoners who remained in custody two years after the commencement of the scheme would be released at that point.
4. The Governments will seek to enact the appropriate legislation to give effect to these arrangements by the end of June 1998.
5. The Governments continue to recognise the importance of measures to facilitate the reintegration of prisoners into the community by providing support both prior to and after release, including assistance directed towards availing of employment opportunities, re-training and/or reskilling, and further education.[31]

This agreement was given effect in the Northern Ireland (Sentences) Act 1998 which also established a Sentencing Commission to consider applications on an individual basis. By March 1999, 248 paramilitary prisoners had been released, including seventy-eight convicted of murder.[32] By 2000 over 400 had been given early release and the numbers have increased since then. So the perception of these prisoners as *de facto* political prisoners has clearly had considerable impact in their treatment post-conflict, including the failure to prosecute those suspected of serious crimes during the conflict when new evidence has emerged.

Under the Act, prisoners were released on licence so they could be returned if they supported an organisation which was not on ceasefire, or were involved in the commission, preparation or instigation of acts of terrorism, or a danger to the public. However, while the reintegration of paramilitary prisoners was also included in the Agreement, it has been difficult in practice with most of the re-integrative work being undertaken by groups and local communities, rather than the state. Ferguson (2014) notes that many ex-prisoners still report problems in gaining access to the job market so have a high unemployment rate, which makes them more exposed to the risk of further involvement in crime, including organised crime. Former prisoners have also encountered difficulties in obtaining visas and bank loans, and problems adopting children.

After the Maze closed in 2000, the remaining politically motivated prisoners were held in the high security prison, Maghaberry. Initially efforts were made to integrate the prisoners from different groups, but they demanded separation from each other and from ordinary prisoners. There were protests in Maghaberry over this issue in 2003, with prisoners going onto the roof. The Steele Report (2003) concluded that, for safety reasons, loyalist and Republican prisoners and politically affiliated prisoners and non-politically affiliated prisoners should all be held separately.

Despite continuing violence on the part of dissident groups and atrocities including the Armagh bombing, the levels of violence are much lower than in the past, with many former political prisoners actively involved in conflict reduction and restorative justice programmes. Northern Ireland is still in transition, with continuing social and economic inequalities and the conflict has had most impact on poor working-class communities, but transitional justice has focused on establishing frameworks of rights, rather than on resolving these underlying inequalities.

What is also interesting, as Behan (2014b) observes, is that despite the experience of imprisonment for those involved in sectarian crimes and the subsequent engagement of leading members of paramilitary groups in democratic politics and positions of power in public life, there has been very little interest on their part in prison conditions, or prisoners' rights, since taking office. In the Irish Republic, very few political leaders campaigned for prison reform or for restoring the vote. As we saw in Chapter 4, the law on prisoners' voting rights was changed there because of the Strasbourg Court's decision in *Hirst*, rather than because of the political leaders' commitment to prisoners' rights, or because those with experience of imprisonment had become involved in a political campaign for enfranchisement. So imprisonment does not necessarily mean that political prisoners find common cause with ordinary prisoners or campaign for them on release from prison.

The relationship between criminal law and counter-terrorism law

A further issue is whether the political motivation of prisoners means that they should be dealt with under separate laws and procedures and whether the use of emergency powers during the conflict was necessary, a question raised by Dickson (2010) and others. The relationship between ordinary criminals and paramilitary groups in the Northern Ireland context is not clear-cut. While, as we have seen, the demands to be treated as political prisoners were central to campaigns leading up to the peace process, there were also links between the activities of the paramilitary groups and ordinary crime, as racketeering was used to raise money for the groups' activities. Nonetheless, terrorists have usually been dealt with by emergency or additional measures, separately from the ordinary criminal law and criminal procedures. Sectarian groups were dealt with differently from ordinary criminals, in many respects, under the Northern Ireland (Emergency Provisions) Act 1987 (EPA) and the Prevention of Terrorism Act 1989 (PTA) which also applied in Northern Ireland.[33] Both were repealed and replaced by the Terrorism Act 2000. The EPA and the PTA then allowed extended detention and denial of the suspect's access to a solicitor for forty-eight hours, and at that time interviews were not routinely recorded as they would be now. Under the PTA, the suspect could be held for seven days without charge. This was successfully challenged in the European Court of Human Rights in *Brogan and others v UK* App Nos. 11209/84, 11234/84 and 11266/84 (29 November 1998) as a breach of Article 5(3). The UK government then derogated from the Convention and the Strasbourg Court upheld this derogation in *Brannigan and McBride v UK* App Nos. 14553/89 and 14554/89 (25 May 1983), because there was an emergency threatening the life of the nation. The Court thought that the problem of terrorist violence was sufficiently serious to justify emergency measures, including extended detention, which breached Article 5, and derogation was appropriate in this case. However, many people were questioned under the PTA in relation to terrorism in Northern Ireland, but were released without charge.

A derogation notice was also filed in 2001 after 9/11 and this was upheld by the Strasbourg Court in *A and others v UK* App No. 3455/05 (19 February 2009). While the court acknowledged that there was an emergency threatening the life of the nation, it found breaches of Article 5 in the detention of the applicants, and that the measure was disproportionate in discriminating between nationals and non-nationals in relation to preventive detention.

Other measures, included Exclusion Orders, to exclude British citizens from England and Wales under the PTA, which were imposed on Gerry Adams and Martin McGuinness, although these were later revoked as part of the peace process. Non-jury trials were also utilised in Northern Ireland in the 1970s and 1980s.

The Diplock Courts were introduced in 1973 and used for scheduled offences and terrorism-related offences, including murder, offences against the person and membership of a proscribed organisation. The offences to which they applied were set out in a Schedule to the 1973 Northern Ireland (Emergency Provisions) Act. Section 1 of the Act stipulated that trial on indictment for a scheduled offence shall be without a jury. They were recommended by the Diplock Report (1972) because of concerns over perverse verdicts and jury intimidation, but arguably these issues these could have been dealt with by special measures to ensure jury anonymity. Research by the Haldane Society found that 40 per cent of the cases heard in the Diplock Courts had no connection with terrorist activity (Haldane Report 1992). Despite the peace process, non-jury trials can still be used if required, if they meet the conditions set out in the Justice and Security (Northern Ireland Act 2007, and there is a risk of the impairment of the administration of justice. These provisions were retained and further extended in 2017.

Of course, repressive measures may be counter-productive and augment public anger and boost support for terrorist groups and thereby increase, rather than decrease, the risk of violence. Internment, for example, garnered support for the IRA. Conversely, if human rights are strengthened and the rule of law observed in the treatment of these groups, then law enforcement measures will have more legitimacy. The issue of legitimacy was crucial in Northern Ireland, because the Catholic community was at that time policed by a principally Protestant and unionist police force and the army was also involved in policing the civilian population. There were also concerns over the role of the security forces, acting in collusion with loyalist groups, involved in homicides, including the murder of the solicitor Pat Finucane. The failure to conduct a proper investigation into allegations of collusion, by security personnel, in the murder of Finucane was deemed to be a breach of Article 2 by the Strasbourg Court in *Finucane v UK* App No. 291788/95 (1 October 2003). The Stevens Enquiry (2003), the Cory Report (2004), and the De Silva Review (2012) also concluded that there was evidence of collusion. There were also concerns over the use of lethal force in Bloody Sunday in 1972, a shoot to kill policy, and the later killings in Gibraltar of Mairead Farrell, Sean Savage and Daniel McCann in 1988. Supergrass evidence was also used in relation to paramilitary activities in the early 1980s, with defendants convicted on the basis of the uncorroborated evidence of accomplices (Gifford 1984). The legitimacy of the criminal justice system had also been undermined by the revelations of miscarriages of justice involving Irish suspects including the Birmingham Six, Guildford Four and Maguire Seven who had been tried on the mainland.[34]

In addition, the Criminal Evidence (Northern Ireland) Order 1988 limited the right to silence. This was the precursor of the changes to the right to silence in England and Wales enacted by the Criminal Justice and Public Order Act in 1994. This was enacted using the Order in Council procedure which blocked any opportunity for a proper Parliamentary debate. Prior to the changes, juries were told that they could not draw adverse inferences or infer guilt from silence in interrogation or at trial, though undoubtedly in many cases juries did precisely this and lawyers rarely advised silence. There had been considerable debate on the right to silence at the time, because it was thought terrorists were 'exploiting' the right. Paramilitaries were trained to withstand interrogation and put up a wall of silence. However, for suspects interrogated by the police at that time in Northern Ireland, the fear of being seen as an informer would have outweighed the worry of adverse inferences being drawn from silence in many cases. In the local communities, there was also a distrust of the police and a history of poor relations with them which discouraged speaking in interrogation.

Although the Colville Report (1987) recommended changes to the right to silence, neither the Diplock Committee (1972), which reviewed the legal procedures to deal with terrorism in Northern Ireland, nor the Gardiner Report (1975), had referred to the need to limit the right to silence. By the late 1980s, the balance between the state and suspect favoured the state, which had an arsenal of weapons, including emergency powers and non-jury trial. However, there had been bombings in mainland Britain in 1988 and a trial of the 'Winchester Three' for conspiracy to murder Tom King who was then Secretary of state for Northern Ireland, although these convictions were later quashed, so by then there was a greater appetite for change.

The need for emergency measures was taken for granted by the Diplock and Gardiner Reports. But, of course, it could be argued that terrorist crimes may be addressed by the ordinary criminal law and a separate system may not be necessary. Moreover, the use of the ordinary criminal law strengthens the rule of law because it treats all suspects treated alike regardless of their political views or religious affiliations and thereby enhances law's legitimacy. In practice emergency and temporary powers may become permanent and measures which are seen as effective may be extended to ordinary crimes. The right to silence changes, for example, could have been limited to terrorist suspects, but have now been extended to all suspects. The reasons given for extended detention, such as checking fingerprints and conducting forensic tests, are part of normal police work and are not unique to terrorism, and so can be addressed through normal procedures. The criminal law on crimes against the person can be used for assaults, while the law of theft and robbery can deal with acquisitive crimes if, for example, armed robberies are committed for the purpose of raising funds for terrorism. So the need for a parallel system is debateable and the former Independent Reviewer on the Operation of the Terrorism Acts has said that terrorism-specific laws should be avoided as far as possible, although the case for some specific terrorism laws has been widely accepted (Anderson 2016: para 11.5). The need for special procedures for terrorism has also been accepted by the Strasbourg Court. In *Sher v UK* App No. 25101/11 (20 October 2015), it acknowledged that:

> Terrorist crime falls into a special category. Because of the attendant risk of loss of life and human suffering, the police are obliged to act with utmost urgency in following up all information, including information from secret sources. Further, the police may frequently have to arrest a suspected terrorist on the basis of information which is reliable but which cannot, without putting in jeopardy the source of the information, be revealed to the suspect or produced in court.
>
> (at para 149)

However, since the mid-1990s, there has been a shift towards aligning procedures in interrogation of terrorist suspects with those in PACE. Emergency laws were replaced by the Terrorism Act 2000, which combined elements of the PTA and EPA, and which has its own Code for Detention and Questioning. Detention beyond forty-eight hours now requires judicial permission to comply with Article 5.

But the state retains considerable powers under the Terrorism Act 2000 and Counter-Terrorism and Security Act 2015 provisions, although the focus in counter-terrorism is now primarily on international terrorism and Islamist extremism. Schedule 7 of the Terrorism Act 2000 is used to question persons at ports or borders and an offence is committed if the person fails to respond to questions and may receive a fine or imprisonment.[35] Section 44 of the Act contained powers to stop and search which, it has been argued, have been used disproportionately against black and minority ethnic groups and Muslims. It was repealed by section 59 of the Protection of Freedoms Act 2012 and replaced with more limited powers in the new section 47A of the Terrorism Act.[36]

The Terrorism Act 2006 contained provisions on the encouragement of terrorism, preparation of a terrorist act, terrorist training and dissemination of publications. It allowed extended detention for twenty-eight days, which was later reduced to fourteen days by section 57 of the Protection of Freedoms Act 2012. The 2008 Counter-Terrorism Act included provisions on gathering and sharing information for counter-terrorism purposes, disclosure of information to and by the intelligence services, powers to combat the financing of terrorism, money-laundering and other activities and notification requirements for those convicted of terrorism-related offences. Control orders were also replaced by Terrorism Prevention and Investigation Measures (TPIMs). The Counter-Terrorism and Security Act 2015 gave the state new powers to take the passports of persons who intend to travel for purposes connected with terrorism and powers for temporary exclusion orders, although the prior permission of the court is needed, and provisions on permission to return, to address the problem of UK citizens returning from fighting in Syria.

Women political prisoners

So far we have focused primarily on the experience of male political prisoners, who have formed the majority of political prisoners and of ordinary prisoners. But the imprisonment of women political prisoners also has a long history as women have waged their own struggles and participated in major conflicts. Women political prisoners have including notable figures such as Rosa Luxemburg, imprisoned in 1904, 1906 and 1916 (Richmond 2017). Emma Goldman, a Russian immigrant anarchist, was also imprisoned in the US for opposing conscription during World War I, and was deported to Russia in December 1919. Women were also held in large numbers under Article 58 in the Gulag in Stalinist Russia. While, as Dearey (2010) notes, women are under-represented in political prison literature, this masks their involvement, as more autobiographical accounts from women have begun to emerge, particularly in relation to Northern Ireland. Within many radical political groups, political activity has been shaped by masculinist ideologies, with political struggle and waging war seen as 'man's work', and women have also been seen as the spoils of war. In radical groups, such as the Weathermen, women members were expected to be sexually available to other members of the group. In the Northern Ireland conflict the leadership was male, as were the student leaders in May 1968.

In the UK, the suffragettes from the Women's Social and Political Union who were imprisoned also went on hunger strike and suffered the pain and the indignities of forced feeding, which led to public outrage (Purvis 1995). The state then responded by allowing them to continue refusing food until they were very weak and then releasing them under a new law, the Prisoners (Temporary Discharge for Ill-health) Act 1913, also known as the Cat and Mouse Act. This meant that if they died, death would occur outside the prison, and if they survived they would be too weak initially to resume their activities.[37] If they did recover their strength and continued with their campaigns, they could be rearrested and the process would begin again. The suffragette prisoners comprised women from a range of backgrounds and ages, including a woman of seventy-eight. In the end the suffragettes suspended their activities when World War I began and limited voting rights for women were granted in the UK in 1918 and full rights in 1928, but in France they were not granted until 1944.[38]

In Northern Ireland, initially during internment, the majority of those interned and detained were male, while women organised protests outside. However, during the 1970s and 1980s, women became more involved as IRA lookouts, and were involved in bombing campaigns. Women political prisoners constituted 5 per cent of political prisoners during the conflict and the majority were Republican. In 1981 in Armagh women's prison, there were twenty-nine Republican prisoners held with twenty-seven ordinary prisoners. Women were allowed to wear their own clothes, so they did not participate in the blanket protest but they did briefly take part in no-wash protests in Armagh prison (Corcoran 2005). There the women formed a company of the Provisional IRA and in one incident took the governor and prison officers hostage in support of men in the Maze who had set fire to their prison. They also campaigned for political status to reject the label of criminal and terrorist, although they did not have to wear prison uniforms. They also participated in a no-wash protest, smearing their cells with menstrual blood as well as excrement. After that ended, three women initially said that they would take part in the second hunger strike, but withdrew and their decision was supported by Bobby Sands.

Women were also held on the mainland. Marian and Dolours Price had earlier gone on hunger strike and were force fed in England, where they were imprisoned in 1973, serving life sentences for their role in the IRA bombing campaign in London. They succeeded in achieving their goal to be transferred to Armagh in 1974. Marian was later released because of health problems, and then returned to prison in 2011, where she was remanded for terrorism-related offences, linked to her involvement with a dissident Republican group. She continued to demand separation from other prisoners until she was released in May 2013. Dolours Price was freed in 1981 on compassionate grounds.

The major miscarriages of justice in the 1970s also included women. Carole Richardson was one of the Guildford Four wrongly convicted in 1975 for the pub bombings at Woolwich and Guildford, whose conviction was quashed in 1989, in light of the fabrication of evidence, problems with the forensic evidence and other procedural defects. Anne Maguire, one of the Maguire 7, was imprisoned for possession of explosive substances in 1976 and her conviction was quashed in 1991, because of the failure of the prosecution to disclose crucial forensic evidence indicating an innocent source of the nitro-glycerine found on the persons and premises of the Maguires.

The peace process, like the conflict, has been viewed primarily as a male affair. But groups such as Women for Peace, whose co-founders Mairead Corrigan and

Betty Williams received a Nobel Peace Prize, and the Northern Ireland Women's Coalition contributed to political change, although they faced problems working within a process and parties whose leadership was dominated by men (DPI 2014).

There is a substantial literature on the way in which women prisoners experience the pain of imprisonment more acutely than male prisoners and the fact that women are often judged more harshly than men, being doubly censured as deviants and for their transgression of traditional female roles. In extreme conditions, such as the Gulag, imprisonment was harder for women than men, because of their sexual exploitation (Solzhenitsyn 2003). Yet women prisoners have until recently been marginalised by both prison regimes, as well as by many commentators. As Corcoran (2006), notes the marginalisation of women in prison continued through the Good Friday Agreement period and during the subsequent transition process. It is only relatively recently that gender-specific policies have been applied in prisons in Northern Ireland, as well as England and Wales, although the current focus on security and staff shortages may undermine that progress. Moreover, women may be affected by responses to the disorder in men's prisons, if security is also enhanced, or their release on temporary licence is limited.

While noting the uniqueness of the experience of incarceration of politically motivated women in Northern Ireland in some respects, Moore and Scraton observe that 'there are clear similarities to the imprisonment of politically motivated women elsewhere' including the marginalisation of regimes for women prisoners and the gendered experience of punishment (2014: 91). These phenomena have been well documented in the prison system in relation to non-political prisoners, so it is not surprising that they are also found in the context of imprisonment of political prisoners.

In some respects the experience of imprisonment for women political prisoners may be even harder than for men. They may suffer additional indignities and humiliations because they are women and it may also be more difficult for them to organise collective protests, as they are fewer in number. Republican women prisoners reported frequent body and strip searches and the brutality of some of the officers, especially during the protests (ibid::47). They also reported their distressing experience of bleeding during searches, when they had been denied sanitary towels. In transit to court and prison, they had to endure offensive and intrusive comments from male prisoners. When Armagh prison closed in 1986, the political prisoners were transferred to the Mourne House unit within Maghaberry Prison which also held non-political prisoners. Two Republican women prisoners held on remand at Mourne House in 2004 demanded separation from other prisoners and were initially refused, although male political prisoners were held in separate units apart from other prisoners and male Republican political prisoners were separated from loyalist political prisoners. The women asked for the same treatment because they said they did not feel safe from reprisals from loyalist prisoners and they also did not want to be on the same wing as ordinary prisoners, which included drug users. One went on hunger strike over this issue of separation, which was then conceded, although, in any case, they were released soon after and the charges against them were withdrawn. Because they had refused to associate with other prisoners during their campaign, they were confined to their cells. The women were concerned at the threat to their safety arising from the closure of Mourne House and the forthcoming transfer of women prisoners to Hydebank Wood, which was seen as a predominantly Protestant prison. The treatment of women prisoners at Mourne House had been criticised by Scraton and Moore (2004) in their report for the Northern Ireland Human Rights Commission. Two women had killed themselves there, Anne Kelly in 2002 and Roseanne Irving in 2004.

Although some women at Mourne wanted separation from ordinary prisoners and thought political status gave them more protection, they were still were aware of the problems ordinary women faced. As one of the Republican women at Mourne said: 'obviously you're always going to have a bit of compassion for everybody – you're always going to want to know if they're ok or what's happening' (ibid: 1 20). They were mindful of the problems of ordinary prisoners and worried about the women remaining in prison after their departure. So women who are political prisoners may find a common cause with non-political women prisoners. If imprisonment is political, in the sense that it is primarily the socially excluded who are incarcerated, women prisoners may represent the extremes of social exclusion in so far as many women prisoners have experienced poverty and have higher rates of mental illness than male prisoners. As we saw earlier, Linda Sue Evans, imprisoned for her activities with the Weathermen, became a prisoners' rights campaigners, while the litigation of the Red Army Faction prisoners in Germany over their conditions of confinement had also highlighted the treatment of prisoners there. Moreover, as we saw in Chapter 2, women prisoners, whether political or non-political, have found many ways to resist their confinement. As well as direct action, riots, strikes and occupations, they may engage in legal action, and seek to resist through asserting new identities through, for example, educational success.

Conclusion

The relationship between political and ordinary prisoners is complex. Both groups may experience the hardships of imprisonment and both may deploy similar strategies of resistance. There is also a sense in which all imprisonment is political in reflecting inequalities of poverty, unemployment and racism. However, political prisoners may also have distinct experiences of imprisonment. Their treatment will be clearly shaped by the local political, historical and cultural context and by their identities as political activists. Being defined as a political prisoner, as we have seen, may have advantages for the prisoner, but from the state's perspective, the criminalisation of political prisoners can give their detention more legitimacy. The state's response to both groups of prisoners will also be shaped by the pressures from public opinion and the media which are considered in Chapter 7.

Notes

1 Report of the Committee on Legal Affairs and Human Rights, rapporteur, Mr Strässer. Text adopted by the Assembly on 3 October 2012 (33rd Sitting).
2 www.amnesty.org/en/what-we-do/detention/
3 See, for example, Duberman (2005) and Messer-Kruse (2011).
4 See Beer (2016) for a discussion of the use of political exile as a punishment in Tsarist Russia.
5 *Debs v US* 249 US 211 (1919).
6 In *Ensslin, Baader and Raspe v Germany* (1978) 14 DR 64.
7 For further discussion of this literature, see Carnochan (1995).
8 See, for example, Bonger (1916).
9 The problems raised by impact mitigation for offenders in relation to social exclusion have been discussed further by von Hirsch and Ashworth (2005), Piper (2007) and Easton (2008).
10 See, for example, Lea and Young (1984) and Matthews (2014).
11 American Federation of Labor and Congress of Industrial Organizations.
12 https://aflcio.org/resolutions/resolution-25-criminal-justice-reform-system-corrections-and-rehabilitation-prioritizes, accessed 23 December 2017.
13 See Jackson (1971), Davis (1971) and (2003) and, Malcolm X (1987).
14 Cited in Seale and McConville (1968: 173).
15 For a history of British anarchism see Quail (1979).
16 https://network23.org/londonabc/about/, accessed 7 August 2017.
17 www.leedsabc.org/john-bowden-time-to-get-him-out, accessed 7 August 2017.
18 www.abcf.net/about-us/, accessed 31 December 2015.
19 While Gulag is an acronym, its spelling in the substantial literature on it varies from GULAG, GULag to Gulag, but for consistency Gulag is used in the following discussion.
20 King (1994) refers to 50 million passing through the Gulag.
21 See Solzhenitsyn (2003: 29).
22 See, for example, H.G. Wells' interview with Stalin, published in the *New Statesman* on 27 October 1934 which was criticised for Wells' deference to Stalin, and Taunton's (2013) discussion of its significance, and see also Christofferson (1999) on the attitudes of the Left in France.
23 See, for example, James et al. (2007) and Ludlow (2014).
24 This figure is for 1 June 2017, Russian Federal State Statistics Service, cited in ICPS (2017) *World Prison Brief.*
25 See, for example, *Maksim Petrov v Russia*, App No. 23185/03 (6 November 2012), *Kulikov v Russia* App No. 48562/06 (27 November 2012), and *Reshetnyak v Russia* App No. 56027/10 (8 January 2013).
26 See for example, *Tarariyeva v Russia* App No. 4353/03 (14 December 2006), *Slyusarev v Russia* App No. 60333/00 (20 April 2010), *Vladimir Vasilyev v Russia* App No. 28370/05 (10 January 2012), *Ivko v Russia* App No. 30575/08 (15 December 2015), *Mozer v The Republic of Moldova and Russia* App No. 11138/10 (23 February 2016) and *Topehkin v Russia* App No. 78774/13 (10 May 2016).
27 The case was heard on 15 May 1980 and reported in 1981, *McFeeley, Nugent, Huntley v UK* (1981) 3 EHRR 161.
28 See discussion in the *Irish Times*, 30 December 2013. However, one prisoner in an English prison reported to me that attempts to encourage families to use Gaelic on visits were not always well received by those spouses who did not have a command of the

language and did not welcome the additional burden of learning Gaelic as well as being the prime carer and having to travel for prison visits.

29 See Beresford (1987) and O'Rawe (2005).

30 For further discussion, see Miller (2016) and Barilan (2017).

31 www.gov.uk/government/uploads/system/uploads/attachment_data/file/136652/ agreement.pdf, accessed 7 July 2017.

32 HL Deb 22 March 1999 Vol. 598, cc135–6WA.

33 The use of emergency powers had initially been authorised by the much-criticised Civil Authorities (Special Powers) Act (Northern Ireland) in 1922.

34 Although its use declined in the 1990s, the Serious Organised Crime and Police Act 2005 which created the Serious Organised Crime Agency, allowed immunity from prosecution or reduction in sentence in certain cases where an offender assists with an investigation (ss 71–75). The evidence of a loyalist supergrass, Gary Haggarty, has been cleared for use in the forthcoming trial of a loyalist suspect accused of two murders in Belfast in 1994. Haggarty received a 75 per cent reduction in his sentence for his own offences which included five murders.

35 See for example. *R (Miranda) v Secretary of State for the Home Department and Commissioner for the Metropolitan Police* [2016] EWCA 6; [2016] 1 WLR 1505. Although there were some changes to Schedule 7 introduced by the Anti-social Behaviour, Crime and Policing Act 2014, for example, reducing the period of detention from nine to six hours, critics thought that they did not go far enough.

36 Following criticism of the provision by the Strasbourg Court in *Gillan and Quinton v UK* App No. 41585/05 (12 January 2010).

37 A similar approach has been used in Turkey, to suspend the sentence of hunger strikes in detention until they recover and then return them to prison, see *Tekin Yildiz v Turkey* App No. 22913/04 (10 November 2005).

38 In France women first exercised this right in the April 1945 election.

7

PRISONERS AS A POLITICAL PROBLEM

Introduction

So far we have focused on the politics of the prison and the prisoner in relation to expressions of citizenship and the prison as a site of political struggle. However, there is in addition a political dimension of the prison which extends outside to the wider society, as prison and prisoners pose a problem for governments and for politicians. This chapter therefore will consider the perception of the prisoner as a problem for politicians negotiating pressures from the media and the public when addressing prisoners' demands. The problem of meeting the public's demands for more punishment and the substantial economic costs of expensive penal options will be considered. As we shall see, this has posed particular problems in the US, as exceptionally high levels of incarceration and shrinking budgets have impacted adversely on the treatment of prisoners. We will also consider the media's treatment of prisoners' with specific reference to rights claims. As well as examining the media's role as a source of knowledge on prisoners and prison life, the question of whether the media can play a positive role in maintaining prisoners' contact with the outside world will be discussed.

The politicisation of punishment

Law and order has been a key concern of governments in the UK and the US since the 1970s. While there may be some differences in the major parties on how issues of crime and punishment should be tackled, they have all been preoccupied with the issue of controlling crime and protecting the public. Certainly governments are cautious in dealing with prison issues as they need to maintain the support of the electorate and therefore their policies have to be seen as legitimate.

In the UK and the US, governments confront the pressures of public opinion, conveyed via the media, while also being constrained by the increasing economic costs of punishment, as well as pressures from international human rights standards. The expansion of prison has dramatically increased the financial burdens of punishment, which have been addressed in the UK through staff cuts and the closure of some older, inefficient prisons, although this has generated problems of instability as we have seen. Moreover, the populist punitiveness of governments reinforces the idea that we can solve crime through punishment, and when this fails, the public demand greater punishment and this may also increase the public's fear of crime.

There is also the question of whether criminal justice policy has been 'over-politicised' since the 1990s. This book began with Lord Woolf's plea that prison should be kept out of politics.[1] It is true that once punishment is construed in terms of political strategy, this may have inflationary effects. The 'politicisation' of punishment may be self-defeating. If demands for punishment are unsatisfied by harsh punishment, then the level of punishment has to increase further. But we know that a rise in punishment may achieve only modest reductions in crime, as has been shown by Tarling (1979, 1993) and others. The alternative to prison of community punishment may not be seen as a sufficiently onerous punishment by either sentencers, or by the public, who may not perceive a community order as punishment at all. However, this drive towards increased punitiveness and penal expansion is not inevitable and some European countries, mostly the Nordic[2] states, have resisted this pressure and relied more heavily on welfarist rather than punitive measures to deal with the problem of crime (Ugelvik and Dullum 2011).

The greater emphasis on risk management and public protection in criminal justice policy places the public at the heart of that policy and the focus has increasingly been on re-balancing the criminal justice system in favour of victims, witnesses and communities. Many of the proposals in the Labour Government's White Paper, *Justice for All* (Home Office 2002) were enacted in the 2003 Criminal Justice Act and the approach was reiterated in the policy paper, *Rebalancing the Criminal Justice System in Favour of the Law-Abiding Majority* (Home Office 2006). The Coalition Government focused on transforming rehabilitation and making greater use of the voluntary sector. It gave new powers to the Secretary of State, on matters including deductions from prisoners' earnings. The current Conservative Government has placed more focus on rehabilitation, education and giving governors greater autonomy, but it has also invested in more prison building and numbers remain very high. The latest projections suggest the number of prisoners will be 88,000 by March 2022 (Ministry of Justice 2017a).

If a government responds to public demands with increases in the severity of punishment, it will lead to penal expansion and will increase financial burdens, as has occurred in the US and the UK, even where the deterrent effect of those punishments is problematic. Public opinion can contribute to penal expansion and longer sentences, if governments respond to those demands. The populist punitiveness of governments reinforces the idea that we can solve crime through punishment and when this does not work, the public want yet more punishment, while also becoming more fearful of crime. This is illustrated dramatically in the case of the US.

Until the 1970s, the US incarceration rate was comparable to other western states, but since then, there has been a substantial expansion reflecting the fact that law and order has been a key political preoccupation with politicians declaring a war on crime and on drugs. The three strikes laws, and the truth in sentencing policies, which require offenders to serve most or all of the sentence they have been given, rather than being paroled part way through their sentence, have contributed to penal expansion. This has meant more offenders receiving custodial sentences and longer sentences (Mauer 2001, Tonry 2004, 2009). While public pressure was a contributory factor to this expansion, with the public demanding tougher policies to deal with rising crime, the policies persisted even when crime rates were falling. The US now has the second highest imprisonment rate worldwide, at 666 per 100,000, exceeded only by the Seychelles (ICPR 2017). The prison population increased in the US from 1.2 million in 1990 to 2.2 million in 2017, peaking at 2.3 million in 2009. This increase has had a substantial disparate impact on young black males as we saw earlier. The survival of the death penalty in the US also, as Garland (2010) notes, allows even life sentences without parole to appear humane by contrast. He has highlighted the devolution of power there to the local level, which means that local politicians are accountable to the local public and this has implications for the retention of the death penalty in those states which still retain it. Barker's (2009) study of the politics of imprisonment in the US also found that public opinion was a key element in penal expansion and in tougher penal sanctions. Barker focuses on the context of local political and institutional structures and patterns of civic engagement at the state level, which affected differential outcomes in the three states she studied, namely California, New York and Washington. However, in the UK, political loyalties are less localised with a more centralised concentration of power.

In the US, it is hard to justify lengthy sentences on the grounds of incapacitation or public protection as third offences punished under three strikes laws may be relatively minor ones. Nonetheless, the impact of prison overcrowding and efforts to manage large volumes of prisoners on shrinking budgets has resulted in criticism from the courts and, in California, has led to court-driven reductions in the prison population. The Californian Court demanded reductions in prison numbers in *Coleman v Schwarznegger/Plata v Schwarznegger* US District Court No. Civ S-90–0520 (4 August 2009), where the state was ordered to reduce prison overcrowding within two years, and this ruling was upheld by the Supreme Court in *Brown* v *Plata* 563 US 493 (2011). Here the issues were discussed in terms of the impact of poor conditions on prisoners' physical and mental health and the failure to provide appropriate medical care to prisoners. The Court ordered that the population be reduced because of concerns over the impact of overcrowding on prisoners' mental health. The decision has been seen as significant in recognising the connection between overcrowding and mental health, and the expectation that prisoners should be treated with dignity and humanity echoes the earlier Pelican Bay case, *Madrid v Gomez* 889 F.Supp 1146 (1995), previously discussed in Chapter 2.

The population did fall in response to *Brown* v *Plata,* although not as much as had been hoped. Changes to the Three Strikes laws in California were also introduced by Proposition 26, so if the offender was convicted of a third offence, they now had the opportunity to show to the court why they were not a risk to public safety. In the context of the massive expansion in the prison population and declining prison conditions, this pressure on the state to decarcerate was welcome. After California was ordered to reduce the population by the Supreme Court, procedures were changed for parole hearings and responsibility for low-level offenders was shifted to the county and some inmates were moved from state prisons to county jails (see Schlanger 2013, Simon 2014). Jails are usually used for those awaiting trial, serving short sentences or awaiting transfer to other institutions, while prisons are for those sentenced to longer periods, from one year to life. Although both have been affected by the penal expansion since the early 1990s, the increase was greater in the prisons. Responsibility for supervision for non-violent offenders and non-sexual offenders was transferred from the state to local level under this 'Realignment' policy. However, the concern is that this may simply displace the problem rather than solve it, if the response is simply to provide more places in county jails, rather than developing alternative community punishments (Lofstrom and Raphael 2013). What also needs to be addressed, especially in the US, is whether long sentences and custodial sentences are necessary in so many cases.

As governments respond to the perceived punitiveness of the public by increasing punishment, this may, in addition, intensify the public's fear of crime, which in the UK and the US, has survived falls in crime rates. But while governments may see the public as punitive, in fact the public's views on punishment may be more nuanced, with demands for strong punishment in relation to some crimes, but not others. Moreover, if a government is committed to penal austerity, it will still have to negotiate pressure from human rights standards, and in Europe from the Strasbourg Court. For example, it is clearly established in international and European human rights law that those suspected and detained for terrorist offences should be detained lawfully and treated fairly, even when the threat from terrorism is severe. In *A and others* v *UK* App Nos. 3455/05 (19 February 2009) the measures used were deemed disproportionate, even though the nation at the relevant time was facing an acute terrorist threat after the 7 July 2007 attacks, and were in breach of Articles 5(1), 5(4) and 5(5) of the Convention, because the detainees were unable to effectively challenge their conditions of detention.

Public opinion and pressures on politicians

Although public opinion may be used by politicians to justify penal policies, it may not be clear what the public's views on crime and punishment are. Their views may not necessarily be inferred from the airing of issues in the media, but more reliable information may be obtained from the Crime Survey and social scientific research, although of course responses may be affected by how questions are framed, so open-ended answers may be more illuminating. The public may not be

well informed regarding the extent of crime or punishment or levels of sentencing. For example, those most fearful of crime may not necessarily run the highest
risk of victimisation and the public may perceive sentencing levels as more lenient
than actual sentencing practice. The measurement of crime is itself problematic,
as rises in crime rates may reflect increased reporting rather than increased crime
and how figures are recorded may change. Differences in police and Crime Survey
statistics, for example, may reflect differences in the ways offences are recorded
and processed and their reference periods. While the police reported an 8 per cent
increase in recorded offences in the year ending March 2016, most of this rise was
due to improvements in recording practices.[3] The latest figures from the Office for
National Statistics[4] suggest an increase in violent crime of 19 per cent from June
2016 to June 2017, which includes increases in homicides and sexual offences and
offences of violence against the person. It is noted that most of this increase accrued
from improved recording practices, but also that rises in the most serious categories
do reflect real increases in violent crime.

Moreover, public attitudes are more complex than politicians may assume. The
research suggests that the public want tough penalties for violent crimes, but may
be more tolerant of lighter punishments for lesser crimes. If the public are given
accurate information, they are more likely to accept existing sentencing practice as
legitimate and in mock sentencing exercises, participants may give lighter sentences,
than suggested by the sentencing guidelines (Mattinson and Mirrlees-Black 2000).
The Sentencing Council has also been more proactive in giving information on its
website to the public to enhance public confidence in sentencing. Even in relation
to the most serious crime of murder, the research of Mitchell and Roberts (2012)
has found less support for a mandatory life sentence for murder than had previously
been thought. Roberts and Hough (2013) also conducted research on the public's
attitudes to sentencing during the 2011 London riots and found the public were
less punitive than the courts in relation to non-violent offences.

The problem, though, is that 'the public' is not a homogenous body and there
may be differences in punitiveness between different sections of the public. For
example, there are also variations in the levels of punitivenesss between men
and women, the young and the old, those with and without higher educational qualifications and with and without religious beliefs. For example, Baker
and Booth (2016) found that religiosity, particularly a belief in transcendent evil,
increased punitiveness and support for the death penalty among the American
public. One study in Sweden found that readers of the tabloid press were the most
punitive (Demker et al. 2008).

The issue of public attitudes towards prisoners is under-researched. However,
press reporting on prisoners' rights is mostly negative, particularly on the voting
rights issue, but also in relation to other issues, such as access to artificial insemin-
ation, the rights of transgender prisoners and awards to prisoners in settlements for
the failure to give access to methadone maintenance programmes. Interestingly, a
Norwegian study of attitudes towards prisoners noted that students' attitudes were
as punitive as prison officers', but student nurses were less punitive than business

studies students (Kjelsberg et al. 2007). Older prison officers were more positive than younger ones and prisoners were more positive than prison officers.

However, there have recently been examples of positive contact between students and prisoners for example in the Learning Together programme at Grendon and Whitemoor prisons and the Inside Out Programme at HMP Durham.[5] Moreover, even on the voting rights issue, as we saw in Chapter 4, there is some limited support for change among some sections of the public, both in the UK and in the US. Thus the public, in some cases, may be more progressive than governments (Manza et al. 2004).

The public, as we have noted, may be ambivalent regarding sentencing issues and may also be sceptical regarding the rehabilitative power of prisons (see Hutton 2005). The impact of terrorist attacks on 'soft' civilian targets which has escalated in recent years has also intensified public anxieties and their sense of insecurity, thereby creating a climate in which substantial penal reform is more difficult. If public attitudes are a barrier to prison reform, especially in the context of recent attacks on the Human Rights Act, publicising the positive aspects of prison regimes and the value of respect for prisoners' rights in specific situations, would be a useful contribution to the debate. More effort could be made by governments to engage the media in focusing on the positive aspects of imprisonment on projects which are constructive and successful in terms of reintegration, but not necessarily puni-tive. If the benefits of rehabilitative or educational programmes in preventing fur-ther offending can be shown, this would also be beneficial. If the public is made aware of why certain measures may be desirable, such as allowing access to TV or methadone treatment, in appropriate cases, this could help to temper penal austerity.

The attitudes of prison officers are also important. One study found that more positive attitudes of prisoner officers towards prisoners was a key issue in successful rehabilitation (Glaser 1969). However, attitudes towards prisoners may vary across different establishments and are more positive in smaller prisons. A small-scale study of attitudes towards prisoners across a range of groups, including prisoners, students, community residents and law enforcement officers, found that prisoners displayed more positive attitudes than the students, or members of the wider community, in the sample (Melvin et al. 1985). The most negative attitudes were found among law enforcement officers.

Willis et al. (2010) considered public attitudes towards offenders and found the most negative attitudes were towards sex offenders, where there is scepticism towards the possibility of rehabilitation or effective treatment and a tendency to overesti-mate re-offending rates. However, as Kerr et al. (2017) point out, attitudes towards sex offenders vary, with forensic staff working with offenders, psychologists and probation officers showing more positive attitudes. The research suggests that more constructive attitudes follow from more contact and from having more accurate information. Volunteers working in prison rehabilitation also have more posi-tive attitudes than prison officers or police officers. Kerr et al. studied a sample of volunteers for Circles of Support and Accountability, a community-based initiative supporting reintegration of offenders and found volunteers held more favourable attitudes towards sex offenders, their treatment and rehabilitation than a sample from the UK general public.

Prisoners' own views on crime and punishment have also been under-researched, so there are few studies on this, but as prisoners are not a homogenous group, we would expect to find a range of views. However, Crewe found that many of the prisoners in his study 'expressed surprisingly punitive dispositions' (Crewe 2009: 429). Some inmates thought that prison was not tough enough to deter offenders and wanted the death penalty for serious offences and saw offenders as responsible for crime. However, the emergence of convict crim-inology, which draws on prisoners and former prisoners' experiences and ideas in developing critical perspectives on crime and punishment, offers a distinct approach within the discipline and an opportunity to give prisoners and former prisoners a contribution to contemporary debates. While the contribution of offenders to our understanding of prison through their writings was found in the nineteenth century, as we saw earlier, for example in relation to Kropotkin's work, convict criminology has recently received a fresh impetus in the UK with the establishment of a British Convict Criminology group in 2011.[6] Earle (2017) sees the contribution of offenders' perspectives as a key resource for our understanding of crime and punishment and charts the development of convict criminology from its origins in the US, in the work of Frank Tannenbaum (1938)[7] and John Irwin (1980) and subsequent developments within the US, the UK and Europe. John Irwin drew on his experiences as an inmate in Soledad in the 1950s, where he was imprisoned for armed robbery, in analysing the tensions in prison, and because of his experience inside, devoted his career to campaigning for prison reform and co-founded the Prisoners Rights Union in California in 1971. *The Canadian Journal of Prisoners on Prison*[8] was established in 1988 and publishes art-icles by prisoners and former prisoners on a wide range of issues, principally on prisons in Canada and the US.[9] Topics covered have included overcrowding, supermax prisons, women's experiences and older prisoners. It has published autobiographical essays, as well as responses to debates within penology, and it is strongly committed to abolitionism.

The increased punitiveness of the public and governments also has to be seen in the context of the role of the media which can inflate demands for punishment The 'toxic cocktail of sensationalised or inaccurate reporting of difficult cases by the media', was one factor in penal expansion referred to by the House of Commons Justice Committee in its report *Cutting Crime: The Case for Justice Reinvestment* (2010: 5). This hyperbolic style of reporting makes it harder to convince the public of the need for reductionist policies.

There are a number of dimensions of the media to consider: first, the media as a source of the public's knowledge of prisoners; secondly, the media's role in the campaigns for and against prisoners' rights, and thirdly, prisoners' own relationship to the media. Much of the academic discussion of the media's role is negative, but the media may also play a positive role in prisoners' lives.

The media as a source of knowledge on crime and punishment

The media is a key source of the public's knowledge of prisoners and prison life and sentencing policy and practice. In the past, some prisons such as Auburn, in upstate New York, did allow visits from outside if visitors could pay. Now prison tours are usually available to the general public only if the prisons are no longer in use. Alcatraz, which closed in 1963, remains a popular tourist attraction. Large sections of the public rely on the media for information on modern functioning prisons and for information on the criminal justice process, through courtroom dramas and in jurisdictions where it is permitted, live criminal trials. Prisons continue to attract public interest and, in the UK, the Clink restaurants attract public interest and support. Increasing public knowledge of the criminal justice system is crucial, otherwise the public may rely more heavily on distorted representations of sentencing and punishment in the media.

The media can shape attitudes towards prisoners and reinforce prejudices, by a cultivation effect, so as people select what to watch, they may thereby reinforce their opinions, but the media also has the potential to challenge attitudes. While the media may exaggerate the amount of crime or prevalence of a particular type of crime, focusing on sexual offences and violent crimes, the low level of the majority of crime is downplayed. Sensationalist reporting of the most grisly crimes can increase fear of crime and of offenders, although these crimes are not the most common ones, but everyday crime is far less likely to attract attention as it is not deemed newsworthy and does not generate bold headlines. As well as focusing on shocking violent crimes, the media also highlights anomalies in sentencing and inconsistencies in sentencing.

However, we know that the fear of crime varies between groups so the audience is not homogenous and different groups may respond differently to the media. With increased access to social media, reliance on tabloid reporting or TV coverage may be less significant for some sections of the public. But high TV consumption correlates with an increased fear of crime. The more TV people watch, the more likely they are to accept the views found there, so if viewers see more violence, they are more likely to have misperceptions on crime and justice, to give too much weight to the role of punishment in crime control, and to see punishment and deterrence as the key goals of the criminal justice system.

The inclusion of the prisoner in civic society, through expanding rights and active citizenship has, however, paralleled a process of social exclusion with a focus on the differences between the offender and the ordinary law-abiding citizen, with media depictions of the offender focusing on violent and sexual offenders, and a depiction of prison life as too soft with frequent references to prisoners' access to TV and play-stations.[10] The disturbances at Ford Prison in 2011 and the consumption of alcohol there attracted much critical reporting in the popular press, with an *Express* exclusive on 'Daily booze-runs, drugs and parties – inside UK's cushiest open prison'.[11] Moral panics on particular crimes or particular groups of offenders, or folk devils, may inflate these fears disproportionately in relation to their actual threat.

The media can influence attitudes towards crime and punishment and ultimately influence penal policies. The role of the media in increasing fear of crime and public concern over crime can make politicians more reluctant to contemplate cutting prison numbers, but rather favour penal expansion. This has been a significant factor in the UK, compared to the Netherlands, for example, which does not have such a strongly sensationalist tabloid press demanding a strong punitive approach (Pakes 2007). Although there has been an increase in punitiveness[12] in the Netherlands in the past few years, its incarceration rate of 59 per 100,000 of the population is much lower than that of England and Wales, which currently stands at 146.[13]

Depictions of prison life

Because knowledge of and contact with prisons by the majority of the public is limited, and in many cases there is no close contact at all, the media plays a key role in shaping understanding and attitudes to prisoners and constructing the reality of prison life. Prisoners are now much more excluded from social life than in the past when punishments were often administered in public, for example, using the stocks. Executions also occurred in public until relatively recently, with the last public execution in 1936 in the US and 1868 in UK, although there have been recurring demands for executions to be televised in the US. Public executions attracted vast crowds in Britain in the nineteenth century and became a form of popular entertainment, with special trains laid on for those who wanted to attend. The crowds also attracted pickpockets and observers were often injured and some even killed in the crush to witness a hanging. A Royal Commission on Capital Punishment in 1864 recommended that executions should be conducted in private but this was not implemented until four years later by the 1868 Capital Punishment (Amendment) Act. But prisons and prisoners are now physically as well as socially excluded from the community, as prisons are closed institutions and are usually inaccessible to the ordinary public unless they are visiting an offender.

Those with no experience of prison life or the criminal justice system are more likely to rely on media depictions, which would apply to large sections of the public (Surette 1997). The accuracy of media depictions is important, but the depiction of prisoners is mostly negative (Pickett et al. 2015). This may have significant implications, as negative reporting may make it is easier to accept the high rates of incarceration, for example, in the US, and regressive penal policies. Page (2004), in his study of attitudes towards Pell grants in the US, found that law-makers, acting with the popular media, garnered support for punitive policies and exploited fears of crime and prejudice towards offenders, which culminated in the loss of these grants, despite the positive benefits of spending on education.

Prison stories are explored in popular culture in music such as, for example, Johnny Cash's *Folsom Prison Blues*, Loretta Lynn's *Women's Prison* and hip hop. A recording of Po Lazarus by prisoners was used in the film *O Brother*

Where Art Thou?. The prison also appears in musical theatre, for example, in *Chicago's Cell Block Tango*. Popular culture is the area in which the practice of imprisonment reaches its largest audience. Criminal justice images, including prisons, may also figure in cartoons and occasionally in advertisements.

However, as Bennett (2006) notes, in his review of prison films, media representations of prisons have been criticised for their trivialising and sensationalist treatment, but also increasing the fear of prisoners and promoting regressive criminal justice policies. The depiction of prison in films has changed from a focus on rehabilitation in the 1940s and 1950s, to studies of power dynamics. Bennett notes that some films may promote prison reform by exposing prison conditions and highlighting problems, for example, Siegel's *Riot in Cell Block 11* shot in Folsom prison. This film was released in 1954, following a period of instability and prison riots. Other films, he says, are more negative, viewing criminals as brutal barbarians and focus on symptoms instead of causes. As we noted earlier, crime reporting disproportionately focuses on violence and sensationalism and this is also found in films on prison life. Netflix's *Orange is the New Black*, which focuses on women's imprisonment and which is very successful in terms of demand and accolades, also contains much sexual and violent content.

Prison films, such as *The Shawshank Redemption,* remain very popular. Cecil (2015) notes that when the film celebrated its twentieth anniversary in 2014, there was a weekend of celebrations including a cocktail party at the now closed prison, Ohio State Reformatory in Mansfield, where it was filmed and which is a major tourist attraction. As she says, 'bad guys make good entertainment', the public is always fascinated by punishment and the spectacle of it, which is why public executions in the past were a form of popular entertainment. Prison films began in the early twentieth century, but the golden era, says Cecil, was in the 1930s when the Federal Bureau of Prisons was established and the Alcatraz flagship prison opened. In the 1960s and 1970s, the number of prison films declined and following the riots in Attica and elsewhere, films depicted a more violent prison population than in the past and the period also saw more prison documentaries. Since the 1980s, prison documentaries have became more sensationalised, paralleling the rise in the prison population and of supermax prisons and the more punitive attitudes of the public. TV prison documentary series, which often focus on new inmates processed into institutions but also on violent offenders out of control in prison, have attracted large audiences, but the number of independent documentaries and prison films has fallen.

Media coverage of prisoners' rights

But as well as charting the experience of imprisonment through dramas and documentaries, the media can contribute to debates on prisoners' rights. Prisoners' voting rights have been a key component of the attack on human rights in recent years, cited in key policy documents and party manifestoes. As well as voting rights, the failure, in some cases, to deport offenders has incensed politicians and the media.

Clashes over the role of rights have led to conflicts between the domestic courts and Strasbourg, as we saw in Chapter 4.[14] Gies (2014) has charted the role of the media in the attack on human rights and on the Convention and the Human Rights Act including its depiction of the Convention in hostile terms as a 'villains' charter'. Wacks (2013) has attributed the media's hostility to the Convention in part to the way the media have been constrained by the courts' recognition of the right to privacy following the enactment of the Human Rights Act and because of recent arguments for a new regime for press regulation.

The contribution of the media to the ongoing debate on human rights is considered by McNulty et al. (2014). They completed a content analysis of media coverage on prisoners' voting rights in the period leading up to and immediately following the debate in the UK Parliament in February 2011. In addition, they conducted a study of the audience's reception to that coverage. From their findings, they argue that the media coverage was heavily skewed towards opposition to restoration of the vote. There were 125 quotes hostile to re-enfranchisement, with only twenty-seven quotes supporting it. The attack on prisoners' votes was contextualised as part of the defence of Parliamentary sovereignty and a rejection of the interference of Strasbourg judges in domestic matters. The media coverage also helped to foster the mistaken perception that the Court was part of the EU and contributed to the aversion to European interference, manifested in the Brexit vote. The debate on the merits of voting rights was swamped by the debate on Britain's relationship to Europe. Even when positive arguments were considered by the media, it was made clear that there were political obstacles to achieving change on enfranchisement. The focus groups interviewed by McNulty et al. shared this hostility, with the majority opposed to restoration and to prisoners' rights in general, and seemed to be strongly influenced by the media discussions of the issue.

In reporting on prisoners' rights claims, the popular press has focused on trivial claims such as prisoners' demands for access to pornography, for example, in the case of Denis Nilsen, or very unpopular claims, such as Abu Qatada's resistance to his deportation. The attack on rights is particularly damaging for prisoners, for, as we have seen, rights instruments may act as a constraint on the principle of less eligibility and limit the impact of public punitiveness. The paradox is that prisoners' rights are needed to protect against public punitiveness and populism, but when rights have been acknowledged, this has added to hostility to prisoners from governments and the public. Politicians are subject to pressure from the public to deal with crime, while rights culture has been under attack from popular media and from governments.

The positive role of the media

Within political theory, the role of the media has often been construed negatively, for example, crude Marxist theories have focused on media propaganda purveying material serving the interests of the dominant class. More sophisticated Marxists, such as Gramsci (1995), see the media as a site for conflict between competing classes. Later writers influenced by his approach have focused on the way the fear of crime can be exploited to justify an authoritarian state and manage economic instability (Hall et al. 1978). For liberal theorists, the media is an arena for airing competing views and it plays a useful role in exposing injustice or poor prison conditions and acting as a check on government. The media has also been crucial in exposing miscarriages of justice.

Within penology, much of the discussion of the media is on its negative impact, as considered above, but its positive impact should not be overlooked. Vandebosch (2005) argues that the media can play a key part in maintaining prisoners' contact with the outside world and effecting a transition for prisoners from the prison to outside, by giving them information on developments in the real world. She surveyed prisoners in two Flemish prisons and conducted in-depth interviews with seventeen prisoners and five ex-prisoners, and found prisoners quite well informed about current affairs. While some prisoners cut themselves off from the outside world, and were more likely be institutionalised inside prison, so they faced problems adjusting to the outside world on release, with implications for their recidivism, others were more focused on the outside world and more likely to reintegrate on their release. For all prisoners it may be difficult to adjust to the noise and pace of the world outside or to having autonomy on decisions in everyday life. Prisoners valued having access to TV as it contributed to normalisation and also gave them information regarding the job market. While the media may sometimes give a distorted view of reality, it can also normalise life in prison and keep inmates informed on social changes. TV and radio can also help to pass the time, offer excitement and escapism, and relieve the stress of imprisonment.

For most prisoners in the UK too, TV is a key media source with access to in-cell TV available as a privilege, under the Incentives and Earned Privileges Scheme, but access can be withdrawn for bad behaviour (Annex E.10, PSI 30/2013). Prisoners also have access to newspapers. But while TV consumption is valued by prisoners, for the most part it is an isolating activity, which means less socialisation with others, which, as we saw earlier, is a significant inhibitor of prisoner politicisation or political resistance. However, TV consumption can facilitate social interaction as discussion of items on TV can be a useful and neutral topic of conversation and help to combat loneliness and can promote re-integration by giving information about life outside. Jewkes (2002) found that prisoners may form sub-groups based on collective enthusiasm for a particular programme. She studied prisoners in four men's prisons, holding category A, B and C prisoners, and conducted individual in-depth interviews with sixty-two prisoners. She argues that the media can provide a source of empowerment for prisoners, as it is offers them a range of material from which they can maintain their former identities or forge new lives. Media resources gave prisoners continuity with their former lives and filled their time, but also offered opportunities for them to create new identities based on popular role models. Some prisoners read broadsheet papers and prisoners generally were quite well informed on current affairs, through watching news programmes. For some prisoners, media resources give them the opportunity to find a solitary space where there were alternatives to the dominant masculine identity in prison, for example, offered by programmes on interior design.

Prisoners' access to the media

TV does play a big part in prisoners' lives, and as well as watching TV and reading newspapers, prisoners may discuss current affairs in classes. EPR 24.10 states that prisoners have the right to be kept informed of public affairs: 'Prisoners shall be allowed to keep themselves informed regularly of public affairs by subscribing to and reading newspapers, periodicals and other publications and by listening to radio or television transmissions', unless there is a specific prohibition on this made by a judicial authority for a specific period. So the media offers a key means of contact with the outside world and contributes to the normalisation of prison life. Normalisation is the principle that prison life should be as close as possible to positive aspects of life outside and is stressed by the European Prison Rules: 'Life in prison shall approximate as closely as possible the positive aspects of life in the community' (EPR 5). So if prisoners keep in touch with the outside world and feel part of the community and prepared for their return to it, this can help with their rehabilitation. Obviously family contact is a key source of external contact, but access to the media is also important. This right to contact is enshrined in the European Prison Rules: 'Prisoners shall be allowed to communicate as often as possible by letter, telephone or other forms of communication with their families, other persons and representatives of outside organizations and to receive visits from these persons' (EPR 24.1). There are also protections for these communications. To ensure that access to lawyers or MPs is not inhibited, correspondence should not normally be opened and this is protected by Articles 6 and 8, but Article 8(2) allows legal correspondence to be read if there is reasonable cause to believe it will affect the security or safety of others.

As well as access to the media as consumers, prisoners may also in limited circumstances have access to the media in order to raise issues concerning prison life. This is protected by Article 10 of the European Convention which stipulates that: 'Everyone has the right to freedom of expression. This right shall include freedom to hold opinions and to receive and impart information and ideas without interference by the public authority.' However, it can be limited under Article 10(2), which allows restrictions 'as are necessary in a democratic society, in the interests of national security, territorial integrity or public safety, for the prevention of disorder or crime, for the protection of health or morals, for the protection of the reputation or the rights of others, for the preventing of the disclosure of information received in confidence, or for maintaining the authority and impartiality of the judiciary.' There are similar provisions in Prison Rule 34, which covers communications between the prisoner and any other person. Any limits should be proportionate to the aim of the restriction.

Prisoners may have access to the media, in person through a prison visit, or by letter or phone call subject to the provisions in PSI 37/2010, *Prisoners' Access to the Media,*[15] and PSO 4410 *Prisoner Communication: Visits* (05/09/2007). The rules regarding access to the media were revised following the cases of *Simms and O'Brien*[16] and *Hirst*[17] and in light of European Convention jurisprudence on Article 10. In *Simms*, the House of Lords had made clear that a blanket ban on prisoners' contact with the media was unlawful, as prisoners may wish to raise matters regarding their alleged wrongful convictions, or to raise issues regarding their treatment in prison. In *Simms and O'Brien's* case, the prisoners wanted to challenge the safety of their convictions and this is a situation where free speech is crucial. So while restrictions on free speech may be justified, they cannot be used to deny prisoners access to justice. It was stressed that the approach in English law and European Convention jurisprudence would be the same. A similar approach was taken in Hirst's case in 2002, where the prisoner gave a phone interview to the media, despite the governor telling him not to do so, where he was speaking as the General Secretary of the Association of Prisoners. The court thought that restricting contact with the media was not part of the prisoner's punishment and the policy, as imposed universally, was unlawful. Prisoners should not be prevented from expressing their views to the media on matters of legitimate public interest.

So prisoners do not need permission in advance to contact the media by letter, but they do for visits and phone calls. If they write to the press, they cannot discuss their own offence or that of other prisoners, unless it is in the context of making a serious comment on crime, the criminal justice process, or penal system, or raising a legitimate question of public interest regarding prisons, or addressing issues concerning their conviction. In doing so, prisoners should not reveal the identity of staff or other prisoners by referring specifically to them. Visits from the media to the prison establishment require an application to the governor, who will pass it on with his view, to the Secretary of State to reach a decision. Such a visit would be granted only if it is necessary to allow the prisoner to challenge his conviction, having exhausted the appeals process, to publicise an alleged miscarriage of justice, or to raise a matter of public concern, and to allow the visit would not pose a threat to security or good order. Only in rare cases are journalists allowed such a visit and the meeting may not be filmed or broadcast and the prisoner cannot be paid. Permission is also needed for telephone calls on the above matters, and may be granted on the condition that identities are not revealed and that those calls will be monitored. However, less latitude is given to prisoners simply publishing their memoirs or salacious reports, on their cases. Denis Nilsen, the notorious serial killer, was not permitted to publish his memoirs recording his crimes, because it would upset the victims' families as well as survivors and the general public.[18]

In the US, prisoners also have the right to contact the media by letter, but not to receive visits from them. A blanket ban on contact would violate the First Amendment, but contact can be restricted, provided the restrictions relate to a legitimate penological interest as was stressed in *Turner v Safley* 482 US 78 (1987). This contrasts with the earlier cases of *Saxbe v Washington Post* 417 (US) 817 (1974) and *Pell v Procunier* 417 (US) 843, where the Supreme Court had permitted prison officials to ban all press interviews with inmates.

What is much harder to control is informal contact with the media on smuggled mobile phones. Despite efforts to control these phones they still remain in circulation and during the 2016 and 2017 riots in UK prisons, pictures of the riots were sent outside and published. Measures being considered include no-fly zones over prisons to prevent drones dropping contraband into exercise areas. In the US some states, for example, Texas, have made it a criminal offence to fly a drone over a prison establishment.[19] In the UK there have been several convictions under section 79 of the Serious Crime Act 2015 for the offence of conspiracy to project an article into a prison without authorisation.

Prisoners of course have access to books and attempts to limit access to books have been resisted. New restrictions on receiving books and other items by post or from visitors were imposed in 2013 by PSI 30/2013, which amended the Incentives and Earned Privilege Scheme. However, this resulted in protests from prisoners and a challenge to this ban was brought by a prisoner to the High Court. Annex F of PSI 30/2013 provided for a maximum of twelve books, but the claimant argued that a limit of twelve was arbitrary and irrational. The defendants argued that the prisoners' access to books was not restricted, because they could use the library and order books they needed. However, the court decided that the 'book ban' was unlawful although it did not rescind the restrictions of other items.[20] The court acknowledged that books are an essential element of rehabilitation rather than merely a privilege. It found that the inclusion of books within the restrictions was unlawful because access through library services is insufficient. The court noted that books requested by prisoners may not be available, library provision varies within the prison estate and libraries may not hold sufficient quality and quantity of books that prisoners may require. So prisoners do rely on books from family and friends outside, which also helps prisoners maintain links with the outside world. The Books for Prisoners Campaign is another example of prisoners' rights litigation which benefits all prisoners.

Conclusion

As we have seen, prisoners are a problem for politicians and governments. There are few political benefits for MPs or political parties, in championing prisoners' rights or prison reform. Furthermore, prisoners' physical separation from society and their invisibility makes them easier to ignore, unless they are capturing the public's attention by rioting. Their 'invisibility' renders them more vulnerable to assault and violations of their rights, including the failure to provide sufficient opportunities for rehabilitation. Politicians who perceive the public to be punitive are more likely to favour penal austerity than to promote prisoners' rights and welfare, as concessions to prisoners may be seen as politically damaging. The Conservative Party Manifesto in the 2015 General Election celebrated its refusal to grant the vote to prisoners as one of its key achievements. While the Strasbourg Court made the point in *Hirst* that rights should not be limited simply because they might offend public opinion, this admonition has had little impact on governments.

Prisoners as non-constituents are not part of the polity, because they lack the vote, so they are politically and socially excluded and effectively in a state of civil death, defined by their alterity or otherness. Conversely, if they had the vote, they would arguably be more engaged in political life and if they were voters possibly would be taken more seriously by their elected representatives. We saw in Chapter 4, the political implications of felon disenfranchisement laws, at its starkest in the US, where these laws, which have a disparate impact on young black males, have affected the outcomes of elections.

It is also ironic that politicians' hostility to the plight of prisoners has persisted when there is now more contact between prisoners and politicians with more MPs in prison because of the expenses scandal and when MPs, as a group, have seen their status in the eyes of the public lowered through their actions and negative media reports. The notion of the *polis* as marked by virtue pursued in this book may seem somewhat rose-tinted, given this recent history of greed and corruption. The public perception of MPs as self-seeking and crooked and the entry into prison of MPs convicted of fraud in relation to their expenses has undermined a positive perception of political life. However, specific MPs have been praised for their altruistic behaviour, for example, the murdered MP Jo Cox, and Tobias Ellwood who assisted a dying police officer at the Commons during the terrorist attack on Westminster Bridge in 2017. Politicians who have served time in prison inevitably become more aware of its problems and we now have a genre of prison memoirs and vignettes recorded by former MPs, who have spent time in prison, including Jeffrey Archer (2003, 2005), Jonathan Aitken (2006) and Denis MacShane (2014). In some cases former politicians who have been incarcerated have subsequently campaigned for penal reform. For example, Jonathan Aitken (2006), who served a short sentence for perjury in 1999, has since worked with charities campaigning for offenders. The economist Vicky Pryce, who was imprisoned for nine weeks for perverting the course of justice by accepting penalty points for her husband, MP and Cabinet minister Chris Huhne, published a book on the economic costs of imprisoning women, *Prisonomics*, and has worked with the charity Working Chance which helps women with a criminal record find work (Pryce 2013). But as disgraced politicians convicted of crimes of dishonesty have rarely been welcomed back into their parties or re-entered Parliament,[21] the impact of their more enlightened views may be limited and outweighed by the views of the majority of their fellow politicians. The lack of respect of the majority of politicians for prisoners may be reciprocated. Crewe (2009) found that prisoners generally had little interest in politics but, like many sections of the public, viewed politicians negatively.

However, an interest in prison reform is not always a consequence of the experience of imprisonment. Peter Kropotkin, as we saw earlier, published work on prison reform following his experience of confinement. Nelson Mandela, who participated in prison strikes during his twenty-seven years in prison, recorded his experiences in his diaries and his autobiography (Mandela 1994). Moreover, as President he oversaw the 1996 South African Constitution which protected prisoners' rights, and enshrines the right to conditions of detention consistent with human dignity (s 35(2)). But in the case of the Irish Republic, as we saw earlier, politicians with a history of past imprisonment displayed little interest in the campaign for voting rights or other prisoners' rights issues.

Rights jurisprudence has assumed greater importance in penal policy and practice, with interventions from the Strasbourg Court and the recognition of prisoners' rights embedded in the European Prison Rules which declare as a basic principle that 'All persons deprived of their liberty shall be treated with respect for their human rights' (EPR 1). The Reports of the European Committee for the Prevention of Torture and Inhuman or Degrading Treatment or Punishment (CPT), have also contributed to improvements in standards in prison as well as other places of detention. The UK has, in addition, signed the Optional Protocol to the Convention against Torture (OPCAT) which requires it to establish a National Preventive Mechanism which makes regular visits to places of detention. Its recent reports have focused on issues including solitary confinement and isolation and children in detention.[22]

We have also defined the prisoner as a *zoon politikon*, and surveyed the efforts of prisoners to reclaim their citizenship status, and assert their rights and the countervailing forces to their politicisation, including efforts to limits rights claims and the fragmenting effects of the modern prison structure and organisation here and elsewhere.[23] The inclusion of prisoners within the rights discourse, at the same time, has been a trigger for the attack on rights. So we find an uneasy relationship between rights, populist punitiveness and prisoner activism, which governments find increasingly difficult to resolve. The expansion of rights has achieved many advances as we have seen, but problems still remain, including an increase in violence in prisons and a failure to reduce recidivism, which imposes economic as well as social costs. The cost of reoffending to the UK economy is estimated to be up to 15 billion per year (Ministry of Justice 2016a: 5). Prison building has continued, with the development of larger prisons, whose size makes it harder to improve dynamic security in prison.

While governments are reluctant to introduce policies unpopular with the public, it is difficult to introduce strong decarceration measures and an abolitionist agenda is unlikely to gain favour. While some modest reductions may be made by focusing on particular categories such as women, this will not make a significant impact on the prison population. More imaginative policies such as Justice Reinvestment, which targets resources on communities affected by high crime rates and high incarceration rates, to prevent entry into the criminal justice system, may have more impact, as would greater use of restorative justice (Allen and Stern 2007). However, shifting attitudes on the part of the public, as well as governments, is a key precondition of change.

Notes

1 *Inside Out*, BBC Northwest (25 May 2015).
2 The imprisonment rates of the Nordic states are much lower than the UK, with Finland at 57, Norway at 74, Sweden 57 and Denmark 59, in contrast to England and Wales at 146, http://prisonstudies.org/world-prison-brief-data, accessed 9 December 2017.

3 www.ons.gov.uk/peoplepopulationandcommunity/crimeandjustice/bulletins/crimein englandandwales/yearendingmar2016

4 www.ons.gov.uk/peoplepopulationandcommunity/crimeandjustice/bulletins/crime inenglandandwales/june2017

5 See Chapter 3 above, Armstrong and Ludlow (2016), Darke and Aresti (2016).

6 www.convictcriminology.org/bcc.htm. See also Earle (2017) and Darke and Aresti (2016).

7 See also Yeager (2011).

8 http://jpp.org

9 See Gaucher (2002) for a selection of writings from the journal from 1988 to 2002.

10 See, for example, 'Are prisons too soft?', *Daily Telegraph* (28 April 2008, 'Prisoners' rights and soft justice are putting the public at risk from re-offenders', *Daily Telegraph* (27 May 2012).

11 10 April 2015. See also 'Ford Fiasco' in *The Sun*, 3 January 2011, and 'Prisoners partying on drugs, vodka and fast food in shocking photos from behind bars', *Mirror*, 7 October 2017.

12 See Boone and van Swaaningen (2013) for a discussion of the recent changes in attitudes.

13 www.prisonstudies.org/map/europe, accessed 7 December 2017.

14 See also Easton (2013).

15 This replaced Prison Service Order 4470 *Prisoners' Access to the Media* (02/09/2005).

16 *R v Secretary of State for the Home Department ex parte Simms and O'Brien* [2000] 2 AC 115.

17 *R (Hirst) v Secretary of State for the Home Department* [2002] EWCH 602 (Admin).

18 *R (Nilsen) v Governor of HMP Full Sutton and Secretary of State for the Home Department* [2003] EWHC 3160 (Admin).

19 Statute HB 1424.

20 *R (on the application of Barbara Gordon-Jones) v Secretary of State for Justice and the Governor of HMP Send* (5 December 2014) EWHC 3997 Admin.

21 Those who are sentenced for more than one year are disqualified from standing for Parliament under the Representation of the People Act 1981.

22 www.nationalpreventivemechanism.org.uk/

23 See, for example, Ratner and Cartwright (1990) for discussion of this in the context of the US.

BIBLIOGRAPHY

Abrams, L.S. Hughes, E., Inderbitzin, M. and Meek, R. (eds) (2016) *The Voluntary Sector in Prisons: Encouraging Personal and Institutional Change*, London, Palgrave Macmillan.

ACLU, NAACP, the Sentencing Project and Others (2013) *Democracy Imprisoned: A Review of the Prevalence and Impact of Felony Disenfranchisement Laws in the United States*, New York, ACLU.

Aitken, J. (2006) *Porridge and Passion*, London, Continuum.

Allen, R. and Stern, V. (eds) (2007) *Justice Reinvestment: A New Approach to Crime and Justice*, London, ICPS.

Althusser, L. (1970) *Lenin and Philosophy*, London, New Left Books.

Amnesty International (2017) *Prisoner Transportation in Russia: Travelling into the Unknown*, London, Amnesty.

Anderson, D. (December 2016) *The Terrorism Acts in 2015: Report of the Independent Reviewer on the Operation of the Terrorism Act 2000 and Part I of the Terrorism Act 2006*, London, HMSO.

Applebaum, A. (2003) *Gulag: A History*, New York, Doubleday.

Arbour, L. (2006) *Commission of Inquiry into Certain Events at the Prison for Women in Kingston*, Ottawa, Canada Communication Group C Publishing.

Archer, J. (2003) *A Prison Diary, Volume I, Hell*, London, Pan Macmillan.

Archer, J. (2003) *A Prison Diary, Volume II, Purgatory*, London, Pan Macmillan.

Archer, J. (2005) *A Prison Diary, Volume III, Heaven*, London, Pan Macmillan.

Aristotle (1962) *Politics*, trans. A. Sinclair, Harmondsworth, Penguin.

Armstrong, R. and Ludlow, A. (2016) 'Educational Partnerships between Universities and Prisons: How Learning Together can be Individually, Socially and Institutionally Transformative' *Prison Service Journal* 225, 9–17.

Bacon, E. (1996) *The Gulag at War: Stalin's Forced Labour System in the Light of the Archives*, London, Palgrave.

Baker, J. and Booth, A. (2016) 'Hell to Pay: Religion and Punitive Ideology among the American Public', *Punishment and Society*, 18(2), 151–76.

Bakunin, M. (1872) *Bakunin on Anarchy*, trans. and ed. S. Dolgoff, New York, Vintage Books (1971).

Ballas, D.A. (October 2010) 'Prisoner Radicalization', *FBI Law Enforcement Bulletin*, 1–3.

Barilan, Y.M. (2017) 'The Role of Doctors in Hunger Strikes', *Kennedy Institute of Ethics Journal*, 27:3, 341–69.

Barker, V. (2009) *The Politics of Imprisonment: How the Democratic Process Shapes the Way America Punishes Offenders*, New York, Oxford University Press.

Barr, S. (2015) *Many ex-felons don't know they can get their right to vote restored*, Washington, DC, The Center for Public Integrity.

Beck, J. (1996) 'Citizenship Education: Problems and Possibilities', *Curriculum Studies*, 4:3, 249–66.

Beer, D. (2016) *The House of the Dead: Siberian Exile under the Tsars*, London, Allen Lane.

Behan, C. (2014a) *Citizen Convicts*, Manchester, Manchester University Press.

Behan, C. (2014b) 'Embracing and Resisting Prisoner Enfranchisement: A Comparative Analysis of the Republic of Ireland and the United Kingdom', *Irish Probation Journal* 11, 156–76.

Behan, C. and O'Donnell, I. (2008) 'Prisoners, Politics and the Polls', *British Journal of Criminology* 48(3), 319–36.

Bennett, J. (2006) 'The Good, the Bad and the Ugly: The Media in Prison Films', *Howard Journal of Crime and Justice*, 45:2, 97–115.

Beresford, D. (1987) *Ten Dead Men: Story of the 1981 Hunger Strike,* London, Grafton.

Bishop, N. (2006) 'Prisoner Participation in Penal Management', *Champ Pénal/Penal Field,* III, 1.

Blankenship, S. (2005) 'Revisiting the Democratic Promise of Prisoners' Labour Unions', in A. Sarat (ed) *Crime and Punishment: Perspectives from the Humanities*, Bingley, Emerald Publishing, 241–69.

Bleich, E., Stonebraker, H., Nisar, H. and Abdelhamid, R. (2015) 'Media Portrayals of Minorities: Muslims in British Newspaper Headlines 2001–2012', *Journal of Ethnic and Migration Studies,* 942–62.

Blunkett, D. (2003) *Civil Renewal: A New Agenda*, London, Home Office.

Boin, A. and Rattray, W.A. (2004) 'Understanding Prison Riots: Towards a Threshold Theory', *Punishment and Society* 6(1), 47–65.

Bonger, W. (1916) *Criminality and Economic Conditions*, Boston, Little, Brown.

Boone, M. and van Swaaningen, R. (2013) 'Regression to the Mean: Punishment in the Netherlands', in V. Ruggiero and M. Ryan (eds) *Punishment in Europe: A Critical Anatomy of Penal Systems*, London, Palgrave, 9–32.

Bosworth, M. (1999) *Engendering Resistance: Agency and Power in Women's Prisons*, London, Routledge.

Bosworth, M. (2014) *Inside Immigration Detention*, Oxford, Oxford University Press.

Bosworth, M. and Carrabine, E. (2001) 'Reassessing Resistance: Race, Gender and Sexuality in Prison', *Punishment and Society*, 3(4), 501–15.

Brown, A. (2007) 'The Amazing Mutiny at the Dartmoor Convict Prison', *British Journal of Criminology*. 47, 276–92.

Buntman, F.L. (2003) *Robben Island and Prisoner Resistance to Apartheid*, Cambridge, Cambridge University Press.

Buntman, F. and Huang, T. (2000) 'The Role of Political Imprisonment in Developing and Enhancing Political Leadership: A Comparative Study of South Africa's and Taiwan's Democratization', *Journal of Asian and African Studies*, 35(1), 43–66.

Burton-Rose, D. (2010) *Guerrilla USA: The George Jackson Brigade and the Anticapitalist Underground of the 1970s*, Oakland, CA, University of California Press.

Carnochan, W.B. (1995) 'The Literature of Confinement', in N. Morris and D.J. Rothman (eds) *The Oxford History of the Prison,* Oxford, Oxford University Press, 427–55.

Carrabine, E. (2004) *Power, Discourse and Resistance: A Genealogy of the Strangeways Prison Riot*, Aldershot, Ashgate.

Carrabine, E. (2005) 'Prison Riots, Social Order and the Problem of Legitimacy', *British Journal of Criminology*, 45, 896–913.

Cecil, D.K. (2015) *Prison Life in Popular Culture: From* The Big House *to* Orange is the New Black, Boulder, CO, Lynne Reinner.

Christie, N. (2000) *Crime Control as Industry: Towards Gulags, Western Style*, London, Routledge.

Christofferson, M.S. (1999), 'An Antitotalitarian History of the French Revolution: François Furet's *Penser la Révolution Française* in the Intellectual Politics of the Late 1970s', *French Historical Studies*, 22(4), 557–611.

Chung, J. (2016) *Felony Disenfranchisement: A Primer*, Washington, The Sentencing Project.

Cichowlas, J.A. and Chen, Y-J. (2010) 'Volunteer Prisoners Provide Hospice to Dying Inmates', *Annals of Health Law*, 19, 127–31.

Clear, T. (2007) *Imprisoning Communities*, New York, Oxford University Press.

Coates, S. (2016) *Unlocking Potential: A Review of Education in Prison*, London, Ministry of Justice.

Cohen, S. and Taylor S. (1972) *Psychological Survival: The Experience of Long-term Imprisonment*, Harmondsworth, Penguin.

Colvin, M. (1982) 'The 1980 New Mexico Prison Riot', *Social Problems*, 29:5, 449–63.

Colvin, M. (1992) *The Penitentiary in Crisis: From Accommodation to Riot in New Mexico*, Albany, NY, State University of New York Press.

Commission on Citizenship (1990) *Encouraging Citizenship: Report of the Commission on Citizenship*, London HMSO.

Conquest, R. (1990) *The Great Terror: A Reassessment*, New York, Oxford University Press.

Conservative Party (2017) *Forward Together: Our Plan for a Stronger Britain and a Prosperous Future: The Conservative and Unionist Party Manifesto 2017*, London, Conservative Party.

Corcoran, M. (2006) *Out of Order: The Political Imprisonment of Women in Northern Ireland 1972–1998*, Cullompton, Willan.

Council of Europe (2017) *Report to the Government of the United Kingdom on the visit to the United Kingdom carried out by the European Committee for the Prevention of Torture and Inhuman or Degrading Treatment or Punishment (CPT) from 30 March to 12 April 2016*, Strasbourg, Council of Europe CPT/Inf, 9.

Crewe, B. (2009) *The Prisoner Society: Power, Adaptation and Social Life in an English Prison*, Oxford, Oxford University Press.

Criminal Justice Joint Inspection (2016) *An Inspection of Through the Gate Resettlement Services for Short-Term Prisoners*, London, HM Inspectorate of Probation.

Cummins, E. (1994) *The Rise and Fall of California's Radical Prison Movement*, Stanford, Stanford University Press.

Darke, S. and Aresti, A. (2016) 'Connecting Prisons and Universities through Higher Education', *Prison Service Journal*, 225, 26–32.

Davis, A.Y. (2003) *Are Prisons Obsolete?* New York, Seven Sisters Press.

Davis, A.Y. and other political prisoners. (1971) *If they Come in the Morning*, London, Orbach and Chambers.

Davis, L.M., Bozick, R., Steele, J.L., Saunders, J. and Miles, J.N.V. (2013) *Evaluating the Effectiveness of Correctional Education: A Meta-Analysis of Programs that Provide Education to Incarcerated Adults*, Santa Monica, CA, RAND Corporation.

Dean, C. (2013) 'Intervening Effectively with Terrorist Offenders', *Prison Service Journal* 203, 31–6.

Dearey, M. (2010) *Radicalization: The Life Writings of Political Prisoners*, London, Routledge.

Demker, A., Towns, A., Duus-Otterström, G. and Sebring, J. (2008) 'Fear and Punishment in Sweden: Exploring Penal Attitudes', *Punishment and Society*, 10(3), 319–32.

Democratic Progress Institute (2014) *The Role of Women in Conflict Resolution: Comparative Study Visit Report: Northern Ireland*, London, DPI.

Department of Constitutional Affairs (2006) Consultation Paper, *Voting Rights of Convicted Prisoners Detained in the UK*, London, DCA.

Desroches, F. (1974) 'The April 1971 Kingston Penitentiary Riot', *Canadian Journal of Criminology and Corrections*, 16(4), 317–31.

Dickson, B. (2010) *The European Convention on Human Rights and the Conflict in Northern Ireland*, Oxford, Oxford University Press.

Dostoevsky, F. (2008) *Memoirs from the House of the Dead*, Oxford, Oxford University Press.

Duberman, M. (2005) *Haymarket*, New York, Seven Stories Press.

Dworkin, R. (1977) *Taking Rights Seriously*, London, Duckworth.

Earle, R. (2017) *Convict Criminology: Inside and Out*, Bristol, Policy Press.

Earle, R. and Phillips, C. (2013) 'Muslim is the New Black – New Ethnicities and New Essentialisms in the Prison', *Race and Justice* 3(2), 114–29.

Easton, S. (2006) 'Electing the Electorate: The Problem of Prisoner Disenfranchisement', *Modern Law Review*, 69(3), 443–52.

Easton, S. (2008) 'Constructing Citizenship: Making Room for Prisoners' Rights', *Journal of Social Welfare and Family Law,* 30:2, 127–46.

Easton, S. (2009) 'The Prisoner's Right to Vote and Civic Responsibility', *Probation Journal*, 56(6), 224–37.

Easton, S. (2011) *Prisoners' Rights: Principles and Practice,* London, Routledge.

Easton, S. (2013) 'Protecting Prisoners: The Impact of International Human Rights Law on the Treatment of Prisoners in the United Kingdom', *The Prison Journal*, 475–92.

Easton, S. (2014) *Silence and Confessions: The Suspect as the Source of Evidence,* London, Palgrave Macmillan.

Easton, S. (2018) 'Older Prisoners, Gender and Family Life' in J. Herring and B. Clough (eds) *Ageing, Gender and Family Law*, London, Routledge, 142–58.

Edgar, K., Jacobson, J. and Biggar, K. (2011) *Time Well Spent: A Practical Guide to Active Citizenship and Volunteering in Prison,* London, Prison Reform Trust.

Electoral Commission (2009) *Electoral Commission Response to the Ministry of Justice Consultation Voting Rights of Convicted Prisoners Detained within the United Kingdom, Second Stage*, London, Electoral Commission.

European Court of Human Rights (2017) *Overview: 1959–2016*, Strasbourg, Council of Europe.

Fazel, S., McMillan, J. and O'Donnell, I. (2002), 'Dementia in Prisons: Ethical and Legal Implications', *Journal of Medical Ethics*, 28: 156–9.

Ferguson, N. (2014) 'Northern Irish Ex-prisoners: The Impact of Imprisonment on Prisoners and the Peace Process in Northern Ireland' in A. Silke (ed) *Prisons, Terrorism and Extremism*, London, Routledge, 270–78.

Fitzgerald, M. (1977) *Prisoners in Revolt*, Harmondsworth, Penguin.

Foucault, M. (1975) *Surveiller et Punir*, Paris, Gallimard.

Foucault, M. (1990) *The History of Sexuality*, Harmondsworth, Penguin.

Fry, D. (2005) 'Managing Older Prisoners at HMP Wymott', *Prison Service Journal* 160, 11–13.

Gardiner Report (1975) *Report of a Committee to Consider in the Context of Civil Liberties and Human Rights, Measures to Deal with Terrorism in Northern Ireland*, London, HMSO.

Garland, D. (2010) *Peculiar Institution: America's Death Penalty in an Age of Abolition,* Oxford, Oxford University Press.

Gaucher, B. (2002) *Writing as Resistance: The Journal of Prisoners on Prison Anthology (1988–2002)*, Toronto, Three O'Clock Press.

Gearty, C. (2016) *On Fantasy Island: Britain, Europe and Human Rights*, Oxford, Oxford University Press.

George Washington University Homeland Security Policy Institute and the University of Virginia Critical Incident Analysis Group (2006) *Out of the Shadows: Getting Ahead of Prisoner Radicalization*, Washington DC, George Washington University.

Gibbons, K. 'Prison Imams Linked to Islamic Radicalisation', *The Times* (14 July 2014).

Gies, L. (2014) *Mediating Human Rights: Media, Culture and Human Rights Law*, London, Routledge.

Gifford, T. (1984) *Supergrasses: The Use of Accomplice Evidence in Northern Ireland*, London, Cobden Press.

Gillat-Ray, S. and Ali, M. (2013) *Understanding Muslim Chaplaincy*, London, Routledge.

Gillespie, M., McLaughlin, E., Adams, S. and Symmonds, A. (2003) *Media and the Shaping of Public Knowledge and Attitudes Towards Crime and Punishment*, London, Esmée Fairbairn Foundation.

Gillies, M. (2011) *The Barbed-Wire University: The Real Lives of Prisoners in the Second World War*, London, Aurum Press.

Glaser, D. (1989) *The Effectiveness of a Prison and Parole System*, Indianapolis, Bobbs-Merrill.

Goldman, L. (2014) 'From Criminals to Terrorists: The US Experience of Prison Radicalisation' in A. Silke (ed) *Prisons, Terrorism and Extremism: Critical Issues in Management, Radicalisation and Reform*, London, Routledge, 47–59.

Gramsci, A. (1995) *Selections from the Prison Notebooks of Antonio Gramsci*, London, Lawrence and Wishart.

Green Party (2015) *For the Common Good: Green Party Manifesto 2015*, London, The Green Party.

Greer, S. (2010) 'Anti-terrorist Laws and the United Kingdom's "Suspect Muslim Community": A Reply to Pantazis and Pemberton', *British Journal of Criminology*, 50, 1171–90.

Hall, S., Critcher, C., Jefferson, T., Clarke, J. and Roberts, B. (1978) *Policing the Crisis: Mugging, the State and Law and Order*, London, Macmillan.

Hamilton, C. and Lines, R. (2009) 'The Campaign for Prisoner Voting Rights in Ireland' in A.C. Ewald and B. Rottinghaus (eds) *Criminal Disenfranchisement in an International Perspective*, Cambridge, Cambridge University Press, 205–20.

Hamm, M. (2009) 'Prison Islam in the Age of Sacred Terror', *British Journal of Criminology*, 49(5), 667–85.

Hamm, M. (2013a) 'Prisoner Radicalisation in the United States', *Prison Service Journal*, 203, 4–8.

Hamm, M. (2013b) *The Spectacular Few: Prisoner Radicalization and the Evolving Terrorist Threat*, New York, New York University Press.

Haney, C. (2003) 'Mental Health Issues in Long-Term Solitary and Supermax Confinement', *Crime & Delinquency*, 49(1), 124–56.

Harcourt, B.E. (2014) 'The Invisibility of the Prison in Democratic Theory: A Problem of "Virtual Democracy"', *The Good Society*, 23:1, 6–16.

Hartung, E. and Floch, M. (1956) 'A Social-Psychological Analysis of Prison Riots: An Hypothesis' 47, *Journal of Criminal Law, Criminology and Police Science*, 51–7.

Haslam, S.A. and Reicher, S.D. (2012). 'When Prisoners Take Over the Prison: A Social Psychology of Resistance', *Personality and Social Psychology Review*, 16, 154–79.

Hay, D., Linebaugh, P., Rule, J.G., Thompson, E.P. and Winslow, C. (1975) *Albion's Fatal Tree: Crime and Society in Eighteenth-Century England*, London, Allen Lane.

Hillyard, P. (1993) *Suspect Community: People's Experiences of the Prevention of Terrorism Acts in Britain*, London, Pluto Press.

von Hirsch, A. and Ashworth, A. (2005) *Proportionate Sentencing: Exploring the Principles*, Oxford, Oxford University Press.

HM Chief Inspector of Prisons (2015) *Annual Report 2014–15*, London HMIP.

HM Chief Inspector of Prisons (2017) *Annual Report 2016–17*, London, HMIP.

HM Inspectorate of Prisons (2005) *Parallel Worlds: A Thematic Review of Race Relations in Prison*, London, HMIP.

HM Inspectorate of Prisons (2010) *Muslim Prisoners' Experiences: A Thematic Review*, London HMIP.

HM Inspectorate of Prisons (2014) *Expectations: Criteria for Assessing the Treatment of and Conditions for Women in Prison*, London, Ministry of Justice.

HM Inspectorate of Prisons (2017) *Life in Prison: Living Conditions*, London, HMIP.

Home Office (2017) *Operation of Police Powers under the Terrorism Act 2000 and Subsequent Legislation: Arrests, Outcomes, and Stop and Search, Great Britain, Financial Year Ending 31 March 2017, Statistical Bulletin 08,* London, Home Office.

Home Office (2002) *Justice for All*, Cm 5563, London, The Stationery Office.

Home Office (2006) *Rebalancing the Criminal Justice System in Favour of the Law-Abiding Majority: Reducing Reoffending and Protecting the Public*, London: Home Office.

Horowitz, I.L. (1964) 'A Postscript to the Anarchists' in I.L. Horowitz (ed) *The Anarchists,* New York, Dell, 581–603.

House of Commons Home Affairs Committee (2014) *Roots of Violent Radicalisation, 19th Report of Session 2010–12,* HC 1446.

House of Commons Justice Committee (2010) *Cutting Crime: The Case for Justice Reinvestment*, London, The Stationery Office.

House of Commons Justice Committee (2013*) Older Prisoners: Fifth Report of Session 2013– 14*, London, House of Commons.

House of Commons Justice Committee (2016) *Prison Safety*, Sixth Report of Session 2015– 16, HC 625, London, House of Commons.

House of Commons Justice Committee (2017) *Prison Reform: Governor Empowerment and Prison Performance, Twelfth Report of Session 2016–17*, HC 1123, London, House of Commons.

Hudson, B. (1998) 'Mitigation for Socially Deprived Offenders' in A. von Hirsch and A. Ashworth (eds) *Principled Sentencing: Readings on Theory and Policy*, Oxford, Hart, 205–8.

Human Rights Joint Committee (2015) *Seventh Report: Human Rights Judgments*, London, The Stationery Office.

Hutton, M.J. (2001) *Russian and West European Women: Dreams, Struggles and Nightmares*, Lanham, MD, Rowman and Littlefield.

Hutton, N. (2005) 'Beyond Popular Punitiveness?', *Punishment and Society*, 73(3), 243–58.

Inderbitzin, M., Cain, J. and Walraven, T. (2016) 'Learning and Practicing Citizenship and Democracy Behind Bars' in L.S. Abrams, E. Hughes, M. Inderbitzin, and R. Meek (eds) *The Voluntary Sector in Prisons: Encouraging Personal and Institutional Change*, London, Palgrave Macmillan, 55–63.

International Centre for Prison Studies (2017) *World Prison Brief*, London, Birkbeck University of London.

Irwin, J. (1980) *Prisons in Turmoil,* Boston, Little, Brown.

Jackson, G. (1972) *Blood in My Eye*, New York, Random House.

Jackson, G. (1973) *Soledad Brother: The Prison Letters of George Jackson*, Harmondsworth, Penguin.

Jaffe, M. (2012) *The Listener Scheme in Prisons: Final Report on the Research Findings,* Ewell, Samaritans.

James, A.L., Bottomley, A.K., Liebling, A. and Clare, E. (1997) *Privatizing Prisons: Rhetoric and Reality*, London, Sage.

Jewkes, Y. (2002) 'The Use of Media in Constructing Identities in the Masculine Environment of Men's Prisons', *European Journal of Communication*, 172, 205–25.

Joint Committee (2013) *Joint Committee – Report on the Draft Voting Eligibility (Prisoners') Bill*, London, The Stationery Office.

Keith, B. (2006) *Report of the Zahid Mubarek Inquiry*, HC 1082, London, The Stationery Office.

Kerr, N., Tully, R. and Völlm, B. (2017) 'Volunteering with Sex Offenders: The Attitudes of Volunteers Towards Sex Offenders, their Treatment and Rehabilitation' *Sexual Abuse: A Journal of Research and Treatment*.

King, R. (1994) 'Russian Prisons after Perestroika: End of the Gulag?' *British Journal of Criminology*, 34, 62–82.

King, R. and McDermott, K. (1990) '"My Geranium is Subversive": Some Notes on the Management of Trouble in Prisons', *British Journal of Sociology*, 41:4, 455–71.

Kjelsberg, E., Skoglund, T.H. and Rustad, A.-B. (2007) 'Attitudes Towards Prisoners, as Reported by Prison Inmates, Prison Employees and College Students', *BMC Public Health* 7(71), 1–9.

Kropotkin, P. (1889) *Memoirs of a Revolutionist*, New York, Grove Press 1968.

Kruttschnitt, C. and Gartner, R. (2005) *Marking Time in the Golden State: Women's Imprisonment in California*, Cambridge, Cambridge University Press.

Labour Party (2017) *For the Many, Not the Few: The Labour Party Manifesto 2017*, London, Labour Party.

Lammy, D. (2017) *The Lammy Review: An Independent Review into the Treatment of, and Outcomes for, Black, Asian and Minority Ethnic Individuals in the Criminal Justice System*, London.

Law Commission (2016) *A New Sentencing Code for England and Wales: Transition – Final Report and Recommendations*, Law Commission No. 365, HC 30, London, Law Commission.

Law, V. (2009) *Resistance Behind Bars: The Struggles of Incarcerated Women*, Oakland, CA, PM Press.

Lea, J. and Young, J. (1984) *What is to be Done about Law and Order?*, Harmondsworth, Penguin.

Levenson, J. and Finola, F. (2002) *Barred Citizens*, London, Prison Reform Trust.

Liberal Democrat Party (2017) *Change Britain's Future: Liberal Democrat Manifesto*, London, Liberal Democrat Party.

Liebling, A. and Straub, C. (2013) 'Identity Challenges and the Risks of Radicalisation in High Security Custody', *Prison Service Journal*, 203, 15–22.

Lloyd, M. (2013) 'Learning from Casework and the Literature', *Prison Service Journal* 203, 23–30.

Lofstrom, M. and Raphael, S. (2013) *Impact of Realignment on County Jail Populations*, Sacramento, CA, Public Policy Institute of California.

Ludlow, A. (2014) *Privatising Prisons*, Oxford, Hart.

Lynd, S. (2004) *Lucasville: The Untold Story of a Prison Uprising*, Philadelphia, Temple University Press.

Mac Ionnrachtaigh, F. (2013) *Language, Resistance and Revival: Republican Prisoners and the Irish Language in the North of Ireland*, London, Pluto Press.

MacShane, D. (2014) *Prison Diaries*, London, Biteback.

Mandela, N. (1994) *Long Walk to Freedom*, Boston, Little, Brown.

Manza, J., Brooks, C. and Uggen, C. (2004) 'Public Attitudes Towards Felon Disenfranchisement in the US', *Public Opinion Quarterly* 68, 276–87.

Marshall, T.H. (1950) *Citizenship and Social Rights*, Cambridge, Cambridge University Press.

Maruna, S. (2001) *Making Good: How Ex-convicts Reform and Rebuild their Lives*, Washington, DC, American Psychological Association.

Marx, K. (1852) 'The Eighteenth Brumaire of Louis Bonaparte in *Marx and Engels: Collected Works*, 11, London, Lawrence and Wishart (1979), 99–181.

Marx, K. (1846) 'The German Ideology', in *Marx and Engels: Collected Works*, 5, London, Lawrence and Wishart (1976), 19–581.

Marx, K. (1853) 'Capital Punishment', *Marx and Engels: Collected Works*, 11, London, Lawrence and Wishart (1979), 495–501.

Marx, K. (1867) 'Capital: Volume I' in *Marx and Engels: Collected Works*, 35, London, Lawrence and Wishart (1996).

Matthews, R. (2014) *Realist Criminology*, London, Palgrave Macmillan.

Mattinson, J. and Mirrlees-Black, C. (2000) *Attitudes to Crime and Criminal Justice: Findings from the 1998 British Crime Survey*, Home Office Research Study No. 200, London, Home Office.

Mauer, M. (2001) 'The Causes and Consequences of Prison Growth in the United States' in D. Garland (ed) *Mass Imprisonment*, London, Sage, 4–14.

McCahon, D.S. (2016) 'Combating Misinformation in the Ex-felon Population: The Role Probation and Parole Agencies Can Play to Facilitate Civic Reintegration in the United States', *Probation Journal,* 63:1, 9–22.

McEvoy, K. (2001) *Paramilitary Imprisonment in Northern Ireland: Resistance, Management and Release*, Oxford, Oxford University Press.

McEvoy, K and Mika, H. (2002) 'Restorative Justice and the Critique of Informalism in Northern Ireland', *British Journal of Criminology*, 43:2, 534–63.

McLennan, R. (2008) *The Crisis of Imprisonment: Protest, Politics and the Making of an American Penal State 1776–1941*, Cambridge, Cambridge University Press.

McNulty, D., Watson, N. and Philo, G. (2014) 'Human Rights and Prisoners' Rights: The British Press and the Shaping of Public Debate', *Howard Journal of Crime and Justice*, 53(4), 360–76.

Melvin, K.B., Gramling, L.K. and Gardner, W.M. (1985) 'A Scale to Measure Attitudes Towards Prisoners', *Criminal Justice and Behaviour*, 12:2, 241–53.

Merton, R. (1938) 'Social Structure and Anomie', *American Sociological Review*, 3, 672–82.

Messer-Kruse, T. (2011) *The Trial of the Haymarket Anarchists: Terrorism and Justice in the Gilded Age*, New York, Palgrave.

Mill, J.S. (1861) *Considerations on Representative Government*, London, Parker, Son and Bourn.

Miller, I. (2016) *A History of Force Feeding: Hunger Strikes, Prisons and Medical Ethics, 1909–1974*, London, Palgrave.

Ministry of Justice (2009) *Voting Rights of Convicted Prisoners Detained within the United Kingdom, Second Stage Consultation*, London, Ministry of Justice.

Ministry of Justice (2010) *Breaking the Cycle: Effective Punishment, Rehabilitation and Sentencing of Offenders,* London, Ministry of Justice.

Ministry of Justice (2013) *Transforming Rehabilitation: A Revolution in the Way We Manage Offenders,* Consultation Paper, Cm 8517, London, Ministry of Justice.

Ministry of Justice (2015) *Justice Data Lab Re-Offending Analysis: Prisoners Education Trust*, London, Ministry of Justice.

Ministry of Justice (2016a) *Prison Safety and Reform,* Cm 9350, London, Ministry of Justice.

Ministry of Justice (2016b) *Summary of the Main Findings of the Review of Islamist Extremism in Prisons, Probation and Youth Justice*, London, Ministry of Justice.

Ministry of Justice (2017a) *Prison Population Projections 2017 to 2022, England and Wales,* London, Ministry of Justice.

Ministry of Justice (2017b) *Offender Management Statistics Bulletin, England and Wales: Quarterly October to December 2016, Annual 2016, Prison Population: 31 March 2017*, London, Ministry of Justice.

Mitchell, B. and Roberts, J.V. (2012) 'Sentencing for Murder: Exploring Public Knowledge and Public Opinion in England and Wales', *British Journal of Criminology*, 52(1), 141–58.

Mochulsky, F.V. (2011) *Gulag Boss: A Soviet Memoir*, trans. and ed. D. Kaple, New York, Oxford University Press.

Moll, A. (2013) *Losing Track of Time: Dementia and the Ageing Prison Population: Treatment Challenges and Examples of Good Practice*, London, Mental Health Foundation.

Moore, L. and Scraton, P. (2014) *The Incarceration of Women: Punishing Bodies: Breaking Spirits*, London, Palgrave Macmillan.

Morrison, J.F. (2014) 'A Time to Think, A Time to Talk: Irish Republican Prisoners in the Northern Irish Peace Process' in A. Silke (ed) *Prisons, Terrorism and Extremism*, London, Routledge, 74–85.

Murdoch, J.J. (1992) 'Encouraging Citizenship: Report of the Commission on Citizenship', *Modern Law Review*, 54:3, 439.

Murphy, E. and Brown, J. (2000) 'Exploring Gender Role Identity, Value Orientation of Occupation and Sex of Respondent in Influencing Attitudes Towards Male and Female Offenders', *Legal and Criminological Psychology*, 5, 285–90.

Murray, C. (2013) 'A Perfect Storm: Parliament and Prisoner Disenfranchisement', *Parliamentary Affairs*, 66, 511–39.

Murray, C. (2014) '"To Punish, Deter and Incapacitate": Incarceration and Radicalisation in UK Prisons after 9/11' in A. Silke (ed) *Prisons, Terrorism and Extremism: Critical Issues in Management, Radicalisation and Reform*, London, Routledge, 16–32.

NACRO (2009) *A Resource Pack for Working with Older Prisoners*, London, NACRO.

Neier, A. (1995) 'Confining Dissent: The Political Prison', in N. Morris and D.J. Rothman (eds) *The Oxford History of the Prison*, Oxford, Oxford University Press, 391–425.

Nellis, A. (2016) *The Color of Justice: Racial and Ethnic Disparity in State Prisons*, Washington, DC, The Sentencing Project.

Nellis, M. (2010) 'Creative Arts and the Cultural Politics of Penal Reform: The Early Years of the Barlinnie Special Unit 1973–1981, *Journal of Scottish Criminal Justice Studies* 20, 118–22.

Neumann, R. (2010) *Prisons and Terrorism: Radicalisation and De-radicalisation in 15 Countries*, London ICSR.

New York State Special Commission on Attica (1972) *Attica: The Official Report of the New York State Special Commission on Attica*, New York, Bantam Books.

Newburn, T. and Stanko, E.A. (1994) *Just Boys Doing Business? Men, Masculinities and Crime*, London, Routledge.

NOMS (2016) *National Offender Management Service Offender Equalities Annual Report 2015/16*, London, Ministry of Justice.

NOMS (2017) *Annual Report and Accounts 2016–2017*, London, The Stationery Office.

O'Rawe, R. (2005) *Blanketmen*, Dublin, New Island.

Page, J. (2004) 'Eliminating the Enemy: The Import of Denying Prisoners Access to Higher Education in Clinton's America', *Punishment and Society* 6(4), 357–78.

Pakes, F. (2007) 'An International Comparative Perspective', in M. Boone and M. Moerings (eds) *Dutch Prisons*, The Hague, B Ju Legal Publishers.

Pantazis, C. and Pemberton, S. (2009) 'From the "Old" to the "New" Suspect Community: Examining the Impacts of Recent UK Counter-Terrorist Legislation', *British Journal of Criminology* 49(5), 646–66.

Pantazis, C. and Pemberton, S. (2011) 'Restating the Case for the "Suspect" Community: A Reply to Greer', *British Journal of Criminology*, 51(6), 1054–62.

Pashukanis, E. (1978) *Law and Marxism: A General Theory of Law*, (ed.) C. Arthur, London, Inklinks.

Perrin, C. and Blagden, N. (2016) 'Movements Towards Desistance via Peer-Support Roles in Prison', in L.S. Abrams, E. Hughes, M., Inderbitzin, and R. Meek (eds) *The Voluntary Sector in Prisons: Encouraging Personal and Institutional Change*, London, Palgrave Macmillan, 115–42.

Phillips, A.J. and Deckard, N. (2016) 'Felon Disenfranchisement Laws and the Feedback Loop of Political Exclusion: the Case of Florida', *Journal of African American Studies*, 20(1), 1–18.

Piacentini, L. (2004) *Surviving Russian Prisons*, London, Routledge.

Piacentini, L. and Pallot, J. (2014) '"In Exile Imprisonment" in Russia', *British Journal of Criminology*, 54:1, 20–37.

Pickett, J.T, Mancini, C., Mears, D.P. and Gertz, M. (2015) 'Public (Mis)Understanding of Crime Policy: The Effects of Criminal Justice Experience and Media Reliance, *Criminal Justice Policy Review*, 26, 500–22.

Pickering, R. (2013) 'Terrorism, Extremism, Radicalisation and The Offender Management System – The Story so Far', *Prison Service Journal*, 203, 9–14.

Pratt, J. (2002) *Punishment and Civilization*, London, Sage.

Pressman, D.E. and Flockton, J. (2014) 'Violent Extremist Risk Assessment: Issues and Applications of the VERA-2 in a High-security Correctional Setting' in A. Silke (ed) *Prisons, Terrorism and Extremism*, London, Routledge, 122–44.

Prisons and Probation Ombudsman (2015) *Learning Lessons Bulletin: Fatal Incident Investigations*, Issue 8, London, PPO.

Prisons and Probation Ombudsman (2016) *Annual Report 2015–16*, London, PPO.

Prisons and Probation Ombudsman (2017) *Annual Report 2016–17*, London, PPO.

PROP (1973) *'Political' Prisoners and Prisoners' Unions: Conflict or Cooperation?*, London, South London PROP Group.

PROP (1976) *Don't Mark his Face: Hull Prison Riot 1976*, London, PROP.

PROP (1979) Wormwood Scrubs: Special Report, London, PROP.

Pryce, V. (2013) *Prisonomics*, London, Biteback.

Pryor, S. (2001) *The Responsible Prisoner: An Exploration of the Extent to Which Imprisonment Removes Responsibility Unnecessarily*, Washington, Prison Fellowship International.

Purvis, J. (1995) 'The Prison Experiences of the Suffragettes in Edwardian Britain', *Women's History Review*, 4:1, 103–133.

Quail, J. (1979) *The Slow-Burning Fuse: The Lost History of the British Anarchists*, London, Paladin.

Ramsay, P. (2013a) 'Faking Democracy with Prisoners' Voting Rights', Law, Society and Economic Working Paper Series 7/2013, Department of Law, London School of Economics and Political Science.

Ramsay, P. (2013b) 'Voters Should not Be in Prison! The Rights of Prisoners in a Democracy', *Critical Review of International Social and Political Philosophy* 16:3, 421–38.

Ratner, R. and Cartwright, B. (1990) 'Politicized Prisoners: From Class Warriors to Faded Rhetoric', *Journal of Human Justice* 2(1), 75–92.

Reicher, S.D. and Haslam, S.A. (2006) 'Rethinking the Psychology of Tyranny: The BBC Prison Study', *British Journal of Social Psychology*, 45, 1–40.

Reiman, J. (2005) 'Liberal and Republican Arguments against the Disenfranchisement of Felons', *Criminal Justice Ethics*, 24:1, 3–18

Richmond, K. (2017) *Women Political Prisoners in Germany: Narratives of Self and Captivity, 1915–91*, London, Institute of Modern Languages Research.

Roberts, J. and Hough, M. (2013) 'Sentencing Riot-related Offending: Where do the Public Stand?', *British Journal of Criminology,* 53(2), 234–56.

Rolland, M. (1997) *Descent into Madness: An Inmate's Experience of the New Mexico State Prison Riot,* Cincinnati, OH, Anderson Publishing Co.

Rubin, A.T. (2015) 'Resistance or Friction: Understanding the Significance of Prisoners' Secondary Adjustments', *Theoretical Criminology,* 19(1), 23–42.

Rubin, A.T. (2017) 'Resistance as Agency? Incorporating the Structural Determinants of Prisoner Behaviour', *British Journal of. Criminology,* 57, 644–63.

Rusche, G. and Kirkheimer, O. (1939) *Punishment and Social Structure,* New York, Russell and Russell.

Ruth, T., Matusitz, J. and Simi, D. (2017) 'Ethics of Disenfranchisement and Voting Rights in the US: Convicted Felons, the Homeless and Immigrants', *American Journal of Criminal Justice,* 42:1, 56–68.

Ryan, M. (2003) *Penal Policy and Political Culture,* Winchester, Waterside Press.

Samaritans (2011) *A History of the Listener Scheme and Samaritans' Prison Support,* Ewell, Samaritans.

Sands, B. (1993) *Writings from Prison,* Cork, Mercier Press.

Sands, B. (1996) *One Day in My Life,* Cork, Mercier Press.

Scalia, J. (2002) *Prisoner Petitions Filed in US District Courts, 2000, with Trends 1980–2000,* Washington, Bureau of Justice.

Schlanger, M. (2003) 'Inmate Litigation', *Harvard Law Review,* 116, 1555–1706.

Schlanger, M. (2013) '*Plata v Brown* and Realignment: Jails, Prisons, Courts and Policies', *Harvard Civil Rights-Civil Liberties Law Review,* 48(1), 165–21.

Schmidt, B.A. (2013) 'User Voice and the Prison Council Model: A Summary of Key Findings from an Ethnographic Exploration of Participatory Governance in Three English Prisons', *Prison Service Journal* 209, 12–17.

Scraton, P. and Moore, L. (2004) *The Hurt Inside: The Imprisonment of Women and Girls in Northern Ireland,* Belfast, Northern Ireland Human Rights Commission.

Scraton, P., Sim, J. and Skidmore, P. (1991) *Prisons under Protest,* Milton Keynes, Open University Press.

Seale, P. and McConville, M. (1968) *French Revolution 1968,* Harmondsworth, Penguin.

Shalev, S. (2009) *Supermax: Controlling Risk through Solitary Confinement,* Cullompton, Willan.

Shalev, S. and Edgar, K. (2015) *Deep Custody: Segregation Units and Close Supervision Centres in England and Wales,* London, Prison Reform Trust.

Silke, A. (2014) 'Risk Assessment of Terrorist and Extremist Prisoners' in A. Silke (ed) *Prisons, Terrorism and Extremism: Critical Issues in Management, Radicalisation and Reform,* London, Routledge, 108–121.

Simon, J. (2014) *Mass Incarceration on Trial: A Remarkable Court Decision and the Future of Prison in America,* New York, The New Press.

Simson Caird, J. (2016) *Prisoners' Voting Rights: Developments since May 2015,* Briefing Paper, CBP 7461, London, House of Commons.

Sinai, J. (2014) 'Developing a Model of Prison Radicalisation' in A. Silke (ed) *Prisons, Terrorism and Extremism: Critical Issues in Management, Radicalisation and Reform,* London, Routledge, 35–46.

Skarbek, D. (2014) *The Social Order of the Underworld: How Prison Gangs Govern the American Penal System,* Oxford, Oxford University Press.

Slade, G. (2016) 'Violence as Information During Prison Reform: Evidence from the Post-Soviet Region', *British Journal of Criminology,* 56, 937–55.

Smith, P.S. (2006) 'The Effects of Solitary Confinement on Prison Inmates: A Brief History and Review of the Literature', *Crime and Justice,* 34(1), 441–528.

Solomon, E. and Edgar, K. (2004) *Having their Say: The Work of Prisoner Councils*, London, Prison Reform Trust.

Solzenitsyn, A. (2003) *The Gulag Archipelago 1918–1956*, London, Harvill Press.

Spalek, B. and El-Hassan, S. (2007) 'Muslim Converts in Prison', *Howard Journal of Crime and Justice*, 46(2), 99–114.

Steele, J. *Review of Safety at HMP Maghaberry* (The Steele Report), August 2003, Belfast, Northern Ireland Office.

Steurer, S.J., Smith L. and Tracy, A. (2001) *Three State Recidivism Study*, Lenham, MD., Correctional Educational Association.

Storgaard, A. (2009) 'The Right to Vote in Danish Prisons' in A.C. Ewald and B. Rottinghaus (eds) *Criminal Disenfranchisement in an International Perspective* Cambridge, Cambridge University Press, 244–58.

Strimple, E. (2003) 'A History of Prison Inmate-Animal Interaction Programs', *American Behavioral Scientist*, 47, 70–78.

Surette, R. (1997) *Media, Crime and Criminal Justice*, 2nd edition, Belmont CA, Wadsworth.

Swavola, E., Riley, K. and Subramanian, R. (2016) *Overlooked: Women and Jails in an Era of Reform*, New York, Vera Institute of Justice.

Sykes, G. (1958) *The Society of Captives: A Study of a Maximum Security Prison*, Princeton, Princeton University Press.

Tannenbaum, F. (1938) *Crime and the Community*, New York, Columbia University Press.

Tarling, R. (1979) *The 'Incapacitation' Effects of Imprisonment*, Home Office Research Bulletin, No. 7, 6–8, London, Home Office.

Tarling, R. (1993) *Analysing Offending Data, Models and Interpretations*, London, HMSO.

Taunton, M. (2013) 'Russia and the British Intellectuals' in R. Beasley and P. Ross Bullock (eds) *Russia in Britain 1880–1940: From Melodrama to Modernism*, Oxford, Oxford University Press, 209–24.

Taylor, C. (2014) *Brain Cells: Listening to Prison Learners*, 3rd edition, London, Prisoners' Education Trust.

Tchnernavin, T. (1934) *Escape from the Soviets*, New York, Dutton.

Tchnernavin, V. (1933) *I Speak for the Silent: Prisoners of the Soviets*, Boston, Half Cushman and Flint.

Thompson, E.P. (1977) *Whigs and Hunters: The Origin of the Black Act*, Harmondsworth, Penguin.

Thompson, H.A. (2016) *Blood in the Water: The Attica Prison Uprising of 1971 and its Legacy*, New York, Pantheon Press.

Tonry, M. (2004) *Thinking about Crime: Sense and Sensibility in American Penal Culture*, New York, Oxford University Press.

Tonry, M. (2009) 'Explanations of American Punishment Policies: A National History', *Punishment and Society,* 11(3), 377–94.

Torres Soriano, M.R. (2014) 'Prison Policy as an Anti-terrorist Tool: Lessons from Spain' in A. Silke (ed) *Prisons, Terrorism and Extremism: Critical Issues in Management, Radicalisation and Reform*, London, Routledge, 243–55.

Ugelvik, T. (2014) *Power and Resistance in Prison: Doing Time, Doing Freedom.* London, Palgrave Macmillan.

Ugelvik, T. and Dullum, J. (eds) (2011) *Penal Exceptionalism: Nordic Prison Policy and Practice,* London, Routledge.

Uggen, C., Larson R. and Shannon, S. (2016) *6 Million Lost Voters: State-Level Estimates of Felony Disenfranchisement,* Washington, The Sentencing Project.

Uggen, C. and Manza, J. (2002) 'Democratic Contraction? The Political Consequences of Felon Disenfranchisement in the United States', *American Sociological Review*, 67, 777–803.

Uggen, C. and Manza, J. (2004) 'Voting and Subsequent Crime and Arrest: Evidence From a Community Sample', *Columbia Human Rights Law Review*, 36(1), 193–216.

Uggen, C., Van Brackle, M. and McLaughlin, M. (2009) 'Punishment and Social Exclusion: National Differences in Prisoner Disenfranchisement', in A.C. Ewald and B. Rottinghaus (eds) *Criminal Disenfranchisement in an International Perspective*, Cambridge, Cambridge University Press, 59–75.

Uhrig, N. (2016) *Black, Asian and Minority Ethnic Disproportionality in the Criminal Justice System in England and Wales*, London, Ministry of Justice.

Useem, B. and Kimball, P. (1991) *States of Siege: US Prison Riots 1971–1986*, New York, Oxford University Press.

Vandebosch, H. (2005) 'The Perceived Role of Mass Media Use during Incarceration in the Light of Prisoners' Re-entry into Society', *Journal of Criminal Justice and Popular Culture*, 12(2), 96–115.

Wacks, R. (2103) *Privacy and Media Freedom*, Oxford, Oxford University Press.

Wacquant, L. (2009) *Prisons of Poverty*, Minneapolis, University of Minnesota Press.

Wacquant, L. (2010) 'Class, Race and Hyperincarceration in Revanchist America', *Daedalus*, 140, 74–90.

Wacquant, L. (2012) 'The Prison as an Outlaw Institution', *Howard Journal of Criminal Justice*, 51(1), 1–15.

Weil Davies, S. and Sherr Roswell, B. (eds) (2013) *Turning Teaching Inside out: A Pedagogy of Transformation for Community-Based Education*, New York, Springer.

Willis, G.M., Levenson, J.S. and Ward, T. (2010) 'Desistance and Attitudes Towards Sex Offenders: Facilitation or Hindrance', *Journal of Family Violence*, 25(6), 545–56.

Wilson, D., Gallagher, C. and Mackenzie, D. (2000) 'A Meta-analysis of Corrections-Based Education, Vocation and Work Programs for Adult Offenders', *Journal of Research on Crime and Delinquency*, 37(4), 347–68.

Wood, E. and Bloom, R. (2008) *De Facto Disenfranchisement*, New York, ACLU/Brennan Center.

Wood, E. and Trivedi, N. (2007) 'The Modern Day Poll Tax: How Economic Sanctions Block Access to the Polls', *Clearinghouse Review Journal of Poverty Law and Policy*, 30–45.

Wood, J. and Kemshall, H. (2007) *The Operation and Experience of Multi-Agency Public Protection Arrangements*, London, Home Office.

Woolf, H. and Tumim, S. (1991) *Prison Disturbances April 1990. Report of an Inquiry*, Cm 1456, London, HMSO.

Woolf, H. (2015) *Strangeways 25 Years On: Achieving Fairness and Justice in Prison*, Lecture, London, Inner Temple, April 2015.

van Wormer, J., Kigerl, A. and Hamilton, Z. (2017) 'Digging Deeper: Exploring the Value of Prison-Based Dog Handler Programs', *The Prison Journal*, 97(4), 520–38.

Wyld, G. and Noble, J. (2017) *Beyond Bars: Maximising the Voluntary Sector's Contribution in Criminal Justice*, London, New Philanthropy Capital.

X, Malcolm (1981) *The Autobiography of Malcolm X*, New York, Ballantine Books.

Yeager, M. (2011) 'Frank Tannenbaum: The Making of a Convict Criminologist', *The Prison Journal*, 91(2), 177–97.

Young, L. (December 2014) *Improving Outcomes for Young Black and/or Muslim Men in the Criminal Justice System*, London, Barrow Cadburys Trust.

Zaitzow, B.H. and Robinson, M.B. (2001) 'Criminologists as Criminals' in A. Thio and T.C. Calhoun (eds) *Readings in Deviant Behaviour*, New York, Allyn and Bacon, 231–33.

van Zyl Smit, D. and Snacken, S. (2009) *Principles of European Law and Policy*, Oxford, Oxford University Press.

INDEX

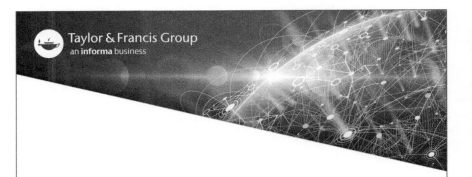